THE HISTORY
OF
TETTENHALL COLLEGE
(1863-2008)

THE HISTORY

OF

TETTENHALL COLLEGE

(1863-2008)

SIMON WHILD

Matador
9 De Montfort Mews
Leicester LE1 7FW, UK
Tel: (+44) 116 255 9311 / 9312
Email: books@troubador.co.uk
Web: www.troubador.co.uk/matador

ISBN 978-1848761-247

A Cataloguing-in-Publication (CIP) catalogue record for this book
is available from the British Library.

Photo Credits
All photography © Tettenhall College/Simon Whild
Except "Alderman Albert Baldwin Bantock" © Wolverhampton Arts Council.

Typeset in 11pt Book Antiqua by Troubador Publishing Ltd, Leicester, UK

Matador is an imprint of Troubador Publishing Ltd

CONTENTS

FOREWORD

L.N. Chown

"Your school days are your best days – the happiest days of your life," or so we were often told by our elders. Although we may have taken little notice at the time, several of us at T.C. in the 30s and early 40s would readily concede that there was much truth in this dictum.

After seventy-four years of contact with Tettenhall College in one capacity or another, I firmly believe that the vast majority of those who have known the school as Pupil, or Teacher, or Cook or Governor, or Groundsman – you name it – have found fulfilment in its service of a sort that they cherish and would not have obtained anywhere else.

What is it about this small independent school that has generated such a lot of regard for nearly 150 years? Can we pinpoint anything definite beyond received wisdom or fuzzy nonsense?

The most ardent supporters of an institution can sometimes also be its severest critics. In my experience this certainly applies to Old Tettenhallians. However, in a thoughtful speech at an Annual Reunion some years ago, the president of the OT Club stated categorically – to use his words – "Tettenhall has always been very fortunate in its staff." A few of his listeners were momentarily startled, but it was clear that almost all agreed without demur. Here it is appropriate to state that in the 80 years since January 1928, to go back no further, we have had just four Headmasters and five Deputies – each providing in his own way that strong leadership and continuity so vital to any business, educational or otherwise, in the private sector. Furthermore, the "atmosphere" of any school or college, an intangible quality pervading a place which visitors quickly sense, can only derive from the collective personalities of everybody in it. "I liked the atmosphere," is a remark made about Tettenhall with great regularity.

That an updated edition of Geoffrey Hancock's gem of a monograph has been awaited for a considerable time says a lot for its author and its subject. Geoff's gift of the common touch when writing or lecturing, his passion for and knowledge of local history made his book instantly popular when it appeared around the school's centenary in 1963. The scale of its development over the last forty-five years has been great enough to fill several chapters. But who was the best person to write them?

To produce a fair picture, a photographer should be the optimum distance from the scene – too near or too far will result in a distorted or blurred image; similarly with a writer. Simon Whild, OT and professional writer, has filled the bill excellently, adding his skills to Geoff's in describing the progress of an extraordinary school. They have together provided a very good read.

L.N. Chown
November 2007

ACKNOWLEDGEMENTS

I am deeply indebted to Mr. G.V. Hancock, not only for turning the potentially prosaic nature of classroom history education into a wonderful pageant of exciting drama, but also for his book *History of Tettenhall College,* which was originally published to commemorate the College's centenary in 1963. This book, as well as the first two thirds of my own, owes a debt of gratitude to Dr. Saunders' notes on the history of the College, and without these, my task (and no doubt Mr. Hancock's) would have been a lot more difficult. I consider it an honour and a privilege to follow in Mr. Hancock's footsteps in producing an updated and published history of Tettenhall College and it is my hope that other College historians will also follow in the years to come.

It would be a lifetime's work to chronicle every event that took place at Tettenhall College during its nearly one hundred and fifty years of life, so this book represents edited highlights, which are intended to be a story that can be read to educate as well as, I hope, delight. This means that a lot of information had to end up on the editing room floor purely for the sake of brevity, and I offer no apologies if I have left anyone out because we have all played our part, no matter how small, in putting the College in the strong position it is in today. Using the word "Tettenhallian" in its broadest possible sense, the College today is an institution of which all Tettenhallians can be justly proud.

No one can write a book of this nature alone, and there are many people who gave up their valuable time to assist me. I'm afraid that space won't allow me to mention everyone, but those people know who they are and they have my heartfelt thanks. However, a special mention should go to both the staff at Tettenhall College and Bantock House, without whose friendly help I would not have been able to complete this project. Special thanks also to L.N. (John) Chown, Dot Stone and Jeremy Walters, because without their valuable assistance and support, this book would definitely not now be in your hands.

S.W.
August 2008

HEADMASTERS OF TETTENHALL COLLEGE

The Rev. R. Halley M.A.	1863-1870
A.W. Young Esq. M.A.	1870-1891
J.H. Haydon Esq. M.A.	1891-1905
R.L. Ager Esq. M.A.	1906-1912
A.H. Angus Esq. BSc. F.R.G.S.	1913-1925
P.W. Day Esq. M.A.	1925-1927
H. Pearson Esq. F.R.G.S.	1928-1941
F.D. Field-Hyde Esq. M.A.	1942-1968
W.J. Dale Esq. M.A.	1968-1994
P. C. Bodkin Esq. BSc. PhD.	1994-

PART ONE

INFANCY

CHAPTER 1

HOW TO BUILD A SCHOOL

Headmaster: The Rev. R. Halley

What is a school? This is a deceptively simple question, but providing an answer is not very simple at all. Many would answer by saying that a school is a building or institution where one acquires learning; others would argue varying shades of definition, whilst others would be prepared to debate the issue for days. All of this points to the difficulty in defining what a school is, and this is why the answers to this question provided by the founders of Tettenhall College must have been very involved indeed.

There are no definite records of a meeting of any sort between Tettenhall College's founders, but one can imagine a group of men observing the first task when setting up any kind of business venture – and that is to define their product. They were all seasoned businessmen and they all wanted to found a school, so once again they must have asked themselves the question: what is a school? In response, the founders of Tettenhall College, may well have defined their proposed school as: "a microcosm of the society prevalent at the time, which exists to serve that society by providing its potential citizens with essential skills to live within it." It is not likely that the founders of the College consciously defined their product as succinctly as this, but with the benefit of hindsight, it is easy to see that this is exactly what they succeeded in creating. Not only this, but they also succeeded in creating an institution that has inspired much love and admiration over successive generations; and this is the story of how it all happened – and how the College managed to survive and prevail through a turbulent roller-coaster ride through some of the most dangerous but interesting times that history has known.

The official date for the origin of Tettenhall College is 1863, although the actual roots that culminated in the College opening its doors in that year are very hard to pin down. Many institutions can say exactly when the idea that formed their origins came from – be it at a meeting between two individuals, or a letter proposing an idea – but this is not the case with Tettenhall College. Many records have long since been lost, and after nearly a century and a

The Rev. R. Halley M.A. (Headmaster 1863-1870)

half they are now not likely to be found – although most surviving sources point to Wolverhampton's Queen Street Congregational Church as the most likely starting point. We do know that most of the College's founders were members of this religious institution, and it is easy to imagine a "Council of War" between several of these men to address the problem of the lack of a good Non-conformist school for their sons. Reading the meagre surviving correspondence of such individuals, we do know that there was a general feeling of frustration among Non-conformists, and especially among the men and women of Queen Street Congregational Church, about the Church of England's overwhelming influence on education in this part of the nineteenth century. We also know that they and many others up and down the country actually set out to do something about it.

For those not familiar with the various divisions in the Christian Church, "Non-conformist" was a term used in England after the Act of Uniformity in 1662 to refer to an English subject belonging to a non-Christian religion or to any non-Anglican church. In modern parlance, the word "Non-conformist" may also refer more narrowly to a person who also advocates religious liberty, atheism or agnosticism, although this was virtually unheard of in the God-fearing times of mid-nineteenth century Britain. In the case of the College's founders (who were Congregationalists), they belonged to a group of people who had gone against the Act of Uniformity, typically by practising or advocating radical, sometimes separatist, dissent with respect to the Established Anglican Church doctrines. Congregationalists may be seen as Protestant Christian churches practicing governance in which each congregation democratically and autonomously runs its own affairs, rather than take direction or money from a centralised authority, such as in the case of Anglican churches taking supervision from a centralised Diocese. This is why the College founders had to take action to form their own school for their children – purely because there was no central Church authority (with its attendant centralised funds) to provide such a school for them.

In the light of this, it must also be remembered that before 1870, education was largely a private affair, with wealthy parents sending their children to fee-paying schools, and others using whatever other local education facilities were available. In choosing an education, there were only two alternatives to engaging a private tutor to teach on a one-to-one basis. The first of these was to send your child to one of the long-established Grammar Schools; the second was to choose one of the equally long-established academies that are popularly known as "Public Schools." In both the latter cases, and especially in Public Schools, the Church of England exerted a firm domination. Religious instruction played a much greater part in school life then than it does today, and this is what caused Tettenhall College's founders to feel frustration and anger. They knew that if they sent their children to such schools, the Non-conformist ideals that they held so dear would not be taught, and those ideals would be supplanted by the theology of another Denomination.

This feeling was widespread, and in an attempt to address the problem, several schools came into being – many of whom only survived a few years, but several still exist today. One other such example is Silcoates School in Wakefield, and reading early correspondence between the founders of this school puts the problem into clear focus: "The want of a respectable school of this kind had long been felt, and with many parents it had often been the subject of serious complaint that they must either allow their sons to grow up imperfectly educated or place them in institutions where their principles would be dishonoured and reviled and therefore endangered, and where through fear or shame they might be induced to abandon the cause of Protestant Nonconformity and either comply with some more worldly or fashionable profession of Christianity, or, what they dreaded more, grow up in sceptical and criminal indifference to religion itself."

One can imagine Tettenhall College's founders saying something similar to each other, living as they did in a society where the conflict of differing religious ideologies could cause bitter divisions in society, effectively dividing communities, organisations, and even families. Clearly though, the religious issues were no less important than the more overtly secular issues of power and money. The Anglican Church held a very powerful political lobby in many organisations, a lot of whom made donations to Church coffers, often at the expense of other religious organisations, including those of the Non-conformist persuasion. In 1887, the "Express & Star" reported a serious battle among the Board of Walsall School where Non-conformists were up in arms about the fact that Anglicans occupied all of the important offices and not only had they introduced a strictly Anglican method of teaching in the school, but were also seeking to prevent Non-conformists from holding teaching posts. The newspaper reports that this not only led to raised voices, but also a lot of table thumping and impassioned arguing.

In the mid nineteenth century, the issue of education was clearly a very important one. The Industrial Revolution had brought a new age of prosperity to the country, and to the Midlands in particular. The rise of a new "middle-class" had ushered in a brave new world that demanded the privileges hitherto only enjoyed by a select few. This new class of people were widespread and wealthy – and behind them stood the various Churches. However, many of these people had not enjoyed much of an education, and they were determined to ensure that their children fared better. This desire was born not so much from the natural desire to provide the best start for their children, but from the knowledge that in this new industrialised and rapidly shrinking world, a sure knowledge of that world and its workings was a vital prerequisite for survival.

However, in the early 1860s the choice for those desiring a Non-conformist education for their sons and daughters was severely limited. The only answer for many was to set up their own schools, and, in the case of schools for boys, this led to the founding of Taunton, Mill

Hill, Caterham, Bishop Stortford, Silcoates – and Tettenhall Proprietary School (later to be renamed Tettenhall College).

And so it was in 1862 that a small group of Congregationalists from Queen Street Church set wheels in motion to found a new Free Church School in the Wolverhampton area. By coincidence, the year 1862 was also the two-hundredth anniversary of the sacking, by King Charles II, of some two thousand Non-conformist ministers – an event that caused a lot of bitterness between the Anglican and Free Churches.

No minutes exist of the first meetings of Tettenhall Proprietary School's founders in 1862 and it is unclear exactly what was done, or who did what. We do know, however, who these founding fathers were, and we do know that they were all important and influential in Wolverhampton society. The school's first Chairman of the Board of Directors was Thomas Wilkinson Shaw, who was a merchant banker along with his brother E.D. Shaw, who was also a member of that first Board. Samuel Dickinson, another merchant was later to be Mayor of Wolverhampton; Thomas Bantock, who founded his family fortune by a contract for delivering the Great Western Railway Company's goods, and like Dickinson, also later served as Mayor. Next was S. Mander, who owned a prominent paint and varnish firm. The Reverend T.G. Horton, Minister at Queen Street, and the Reverend S.P. Carey of Waterloo Road Baptist Church also played a prominent part in the school's founding, as did Dr. R. W. Dale of Birmingham, E. T. Holden of Walsall, Samuel Morley of London, F. Keep of Birmingham, and Joseph Thompson of Manchester.

In 1863, the Midland Counties Proprietary School Company was founded with a declared share capital of twenty thousand pounds. As such, the company was a Joint Stock Company – a popular device in Britain of the nineteenth century – and it was evidently hoped that supporters of what would later be known as Tettenhall College would buy stock in the hope of being paid a dividend, should the school be successful in returning a profit. A joint stock company is a type of corporation or partnership. Certificates of ownership or stocks are issued by the company in return for each contribution, and the shareholders are free to transfer their ownership interest at any time by selling their stockholding to others. In Britain, and elsewhere, there are two kinds of Joint Stock Company. The private company (sometimes called an "unlisted company"), such as the Midland Counties Proprietary School Company, is one in which the shares are not offered for sale on the open market – the shares are usually only held by the Directors and Company Secretary, or by other private shareholders. The purpose of shareholding in such a company is to confer the financial protection of limited liability upon the owners since the shareholders are usually liable for any company debts that exceed the company's ability to pay. However, the limit of their liability only extends to the face value of their shareholding. This concept of limited liability largely accounts for the success of this form of business organization. Ordinary shares entitle the owner to a share in the company's net profit. This is calculated in the following way: the net profit is divided by the total number of owned shares, producing a notional value per share, known as a dividend. The individual's share of the profit is thus the dividend multiplied by the number of shares that they own. It seems that the College's founders were keen to follow the example of other schools in Britain that were also set up in this way, and, like those other institutions, the school's founders were also to discover many severe drawbacks along the way.

All this meant that the first major task of the Board of Directors was to find investors in the project. This proved to be a difficult task, and when the school eventually opened on 1st August 1863, only £5,225 worth of shares had been taken up. A year later £8,700 had been sold, and a year later still, when building began in earnest, £12,300 was the total promised. According to the shares register, shares were sold all over the country, but West Midlanders bought the majority. The largest individual contributor was John Crossley, a Halifax carpet manufacturer, who invested a thousand pounds. The Shaw brothers and S.S. Mander each invested £750. The majority of those who invested came from the merchant classes, although there were a handful of professional men, a few ministers of the Church, and one or two who described themselves simply as "Gentlemen."

On the face of it, there were an encouraging number of investors, but the amount invested fell short of the mark, and this was to be a harbinger of the school's insecure financial situation for many years to come. It must be noted that the school was not alone in its financial difficulties. Many other similar schools suffered from the same problem and many did not survive them. In the case of Tettenhall, however, it came very close to bankruptcy many times, but on every occasion what seemed like a miracle came along to save the day.

There is little doubt that fortune has smiled on the school many times during its history, but one factor that has always acted in its favour is the spirit of enthusiasm on the part of those involved. It is easy to suppose that the religious faith shared by those first Directors spilled over into school business in a way that kept everyone together and focused on the essential goal of providing an education for generations to come. And so it was in such a spirit of determination and faith in the rightness of the project that the first Directors pressed on and built the school, despite the financial shortfall.

On several occasions, the Board made clear the aims of the proposed school, and these were later clearly defined as follows: "…to provide a liberal education for the sons of Non-conformists, and others. First the pupils are subject to such a thorough mental discipline as may qualify them for any pursuit in future life, whether professional of commercial. Second… it is thought to secure for them that robust health which is so essential a condition of success, whether in study or in business. Third, the aim of the Directors and masters is the formation of good habits, the encouraging of right principles, and the awakening of generous and noble aspirations." These were definitely lofty aims, and it is to the school's good fortune that its founding fathers were the sort of men who had the ability and determination to make it all happen.

All self-respecting academies of learning in the nineteenth century needed dedicated premises, so the first major task facing the founders was to find a site for the school. The original intention had been to rent existing premises until a suitable site became available to buy and develop, and while the modern definition of Tettenhall College remains firmly founded in Tettenhall, it could easily have been founded elsewhere. As chance would have it though, a "Gentleman's Residence" that suited the school's requirements became available in Tettenhall and the Directors bought it for the sum of £3,700, and the institution we now know as "Tettenhall College" was born.

The house was an imposing Georgian residence with numerous outbuildings including a large barn situated on the site of what is now the Groundsman's Lodge. Of course, the house itself would later become the house occupied exclusively by the Headmaster, but in those days it stood in about six and a half acres of grounds including a large pear tree and further woodland that sloped down to a field near to what is now Henwood Road.

This meant that the Directors had plenty of land on which to build, and it is clear that their optimistic vision held no doubt that the school would flourish and grow. As it stood though, the house had numerous large rooms, suitable for classrooms, and there is little doubt that the proximity to the well-populated West Midlands, as well as the overall desirability of the village of Tettenhall, appealed to the founders. They were so delighted in acquiring the premises, that in their initial advertisement in the Wolverhampton Chronicle on 29th July 1863, they referred with enthusiasm to the school's site in "the picturesque and highly salubrious village of Tettenhall". The advertisement went on to say that the subjects taught at the school would include "all the usual branches of an English and Classical Education, together with the French language and the rudiments of Drawing and Vocal Music; besides which, regular instruction will be given in the Holy Scriptures and the elements of Natural, Moral and Social Science." "Chemistry in the laboratory" was, however, to be an optional extra.

The next task facing the Directors was the appointment of a Headmaster, since without a good Headmaster, the fledgling school would not last long. It has always been the figurehead of the Headmaster that has been instrumental in determining the school's fortunes, and whilst he would not necessarily be a shareholder or even a Director, he would occupy a position that many would see today as that of C.E.O., and he would be the visible face of the school to all its customers.

This meant that the Headmaster had to embody the ethos of the school, which meant he should be a Non-conformist man of the cloth, or at least someone with a devout belief in the need for a Non-conformist school. It was also important that the new Headmaster come with good references and be a man "of good standing." One candidate that stood out was the Reverend Robert Halley M.A., who was at the time the Principal of the Doveton Protestant College in Madras, India. He was anxious to return to England because of the poor health of his wife, and he readily accepted the Board's invitation to become the school's first Headmaster.

Robert Halley was the son of Dr. Halley – a man, who in 1835, had been invited to make an inspection of Caterham School. The young Robert had been born seven years previously in 1827 and came to Tettenhall at the age of 36. He had been educated partly by his father, and in later years at Totteridge School. A graduate of Coward College, London University, he took his M.A. in 1847, and spent a year at the University of Bonn. He became Professor of Literature in the Lancashire Independent College at the age of 23, shortly before he was ordained, and soon after he was appointed to Madras, spending seven years there before coming to Tettenhall.

And so, on 1st August 1863, Tettenhall Proprietary School first opened its gates. In those days, the school year was divided into two terms, each of twenty weeks beginning on 1st August and 1st February. There were fifteen boys, two of them sons of the Headmaster, and the remainder coming from eight other families. In addition to this, there was a cow, purchased for £24, whose task it was to supply boys with milk. Records show that the cow lasted three years before being sold. Whether she was replaced or not is unclear, but we do know that she was much loved by the early boys.

In those early days, the boys lived with the teaching staff in the building that later became the Headmaster's House, and today is known as the Old House. Numbers soon rose to 38 and one can only begin to imagine what those crowded conditions must have been like. However, a clear account of those days can be gleaned from the memoirs of Tom Edwards, one of those first fifteen boys: "The dormitories were the two rooms over the lawn," he writes. "Mr Frazer (a Scot, red bearded, took huge quantities of snuff) slept in the room between over the porch. Many times he must have pretended to be asleep (he used to snore horribly) when the occupants of the two opposite rooms desired to express their contempt of each other by means of a pillow fight or to catch spies with a booby trap.

"We rose at 6.30 and did half an hour's prep from 7.00 to 7.30. At 8 o'clock. We all had to call out our numbers; then the order came: 'Attention, eyes right, dress, right, half turn, by your left quick march,' and we all marched into breakfast – plenty of good, plain bread and butter, and excellent coffee. Half an hour's drill and half an hour's play followed before lessons began at 9.30 in the Barn, which had been converted into a classroom."

At the end of the day, when evening Prep was over, there would be Prayers in the barn, and then: "The custom was for the Headmaster to stand by his desk, wearing an old faded mortar board and a very short torn gown, while we filed out, the Head Boy going first and so on until the last small boy's turn came, each one shaking hands with Mr. Halley, then with Mr. Pommitz, who stood by the large slate, and, last of all, halting and giving the salute to old Sergeant Mortimer, who stood at the door. If any fellow did not salute smartly, he was immediately called back and made to salute again in a proper manner."

Edwards has much to say about Sergeant Mortimer, who was a great favourite among the boys. A Royal Marine pensioner, he must have been a most impressive figure with his navy blue uniform and silver buttons, his peaked cap and, for evening prayers in the barn schoolroom, his patent leather belt, sword straps and white gloves. He was, says Edwards, "a fine looking man with an honest open face, surrounded by old time Navy whiskers of a carroty colour."

Whilst the Directors had provided what were then ample facilities for a good physical education, there wasn't much in the way of organised games in those early days. However, those first boys had a great deal of fun from boxing, gymnastics, bird nesting, and playing cowboys in the wood. From time to time, boys from the village, with whom those of the school were often on bad terms, used to take the clothes of the College boys as they bathed, and this often led to many fights.

On Sundays, the boys went to Queen Street for morning service. They marched "in true military style, either two deep or formed fours with Sergeant in full uniform and wearing sword belt, walking abreast of the two or four leaders – all in perfect step and very smart, so slouching was most definitely not allowed. At the rear followed the Headmaster in cap and gown, and with him the other masters." On such journeys, all the boys wore mortarboards with black and velvet bands and distinguishing tassels for juniors, seniors, monitors, and those who had distinguished themselves in examination. There is no doubt that these processions did make an impression on local residents and one cannot help but conjecture how much this was contributing to laying the foundations of the school's present day reputation in the Wolverhampton area. Certainly, many accounts recall these Sunday processions by the College boys, so they must have done a lot to spread the word.

Despite the reminiscences of Tom Edwards, official accounts of that first year are scanty. Minutes of the Board of Directors do not begin until 1864, although we do know from other sources that the school was the subject of a lot of local hostility. It is said that some of the residents of Tettenhall took legal advice as to whether the school's opening could be prevented. One of the school's most ardent foes at this time was none other than Colonel Thorneycroft – the owner of the Towers, the school's next-door neighbour. In order to prevent annoyance to the Colonel, what is now the fives wall was built in 1864, ostensibly to be a screen, but later to become the site of "fives" – one of the school's best-loved informal sports. The game has also been known as hand-tennis and historically was often played between the buttresses of church buildings in England. Its name was derived from the slang expression

An artist's impression of Main School as it might have appeared around 1870

"a bunch of fives" (meaning a fist). The most popular versions played in England are traditionally Eton fives or Rugby fives, and the version played at Tettenhall is a variant of both Eton and Rugby fives in that the gloves used are thin (like in Rugby fives) and the ball is very much like that used for Eton fives. The fives court at Tettenhall is very much like that at Eton College, but slightly different court layout. It seems then that these early boys had invented their own variation of the fives game, so let this henceforth be known as "Tettenhall fives."

However, the fives wall was not the first development carried out by the Directors. In late 1863 and early 1864, the Gymnasium was built and equipped. In addition to this, a covered play shed was built (at the not inconsiderable cost of £384) on the site of what is now the Swimming Pool. All of this illustrates the desire of the Board of Directors to ensure the physical well being of those early boys – a priority not often found in schools of this period.

By 1864, the Directors had fixed upon "a medium rate" for fees (50 guineas a year for boys over fifteen) "calculated at once to ensure a large number of scholars, and at the same time maintain for the school a high standard of social respectability". The Directors' report goes on to say: "It is gratifying to the Board that they are enabled to announce that the important undertaking has been auspiciously inaugurated, makes satisfactory progress, and is now placed upon a foundation so stable and sure as with the Divine blessing to secure its certain and long continued prosperity."

"Income" said the Directors' report was "very nearly" sufficient to cover expenditure. "With a slight increase in the number of scholars, the School will no doubt begin to be remunerative." These words turned out to be prophetic, since it was the act of keeping numbers at the school up that would prove crucial in later years. There had been seventeen boys altogether in the first year; in the second the numbers rose to 32, and in 1865 to 38. Whilst this seems a large increase in percentage terms, the actual revenue generated, from a pure cash-flow point of view, was not sufficient when one bears in mind that only a fraction of the school's share capital had been taken up. At this time, the Secretary to the Board was a Rev. J. Watts, whose no doubt thankless task it was to travel all over the country persuading people either to buy shares in the school, or at least send their sons there.

However, it is clear from what Tom Edwards has to say, that none of these matters interfered with what he describes as four of the happiest years of his life. The accounts show too, that on May 24th in 1864, £6 5s 9d was spent on a trip to the Wrekin, and in November of the same year, 5s went on fireworks.

There were also regular walks to local villages and perhaps the most interesting of these was the walk to Albrighton. "When the number was comparatively small," writes Edwards, "we had a quaint custom called "christening" the new boys. It was done at a well near Albrighton. "Old Bob" (The Headmaster) used to put on his greeny-black cap and gown, with Sergeant Mortimer dressed on his uniform acting as whipper-in, and we were walked off over Kingswood Common to Albrighton. Arrived there. 'Old Bob' would take us into Tomkins' sweet shop and stand biscuits, toffee or bulls eyes, after which we all walked to St. Dunstan's well. It was over a small bridge or wall, near a pool and a church, in a field by the roadside. There the new boy had his face dipped three times into the well and he then became a fully fledged Tettenhallian."

CHAPTER 2

A GROWING SCHOOL

Headmaster: Reverend R. Halley

By the end of 1864, Tettenhall Proprietary School had 32 boys. However, the Board knew that this number was about to diminish due to the amount of boys leaving, and to attract more pupils they could not continue to provide a school in what was just an old house and a collection of outbuildings. This was balanced against the fact that share capital still had not all been sold and the risk of developing the school's building infrastructure had to be compared with the sheer cost of doing so.

Despite the risk of this delicate balancing act, the Directors decided to develop the school's facilities by creating new buildings. In February 1865, they accepted the tender of John Barnsley and Sons, Birmingham, for the first part of what was later to become known as Main School. At £4,288, it was the lowest of three tenders submitted. It had been the Board's intention to begin with one wing, and then proceed with a second several years later, thereby spreading out the cost over a long period. However, it soon became apparent that it would be necessary to build Main School in one go because it would be impossible for the school to function when only part of the proposed development had been completed.

And so, on 6th March 1865, building work began. To justify their decision to the shareholders, the Directors said that they "had the question forced upon them whether they could conduct the school in all respects satisfactorily without the whole of the buildings already designed, and were compelled to admit that not to go forward would be equivalent to seriously going backwards." No doubt the willingness of the builders to lend much of the money required for the work was also a contributing factor in the decision to press on with building. This notwithstanding, the builders carried out the work under the threat of penalty clauses in their contract that imposed fines of twenty-five pounds a week for non-completion. The architect for Main School was George Bidlake, who also built, among other things, town halls at Bilston, Pontypool and Oswestry. He also designed Queen Street Chapel in Wolverhampton and the Congregational Church at Tettenhall Wood.

While the building works were in progress the boys took full advantage of the many opportunities to create their own adventures. Tom Edwards tells us of the many feasts the boys enjoyed including rashers of bacon cooked on the sharpened end of a plasterer's lath, and the eggs boiled hard in an old tin can. These meals were often consumed in dens constructed from building materials. Climbing up the scaffolding was another popular pastime; one boy, clad only in a nightshirt, is said to have climbed at night to the top of the scaffolding and carved his initials on one of the rafters in the turret. Not surprisingly, no one has ever been up there to check this contention.

Despite this, the building works progressed rapidly and the centre left wing (as viewed from the playground) and the domestic wing were completed by the summer of 1866, and the remainder was completed in March of 1867. Main School was formally opened on April 16th of that year, and the total cost of it all, including the caretaker's lodge, was £16,769 14s 5d. The event was celebrated by a service in the Chapel followed by what the "Wolverhampton Chronicle" calls a "sumptuous" dinner in the new Dining Hall. The guests, who included Henry H. Fowler, later the first Lord Wolverhampton (Secretary to the Treasury, President of the Local Government Board and Secretary of State for India), heard speeches from T.W. Shaw, Dr. Halley, Samuel Morley, and a number of others. Many remember Mr. Halley's speech that evening on the subject of education. "All education," said Mr. Halley, "should be based on religion. Whether Minister or layman, it is the duty of the schoolmaster to exhibit and to excite personal holiness, to keep within the view of his pupils the great interests of eternity, and basing his own actions on Christian principle to teach them to do the same.

"Education has for its object not the imparting of particular facts and rules, but the calling forth of mental powers, the strengthening of the mind by exercise, the cultivation of its various faculties and the controlling of its wayward tendencies. We seek to train the mind; if I may so speak, to sharpen and to cleanse and to put into working order every part of the instrument, confident that it will do its work hereafter when supplied with raw material in the world's factory. I doubt not but that the doctor, the lawyer, the merchant's clerk will each learn his business better in its appropriate place than he could have done at school, but always on one condition – that he carries to his subsequent education a mind, well trained, active and vigorous."

The essence of Mr. Halley's speech was an attack on the idea of a utilitarian education, which can be defined as an education aimed at learning skills needed to earn a living. Mr. Halley clearly believed that it was more important instead to teach boys the essential skills that would enable them to live in contemporary society. He said: "We have not a number of empty bottles put before us to be filled; it is not our part to cram into the mind a given number of useful facts or a given series of useful rules; neither is any branch of education to be condemned because it cannot be adapted to the after-pursuits of the man. The whole purpose of education is to call forth the mental and the moral powers – to teach a boy to use the mental gifts with which his maker has endowed him – to cherish humility of spirit, earnestness of purpose, a right appreciation of the relations between the present and the future, between boyhood and manhood, between manhood and eternity."

While Mr. Halley saw the need for the boys to learn the Classics, he did not approve of the practice of teaching boys to compose either ancient Greek or Latin verse. To support this, he ordered that Mathematics should form as important a role in the school timetable as the Classics. He also recognised the increasing importance of science in education. He said: "It is a scandal when a man, well taught after the fashion of the education of his day, is ignorant of the first laws of nature, which govern the various functions of the bodily frame." The Headmaster ended his address with these words: "We propose to give a religious education, religious in its principles rather than in its dogmas – and education, so far as we shall have wisdom granted to discern it, of all the powers and faculties of the mind – to fit our boys not specially for professions or for commerce, but to take their place in the world, able to grasp whatever they may be called upon to study. We wish to see them grow up God-fearing men, liberal and yet with firm principles, loving right and truth, manly and independent – yet not eccentric in their independence, understanding what is due to themselves, but even more what is due to others, taking their full share in the world's business – citizens able to command the respect and confidence of their fellows – politicians, discerning what is wisest and best, and above all members of Christ's Church owing allegiance to Him, and refusing it to priests and emperors alike – owning neither civil nor ecclesiastical pretenders when they stand between the soul and its Maker."

It is clear from this that Mr. Halley held advanced views for the time. There are many educationalists today that hold similar views – indeed the basic principles propounded by Mr. Halley would continue to be a cornerstone for the school's principles of education for some time. Despite this though, Mr. Halley resigned as Headmaster just three years later. There are no records that clearly say why he resigned, although it is easy to suppose that it was mainly down to the myriad difficulties in founding a school. These problems included financial difficulties as well as the sheer burden of having to make such a new venture pay, both in terms of education standards and finance. It is possible also that the turmoil created by the erection of new buildings did not help matters either. It is unlikely that lack of academic achievement contributed to Mr. Halley's early departure since an independent examiner's report on the work of the school in June of 1868 was extremely favourable. However, the Director's report of 1870 did mention "unfavourable impressions prevailing among the parents," and the next year's report spoke of problems concerning the internal management of the school. This indicates that it was administrative and disciplinary matters, rather than academic shortcomings, that caused Mr. Halley to leave.

These "administrative and disciplinary" matters can be traced back to the year 1866, when the Directors made a report saying that only £15,000 of the hoped for £20,000 of share capital had been taken up. This meant that fees had to be raised by ten guineas to help make up the shortfall. In April of the same year, a new boy ran away, and in June a temporary teacher was dismissed because he had "ill used some of the boys and severely hurt one of them." In January of 1867, the school's secretary, the Reverend Watts, was told that he would have to go unless more shares were sold and more boys admitted. Mr. Mander, one of the Directors, urged drastic economies, including the reduction of salaries. In March the Secretary lost all of his salary, but was promised ten per cent of the value of all the shares he sold, and five per cent of the fees of all the boys he secured for the school. In their report of the same month, the Directors blamed the "depressed state of trade throughout the country" for the failure to recruit more boys than the 65 on roll at that time, although it is clear that the difficulties were as much internal as external.

In June of 1868 the Directors found themselves searching for ways of raising a mortgage to pay off the builders. Reports indicate that the cost of the building had considerably exceeded the amount originally estimated, and this caused the Directors to instruct the Headmaster to replace members of staff "to reduce the salaries as far as he may find possible without detracting from the efficiency of the teaching." In response to this, the Second Master and the Reverend Jackson were dismissed. Other income generating measures, such as the admission of Day Boarders and Day Boys, were passed by the Board, although they could not prevent numbers falling from 68 to 39, as recorded in the Directors' report of 1870. All of this must have been too much for Mr. Halley to bear, so he offered his resignation to the Board, who accepted it, in November of 1869.

Mr. Halley moved to Arundel in Sussex, where he remained for the rest of his life as Minister in charge of the Independent Church. He died on 24th February 1885, and is buried in Littlehampton cemetery. The Reverend Halley appears in the memoirs of Tom Edwards as a kindly, likable man – "Old Bob," they called him – and his wife "an exceedingly nice lady in the true sense of the word."

No word of thanks for Mr. Halley's services is recorded either in the minute books of the Board, or in the Directors' report for 1870. However, the same document does announce with great enthusiasm the appointment of a new headmaster. This indicates that blame for the "failure" of the school to generate profit for shareholders was at least in part laid at Mr. Halley's door, and it seems that the Directors were seeking to reassure the shareholders that the infusion of new blood would herald the introduction of a new more prosperous era.

CHAPTER 3

THE GOLDEN AGE

Headmaster: A. W. Young, Esq.

Following Mr. Halley's departure, things looked bleak. Many sources reveal that there were many that thought the school would have to be wound up after only seven years of life, although reading through several letters, it is clear that the indomitable spirit that has saved the day so many times for the College was no less prevalent in 1870 than it has been ever since. There was a massive debt owing to John Barnsley and Sons – the company that had built Main School; staffing levels were low, as was the number of boys – there were numerous other debts owing to suppliers and perhaps worse still, there was no Headmaster. Despite this, the Directors opted to press on regardless. Records reveal that they opted for a methodical approach to solving their many problems, and the first item on the agenda was to find a new Headmaster. There were no set criteria for Mr. Halley's successor, although it is clear that the Directors wanted a man with strong Non-conformist convictions, a strong record of academic achievement together with a dynamic personality to lead the school out of its troubles.

They found such a man "after careful inquiries in many quarters," and although several candidates were considered, one stood out head and shoulders above the others. That man was Alexander Waugh Young – who came from a staunch Presbyterian family and held a first class record of academic achievement, firstly from City of London School and later from University College, London, where he was awarded the Andrews Scholarship – the most important honour the university could bestow. After taking his degree, he was appointed a Fellow of University College. On leaving London he became Principal of the Coleraine Academical Institute in Northern Ireland, a post he filled with great distinction for ten years before moving to Tettenhall in 1870 at the age of 34. He brought with him impeccable testimonials from those who had taught him, as well as from those that knew of his teaching ability. His specialist subjects were Classics, Maths and Philosophy, and it is clear that the Directors were confident that he had the strong personality needed to turn the school's fortunes around.

Alexander Waugh Young Esq. M.A. (Headmaster 1870-1891)

The post of Headmaster had been advertised at a salary of £300 per annum, together with residence inclusive of rates, gas and coal. In addition to this, the Headmaster was to be paid a fee of £3 per annum for each boy in excess of fifty. However, it seems that Mr. Young displayed sufficient strength of character to negotiate with the Directors, and he ended up with a salary of £400 per annum plus all the other additions. His contract also contained a clause that made his continued employment "subject to continued existence of the school," which was clearly a reference to the College's dire financial plight.

Having obtained their new Headmaster, the Directors then turned their attention to this problem of the school's finances, or lack thereof. The expected £20,000 of share capital still had not been taken up, so the Directors decided to increase share capital to £30,000 and secure a mortgage to raise the money to pay off the builders, who by 1870 were more than anxious to be paid, and sent frequent deputations to siege the school gates demanding their money. Matron was also demanding more money, and asked for a salary of £50 per annum, plus one pound for each boy in excess of 70. However, the Directors turned this down, although they did offer a £5 bounty to any clergyman who could persuade a parent to send a boy to the school, and they also bought a pulpit for the Chapel, which was soon to be followed by an organ, which they bought for £78 in 1871. To save money, they decided to rent out the Headmaster's House for £60 a year. Of greater importance was £4,000 guarantee given to the bank by the Shaw brothers, Mander, Dickinson and Bantock – a guarantee not surrendered until 1882.

It wasn't long before the new Headmaster made his appraisal of the school in a formal report to the Board of Directors. Mr. Young was most critical of the appearance of many of the rooms, and the general unfinished state of much of the building. He deplored the lack of a proper cricket field, and most especially, the lack of any kind of scholarships that would encourage boys to stay longer. The Board promised to do what it could, and Messrs. T.W. Shaw and S.S. Mander each offered £30 a year for scholarships. During 1870, the Board introduced two important changes. They accepted the Reverend T.G. Horton's suggestion that the name of the school should be changed from the "Tettenhall Proprietary School" to "Tettenhall College," and they also agreed that in future, the school year should consist of three terms instead of two. These are two changes that have clearly stood the test of time since they are here to this day.

Despite his austere report of the state of the College, the Board was clearly pleased with the new Headmaster. In their report of 1871 they said "they could not speak too favourably of the present condition and internal management of the school. The new Headmaster had fully realised their expectations, and they deem it almost impossible that the general condition of any school can be more favourable." Despite this, there was still the problem of the builders, who persisted in their demands to be paid. There is no doubt that the Directors were anxious to solve this problem, but an attempt to secure a bank loan was unsuccessful, and any possibility of paying the monies out of share capital was not possible due to the slow uptake. It seems that the builders would have to be patient.

In October 1872, the Reverend P.P. Rowe, who in February of that year had been asked to take services in the Chapel at fifteen shillings a time, was appointed Secretary, and he at once set about his duties with a fanatical gleam in his eye. It is clear that he was chosen for his formidable personality and his uncanny ability to sniff out any inefficiency in the system. His economies did much to introduce some kind of financial stability to the newly renamed Tettenhall College, but there is little doubt that his many reforms proved unpopular with the domestic staff, whose budgets were viciously slashed.

It is clear to see from those early minutes that there was a more business-like air at Board meetings with the Reverend Rowe as Secretary. Minutes from this period record his sharp ability to cut through any waffle and press on to the next matter in hand. As far as the accounts were concerned, it is also clear to see that finances started to improve, although this was to be a gradual thing. In their 1871 report to the shareholders, the Directors had blamed the current depression in trade for the failure to get much of the £10,000 increase in capital taken up, although after a loss of £307 in the following year, they enthusiastically pointed out that this was the smallest annual loss yet sustained in the nine year history of Tettenhall College. The fact that "Tettenhall College" (as such) had only existed a few weeks obviously escaped the attention of all but a few, and the murmurings of approval silenced any naysayers.

To bolster up this contention, the Directors were keen to point out to shareholders that eleven out of sixteen boys had passed the Cambridge Local Examination, five of them with honours, and that parents were writing in praising "the high moral and gentlemanly tone, as well as the educational efficiency of the College." However, the long-suffering shareholders had to wait until March of 1873 before the number of boys increased from to 85 and the annual loss was reduced to £166. No doubt the increase in numbers was due in some small part to the fact that Mr. Young had brought a number of boys with him from Coleraine, although there is little doubt that the Rev. Rowe's many reforms and economies contributed greatly to the decreased loss. Eventually, in 1874, Tettenhall College made its first annual profit of £607, and achieved eighteen out of twenty passes in the Cambridge Local, six with honours.

But still the spectre of the unpaid builders loomed over the College. Efforts to raise money in sufficient quantities had failed – the Secretary had written some letters worthy of Dickens himself to many insurance companies in the hopes of gaining a mortgage, but all without success. All the Board could do was instruct the Secretary to pay the builders instalments from time to time with whatever small sums remained in the current account when all other expenses had been met.

In an effort to make things more and more efficient, Rev. Rowe continued to put pressure on domestic staff to make whatever economies they could. He sent strict instructions that less money should be spent on food, and Matron was instructed that half a pound of meat a day was ample for each boy. She was also advised to adopt "a system of estimating beforehand in relation to all articles of food, what amount would be necessary to supply the wants of each person, and then providing, as nearly as possible, that amount" – a fact that shows how inefficiently the domestic side had been run before Mr. Rowe's time. The Secretary was told by the Board *not* to mention luncheon on the invitations sent out for Speech Day, and Matron was instructed to provide on that occasion "a round of beef, and bread and cheese, and *nothing* more." Butchers were soon being invited to submit tenders for the supply of meat, and concern was being expressed once more at the consumption of beer. In this regard, Matron was instructed not to let the key of the barrel out of her possession. Such efforts produced results, and for several years, Mr. Rowe was able to point to a reduction in expenditure. In 1875 he claimed a saving of £300 over the previous year's expenses. It is possible though that at least some of this reduction had been down to a change of Matron in 1874.

Despite this, the Directors complained on two occasions in 1876 of increases in the amounts spent on food: meat and bread especially. Matron claimed that this was largely down to the custom of foraging, where boys would slip into the kitchen and help themselves. There are several records of the day that mention how wasteful the food situation was, and in particular, how low the quality of food was. One individual goes on record as saying: "the swill" he had seen carried from the College indicated "the most extravagant waste." This prompted the Board to instruct the Secretary in 1880 to write for meat tenders and accept the lowest. This may have been a factor that influenced several complaints about the food. One boy complained that there weren't always sufficient vegetables, and J.E. Few remembers the Headmaster inviting some of the seniors to join him in eating cold mutton, which a number of boys had complained was bad when served hot earlier in the day. Despite this though, there were some that considered the food "sufficient and well cooked without being fanciful."

Savings in expenditure were only part of the effort to establish financial stability at the College, and the main aim was to get more boys. To this end circulars were sent to delegates at Congregational Union conventions and advertisements were placed in many periodicals. There was even a proposal to hang a lithograph of the school made by a certain Dydipiski in railway waiting rooms. However, it is doubtful that such measures as these contributed much to the eventual increase in numbers at the College, which rose from 44 to 97 between 1871 and 1873, and then to 108 in 1877. There is much correspondence between individuals of the 1870s that clearly indicates that the good reputation of the College was rapidly spreading. This

Mr. Young, his family and servants, pictured outside the
Headmaster's House with Main School in the background.

was largely down to increasing level of academic achievement, as well as a vast improvement
in the school's ability to provide a "well-rounded education of good moral standing." This
was almost certainly a major factor in the school's improved ability to attract pupils, and
certainly bears out the then contemporary writer Sir Arthur Helps' contention in his book
Realmah (1868) that "nothing succeeds like success."

And so Tettenhall College entered into what the Jubilee edition of "The Tettenhallian" retrospectively calls the "Golden Age." During this period of Mr. Young's Headmastership there were some very good academic achievements. In 1870, R.F. Horton, one of the most brilliant scholars produced by the College, was placed first in the country in the junior section of the Cambridge Local examination, a result, of course for which Mr. Halley must be awarded at least some of the credit. In 1876 Allan Young, the Headmaster's cousin, was placed first in the country in the senior part of the examination. In 1877 W.I. Watson was first in Natural Philosophy; in 1878, A. Gunn achieved a similar distinction in Drawing and in 1888, E.E. Parrett was first in Music, being also the first boy from *any* school who had obtained full marks. In their Annual Report of 1886, the Directors reported that 7,000 candidates had sat the examination in that year, and that boys from the College had been placed fifth and twenty-fourth in Latin, twenty-first and twenty-ninth in Greek, fifteenth, twenty-fifth and fortieth in Religious Knowledge, twenty-sixth in English, twenty-ninth in Mathematics, thirty-ninth in Music, and first in Drawing.

Such remarkable results point clearly to the good Headmastership of Mr. Young, although mention must also be made of his team of supporting staff that were no less instrumental in the College's new-found academic success. Second Master, James Shaw, had come with Mr. Young from Coleraine, and he had gained first class honours in classics at London. He was also at the College for the better part of ten years. Robert Whitby, Paul Matthews and A.H. Summers – all Cambridge men – followed him as Second Master. Another member of staff who was much thought of was Henry Taylor, whose teaching of English so impressed his pupils that after his death, some of them endowed a prize.

During Mr. Young's tenure, discipline at the College was firm, and yet based on kindness and a genuine affection for the boys, together with an earnest desire for their moral welfare. "We youngsters," wrote one of his pupils, "were of course very much in awe of him. Why, I cannot say, as though he was a splendid disciplinarian, it was his kindliness that made the deepest impression upon me." Mr. Young was clearly an impressive figure of a man who looked every inch the Victorian Headmaster that he was. He established a strong tradition of telling the truth among his boys, and one of them later wrote that "it was very rare for boys not to own up to misdemeanours." Two boys of whose conduct he disapproved were expelled, and on both occasions he had the full backing of the Board. It is a testament to the amount of respect that Mr. Young commanded that the Board supported him in almost everything he did. In their annual report of 1877, his services were described as "INVALUABLE" (their capitals). In 1878 when Mr. Young announced his intention to marry, and his need for a stable and coach house, the Board immediately rented premises for him. It is no surprise therefore that Mr. Young was the first Headmaster to attend Directors' meetings, such was the respect he commanded.

However, a shadow fell over the Directors' table in 1876 when Mr. Young applied for the position of Headmaster of University College Schools London. One can imagine the Directors' collective sigh of relief when the application proved unsuccessful. No doubt there were many Board members that saw this as an object lesson not to take the Headmaster for granted.

Following hard on the heels of this was another crisis in the form of an epidemic of measles. This proved to be serious enough for the Board to rent premises in the village to house the sick in isolation. This scare prompted the Board to recommend to parents that they buy flannel garments for their boys.

Soon after this, the College's neighbour, Colonel Thorneycroft, complained of damage done to his roofs by boys climbing over them in search of lost balls. He usually followed each complaint with a bill for damages, although as relations improved, these became fewer and fewer as the years progressed. Despite these relatively minor problems though, the College's improved fortunes had allowed the Shareholders to hold some hope of receiving a dividend in the future. An official document served to remind them that "Tettenhall College does not exist so much for commercial success – although that is always strenuously aimed at – as for the sake of providing a RELIABLE school for the sons of Non-conformist gentlemen, in which the constant endeavour shall be to link the highest of education with manly energy and a religious life."

This was also the year when the Board succeeded in finally paying off the builders! It will be remembered that the Board had been paying for the construction of Main School in sporadic instalments, and by 1876 only £1,357 remained to be paid of the original total cost of £16,769 14s. 5d. One can only imagine the jubilation when the Board finally instructed Rev. Rowe to make out a cheque in full and final settlement.

In addition to this, the Board had (thanks to the energetic fundraising efforts of Rev. Rowe) managed to build a new covered playroom and, incredibly, a covered Swimming Pool at a total cost of £1,100. The Swimming Pool was the first of its kind in a British school and although it didn't have the benefit of a modern filtration plant, it was certainly a positive asset for attracting prospective parents, and especially those who wanted their boys to learn to swim. It is easy to imagine that the pool in its early days is much like it is today, but this is certainly not the case. It was little more than a crafted hole in the ground, and it was in fact a punishable offence at one time for boys to stir up the mud on the bottom. H.F. Straker remembers that one occasion when Mr. Young was showing some prospective parents around the school, the Headmaster proudly showed the visitors the pool, although to his certain embarrassment there was, written on the slime at the bottom: "This bath is dirty!"

It was also 1876 when Tettenhall College was examined by Professor Massie and H. Nesbitt, who awarded a most favourable report, in which the examination results of that year – 21 passes out of 26 – 8 with honours and 11 with distinction – stand out quite clearly. Moreover, the Headmaster had raised funds "free of expense to the company" to purchase

The Tettenhall College Swimming Pool around 1896 – one of the first
such pools to be offered at a British school.

a new organ for the Chapel. The new organ was a three manual model, and was bought at a
cost of £200, although £50 was received for the old one. This organ remained in use in the
Chapel until 1970, when it was replaced, through the good offices of Rev. J.L. Chown, by the
one in Waterloo Road Baptist Church – a building that was due to be demolished to make
way for the construction of the Wolverhampton Ring Road.

And so the College passed from strength to strength during its "Golden Age." The Board
described 1877, the following year, as "the most successful and encouraging year in the
educational history of the College," and emboldened by their new-found affluence, resolved,
at the request of Colonel Thorneycroft, to contribute one pound a year to the cost of a new
lamp post outside the Village Institute. This event is also notable as the beginning of more
cordial relations between the College and its neighbour Colonel Thorneycroft. It's clear
though that no one at the time could possibly have any idea as to how tremendously
significant to the fortunes of the College this positive turn of relations between the College
and its neighbour would make in the years to come.

The following year was a bad one for the West Midlands as a whole. The iron trade
suffered a great depression, so much so that Colonel Thorneycroft closed down the ironworks

that had made his family's fortune. Had this happened ten years earlier, the College might well have collapsed, but the great reputation enjoyed by the school under Mr. Young enabled it to weather the worst of the storm. In these early days, the fortunes of the College were very strongly geared to the fortunes of the local economy and numbers began to drop steadily from the peak of 108 in 1877 to 65 in 1885. Although they picked up again in the last few years of Mr. Young's administration, they never again reached the peak of 1877.

Despite this, the profit in March 1879 was the largest on record and the Directors were moved, in their annual report, to recollect how near to disaster the College had been in the year before Mr. Young had taken over as Headmaster. The report says: "At one period further endeavours after success appeared quite hopeless to many, perhaps indeed to all but some half dozen gentlemen who resolved to be faithful to the uttermost to the sacred cause your school was established to uphold and advance. In looking back, therefore, your *Directors* feel, along with thankfulness, some surprise that so much has been accomplished."

The significant thing is that although the bad state of the local economy caused numbers to fall, the College continued to make a profit, and this can only be attributed to the efficient administration of the Headmaster, and, of course to the zeal of Rev. Rowe, who continued his relentless reforms to the domestic side of the school with unbounded energy. In December 1879 he was inquiring into the large number of breakages, and the extravagance of the use of penholders. But Mr. Rowe's time was running out now, and in the beginning of 1882, when the Board sought to lay still more duties upon his already overburdened back, he felt moved to resign. No doubt he had upset a lot of people, but the College owes a great deal to the energy and ability of this extremely devoted man, who lent the word "zeal" a whole new meaning.

But Rev. Rowe's departure did not mean any relaxing of the policies he had put in place. Matron had to secure the special permission of the Board to buy some enamelled pie dishes and pudding bowls, and after a great deal of pressure, the washerwoman was forced to accept a reduction from one shilling per dozen articles to eleven pence for the washing she did for the College. Six years later she had the temerity to ask for an extra halfpenny, which she didn't get, and soon after resigned her post claiming ill health. Her successor had to be satisfied with nine pence a dozen. Even Matron's shoe account was tested and found to be unsatisfactory. Henceforth, the Board decreed she should keep a separate account for shoelaces. The new Secretary's request for an increase in salary was rejected, and when the College plumber offered to supply a ladder at nine pence a rung, his offer was rejected when it was discovered that seven pence a rung was the going price in Wolverhampton.

Even after his departure, it is clear that the spirit of Rev. Rowe lived on at Tettenhall, and it wasn't just the domestic staff that felt the economising lash of the Board's cutbacks. In 1888, the Directors discovered that both the water and ale accounts were considerably higher than previously, and the Secretary was instructed to examine all the water taps and to enquire if the masters drank beer at other times than with their meals. A full investigation was launched into the possibility that there was somewhere on the College grounds a "phantom beer drinker," although the culprit was never found.

Wherever possible, the Board sought to get discounts from firms for the goods they bought, and invariably the Secretary was instructed to write for tenders, and always accept the lowest. One evening during prep (which was usually held in Big School), the Headmaster appeared, and according to one Old Tettenhallian, said: "You boys are a set of walking bellies. You go down to the village, you guzzle and gorge, and fill yourselves with halfpenny buns, cream horns and vanilla slices, and you come back to school and turn up your noses at good wholesome food, which I eat, my wife eats, the matron eats and the masters eat, and you, forsooth, a set of miserable blackguards, complain."

But such policies served to give the College the financial stability it very much needed. In 1882, when the College threatened to secure a new mortgage from a different lender, the holders of the old mortgage reduced the interest rate to 4 per cent, and in the following two years the Board was able to invest £500 in Wolverhampton Corporation stock. It must also be mentioned that in 1880, Mr. Young had demonstrated his confidence in the College by buying a large number of shares. In the following year his confidence was vindicated by the excellent examination results in which Tettenhall College was the only school sitting for the Cambridge Locals that could show two boys with five distinctions each. H.L. Joseland was one of these and the other was A. Harden, who was later to win a Nobel Prize for Chemistry.

However, in the spring of 1883 an epidemic of diphtheria in which several boys died threatened to undo all the progress made to date. This forced the Board once more to rent a house in the village where the sick might be isolated. It is likely that the cause of the sickness was the College drainage system in which the main sewer – which was insufficiently ventilated – went under the school buildings. This meant that sewer gas tended to linger in the building, and this was made worse when a workman put a spade through one of the pipes. Despite the fact that the Board spent over £200 on putting the system right, it is easy to imagine the alarm of parents, some of whom took their sons away from the College. Whilst the exact reasons are not clear, some 16 boys were withdrawn, and the retrospective view is that such withdrawal was at least due in part to the diphtheria outbreak. It is easy to imagine that this crisis could have been a lot worse, and it is a testament to the school's improved reputation that this crisis could be endured without any lasting damage.

In 1886, after twenty-three years of financial struggling, the Midland Counties Proprietary School Company paid its first dividend to its long-suffering Shareholders. It paid out a modest 1¼ per cent, which cost the company only £250 but nevertheless was a great financial step forward. In the following six years the Board paid this same dividend, and in 1888 the company was able to pay off £2,000 of its £6,000 mortgage.

The only cloud on the horizon was dwindling numbers, and the Board tackled this problem in several ways. Rev. H.J. Heathcote was given the task of getting in touch with Non-conformist ministers in the big towns of Britain with the object of securing more boys. For each boy, the Minister would get two guineas and Heathcote would get one. In 1885 as many as 3,600 copies of the school prospectus were sent out, but in the following year, the Board was able to spend £138 on a Chemistry Laboratory and lecture room alongside the playground. In addition to this, the Board sent out a circular letter with dividend cheques asking shareholders to make an effort to secure more boys for the College. The obvious incentive for Shareholders to do this is contained in the letter's final paragraph, which says: "The Directors are strongly of opinion that if the Shareholders took the matter up they could very soon fill the school, and then the Directors would have no difficulty in speedily recommending larger annual dividends."

By 1887, numbers looked a little more optimistic, and the Directors determined to swell their numbers with more influential people that could only benefit the long-term future of the College.

The original Chemistry Laboratory in what later became the
Art Room facing the Playground.

CHAPTER 4

THE BANTOCK ERA BEGINS

Headmaster: A. W. Young, Esq.

In 1888, Albert Baldwin Bantock – the greatest benefactor Tettenhall College has ever known – was appointed to the school's Board of Directors. It must be remembered that one of the College's main aims was and still is "the formation of good habits, the encouraging of right principles, and the awakening of generous and noble aspirations..." and throughout a long and distinguished career, Mr. Bantock, like his father Thomas Bantock – one of the College's founding fathers – frequently preached the training of character as an essential aim of any school. The young Mr. Bantock joined the Board of Tettenhall College at the age of twenty-six, and at this time, he had been a partner in his family business, Thomas Bantock and Company, for two years. His father had founded the family haulage business from nothing, and believed strongly that he owed much of his success to a good education, which he received courtesy of his father's employer and patron, the Duke of Sutherland. It is fortunate that the young Baldwin Bantock shared his father's convictions about the benefits of a good education, since it was this belief that drove him to become a strong force in the ultimate survival of Tettenhall College.

Born in 1862, the year before the College was founded, Mr. Bantock was, of course, educated at Tettenhall College, and had gone on to became a partner in his father's business in 1886. Like his father, he was an active member of Queen Street Congregational Church (where he eventually became Senior Deacon) and took an interest in local politics from an early age. As well as his efforts for Tettenhall College, he also worked hard to found a school in Lea Road and for 17 years he was the Superintendent of the Sunday School at Lea Road Church.

College records about the young Mr. Bantock's academic achievements at school are scanty, but we do learn that he was a keen sportsman, especially at cricket and golf, and he "showed a shrewd interest everything and all those around him." Like his father, this "shrewd interest" led to Mr. Bantock becoming the representative of St James' Ward in 1900, and his eventual election as Mayor of Wolverhampton in 1905, again in 1906 and once again on the outbreak of war in 1914. This distinction of being elected Mayor of the town three

Alderman Albert Baldwin Bantock
(Chairman and member of the Governing Body 1888-1938)

times, and two of them in succession, is unique to Mr. Bantock and shows the high regard in which he was held by his fellow members of Wolverhampton Council. This is also reflected in the fact that he was also the Chairman of the Corporation Finance Committee for many years.

When his father died in July 1895, Mr. Bantock inherited his father's share of the family business along with the family home in Merridale, where it still stands, very much as it was in 1888, but now looked after by Wolverhampton Council to whom it was left in Trust by Bantock's wife. Despite the demands of a very busy life, Mr. Bantock remained a firm and active supporter of his old school, and his rise to become one of the most influential benefactors in the course of the College's history is legendary.

Several letters from this period recall Mr. Bantock's first impression of his old school the day he first re-entered the doors as a Director. He was much taken, it seems, by a large bowl of flowers; placed by order of the Headmaster in the main reception – a "spray of colour in what [is] otherwise a fairly dark hallway," he commented in a significant observation, since it was later to be Mr. Bantock's generosity and drive that would light the College's path through some very dark times in the years ahead.

The year that Mr. Bantock joined the Board of Tettenhall College is also significant in the school's history because it was also the year when the school magazine "The Tettenhallian" was founded. There is little doubt that the book you now hold in your hands would not have been possible without the detailed and often witty observations contained in the numerous editions of this magazine. Having read this far, there might be those that would consider this no small loss, but there is absolutely no doubt that a strong factor in the College's continued survival has had its roots in the school's strong connection with its past. As will be seen in the troubled years to come, there were to be occasions in the not too distant future when the only things separating the College from certain destruction were the decades of colourful history propping it up, and the strong desire among the College's members to make those years live on well into the future.

But the founders of the school magazine surely could not be aware of all this back in the heady days of 1888. Like the College's beginnings, no one can really point to any single event that precipitated the birth of "The Tettenhallian," although if anyone can be deemed to be the "father" of "The Tettenhallian", it would be A.H. Summers, who suggested that one of the other boys at the College should write an article recording a particularly memorable rugger victory over the Wolverhampton Grammar School. In those days, hardly any self-respecting public school would consider playing anything but rugby, and it has long been thought that the reason why the Grammar School gave up rugby in favour of soccer was down to their continued humiliating defeats at the hands of Tettenhall College. Consequently, A.H. Summers felt that this particular drubbing of the Colleges' archrivals needed to be recorded for posterity. The fact that later generations of Tettenhallians could use these lovingly detailed records to wave in the face of the Grammar School clearly could not have entered his mind.

And so it was in February of that year that the first pale green issue of "The Tettenhallian" rolled off the presses to a small but enthusiastic audience of Tettenhallians. It is disappointing that history does not record whether any complimentary copies were sent to the Grammar School, although one can image that by now that that particular educational establishment was pretty much used to being defeated by the College and having their nose rubbed in it. In any event, that first issue of the magazine states proudly: "A School without its records is like a nation without its history, and it is in the pages of the magazine that will be found the records of the school." In addition to these notable "records" though, that first issue contained articles on games, a very amusing item on the Norfolk Broads, a very insightful piece of journalism on the ins and outs of commercial education and numerous puzzles and pastimes including a particularly tricky chess problem – courtesy of the newly formed Chess Club. For many years, "The Tettenhallian" was published twice per term, making six issues per year in total.

Rather than be a "company report" type magazine with articles from all department heads brimming with facts and figures, those early editions of the school periodical contained an eclectic mix of articles that range from accounts of everyday life at the College to creative writing (including poetry), as well as various other literary forms. Very often, the more informative side of the magazine would give accounts of amusing anecdotes from school life – often told with a large dollop of relish. A popular subject was the Saturday night entertainment for the boys, and notable events from those early days were the frequent visits from a Mr. Stanley who gave recitations, and also from Professor Evansio who was a conjurer and ventriloquist. There were transcriptions and articles about songs sung around the piano, together with lovingly written reviews of sketch shows produced in Big School. In the days when entertainment was almost always live and very often improvised, one can imagine the satisfaction that these early "Tettenhallian" journalists had when regaling their audience with the inventiveness and variety that often resulted.

In 1888, Jack the Ripper had claimed his first victims in London's smoggy streets, John Logie Baird, the inventor of the television, was born (as was T.S. Eliot), Vincent van Gogh cut off his left ear, and everyone in Britain was obsessed with cycling. Ever since the first recorded appearance of the penny-farthing bicycle in 1870, the sport had fallen just short of a national obsession, and those early Tettenhallians were certainly not immune to this. A keen Bicycle Club had been formed, and its numerous exploits appear in detail in these early editions of the school magazine. This is probably because of the high level of accidents experienced by those early cycling pioneers, and stories of accident and misfortune were no less popular among the reading public then than they are today. The club was equipped with six "ordinary" penny-farthings, one "safety" and one tandem version of the vehicle. One account records the perilous journey made to Birmingham on one of the "ordinaries," with all the attendant perils of negotiating cable, steam and horse tram lines. B. Seth-Smith recounts his first ride on a penny-farthing down the slope of the playground (now the car park). This was obviously an ill-advised downhill journey, since by his own admission Seth-Smith didn't know how to stop the thing. The result was a "white knuckle" ride down the length of the playground, followed by a headlong flight (*sans* bicycle) into a conveniently placed pile of ashes. All of this, of course, was to the great amusement of all those present, and subsequently to the readership of the school magazine. There are many letters of the time that recount huddles of boys around a copy of the school magazine "having a good chortle."

All of this gives a valuable insight into these inner workings of life at Tettenhall College in ways that a detailed study of the Directors' minutes cannot. "The Tettenhallian" was not only a wonderful vehicle for recording daily life, but also a good insight into the personalities that guided the school through what later proved to be some very turbulent times.

Times were indeed good in 1888, or at least so the people at the College thought. Despite the advances of the Industrial Revolution, there was still in England a palpable feeling of the country's rustic past, even in those closing years of the nineteenth century. This was a time when nature rambles were eagerly anticipated outings, and simple toys like the hoop & stick and the whip & top could give hours of fun. To keep a top or hoop spinning required much dedication, dexterity and commitment to the task in hand, so it is easy to see the benefits of such a seemingly simple pastime. The same could also be said for many of the myriad other activities promoted by the College, and this idea that "living skills" were just as important as the three "R"s was indeed rare and innovative thinking at that time. To our eyes, these people lived unsophisticated lives, but it must be remembered that for all their lack of comparative technological advancement, the Tettenhallians of 1888 were very aware of all of the realities of the world around them, and without Tettenhall College they would not have received the moral fortitude to survive the seemingly inimical world outside the College's gates.

There are many accounts of the school's annual outing to Sutton Park, several of which appear in the pages of "The Tettenhallian," along with energetic accounts of the special swimming sports provided for those who were unable to go home during the spring term break. These latter events involved many things, but the one that stands out is the event that involved scrambling along a greasy pole suspended over the swimming pool with the intention of reaching a bottle of sweets fastened onto the end of a pole. The magazine praises those boys that managed to reach the bottle of sweets, and it also pokes dry amusement at the many that fell into the pool's dark and murky depths. Accounts of the various nature rambles at Sutton Park, recount Mr. Young's knowledge and love of nature, and it seems that his knowledge of British flowers and fauna was accordingly impressive.

Those editions of the magazine also speak of the somewhat sinister-sounding "Exalted Order of St. Barnabas". The Order doesn't seem to have done much apart from indulging in an initiation ceremony involving a great deal of Latin, a rather frightening rite involving bloodletting, and the swallowing of an unspeakable draught of nausea-creating ingredients. Unfortunately, one Grand Master left with all the documents of the Exalted Order of St. Barnabas, and so the order rapidly dissolved. Not surprisingly, the College authorities officially discouraged such practices, although many private letters do recount other similar unofficial schoolboy "orders," the nature of which has been sadly lost.

During these years a tradition grew up of boys who were soon due to leave holding a dinner for all their colleagues, although this was soon prohibited due to the extravagant nature that these events eventually became. At roughly the same time, "The Tettenhallian" recalls with great dismay the outlawing of the practice of sliding down the school banisters – a practice still thoroughly discouraged to this day.

Even in these early days, the College was an excellent place to go if one liked sport. As a mirror of school culture, the early issues of "The Tettenhallian" were no less keen to talk about the subject than every issue that followed them. In those days, sporting activities were held on the cricket ground, which was a field rented for the purpose by the College, since the premises at the time didn't have sufficient or suitable grounds where boys could play sports like cricket or rugby. It seems that those occasions were considered fun events that involved the College's newest supporter, Colonel Thorneycroft, as referee. For quite a long time the Colonel had been an ardent opponent of the school, often writing blistering letters to the Express & Star and occasionally instructing his lawyers to take action over even the most trivial issues. Long letters of complaint to the Headmaster were commonplace, and the events that led to the Colonel becoming a firm friend of the College are sadly lost to time, but the evidence available suggests strongly that it was the Headmaster's insistence that the Colonel be invited to join in with the school's sporting activities that at least went some way to creating the strong bond of friendship that would later, after the Colonel's death, have massive positive effects on the fortunes of Tettenhall College.

There is no doubt that the Tettenhallians of 1888 had no idea that they were setting the foundations for their school's continued existence, and all they wanted was to enjoy their sport in an atmosphere of harmony. Colonel Thorneycroft obviously had no trouble burying the hatchet so that he could accept the College's invitation to referee their cricket matches, and "The Tettenhallian" records his "robust sense of humour and unswerving love of fair play." These sporting events were presided over by the Headmaster's wife, who took delight in presenting the prizes. These were the days when Tettenhallians were proud to clear a mile in five minutes twenty-two seconds, and one boy even managed to swim three lengths underwater in the school pool – an impressive feat of endurance considering the water's "thick, green and murky consistency" back then.

Tug 'O War contests were popular, and it seems that the two teams taking part in these events usually consisted of the "Classicals" and the "Moderns." Whilst there was usually a prize for the winning team, the losers often suffered the humiliation of being thrown in the swimming pool fully clothed. No doubt the presence of a large number of boys in the pool all at once all caused the mud at the bottom to be stirred up, and no doubt the appropriate punishment was accordingly dished out. Modern sensibilities would probably frown on the official endorsement of such practices, but in those days of the late Industrial Revolution, society was undergoing massive change, and commercial competition (either within Britain, or with her foreign economic competitors) was fierce. The practice of the Tug 'O War instilled in boys the sense of necessity of working together toward a common aim, and the need to prevail – failure to do this often meant destruction, and the motive to "come out on top" with no credence for second place was considered a prime requisite for survival in late Victorian society.

This meant that sport at the College was hugely popular, both with staff and boys alike. There were the usual staples of cricket and rugger, although the latter was played with slightly different rules to those in force today. Points were awarded not only for goals and tries, but also for "minors." These latter were points awarded when the opposing side was forced to touch down behind its own lines, and only counted in some "Cup" matches when the two teams were level in points for tries and goals. This often led to a much tenser match with less likelihood of a draw. Again, the need for a clear-cut winner in sport was far more pronounced than perhaps it is today where the philosophy sometimes prevails that the "taking part" is more important than the "winning."

And it was not just sport that thrived – there were many other character-building activities to choose from. One Old Tettenhallian recalls in later years: "…perhaps I didn't learn a great deal from books there, but I could make a boat as well as any in the School." It is interesting to note that this boy went on to become a marine engineer of considerable note. This emphasis on vocational pastimes was true of many of the school's large array of activities, which ranged from bird nesting to stamp collecting. Whilst the importance of schoolroom learning was never neglected, it was always important to round off these activities with things that encouraged an enquiring mind about life and society in general. This included many excursions aimed at giving the boys a "hands-on" experience of life in the "real world" above and beyond what could be taught in the classroom. This is no less a priority at the College now than it was in those early days. However, in the nineteenth century, the idea of opting out of such activities was severely frowned on, and this practice now known as "goofing off" frequently received the lash of "The Tettenhallian's" literary whip. The December 1888 edition said of pupils shirking organised activities on half-term Monday: "…a good number went on the usual excursions while some, far more than there ought to be, adopted the feeble plan of loitering about the College, a most reprehensible and lazy habit."

"The Tettenhallian" in those days was a great deal more outspoken than it has become of late. In those days, the magazine was not only a mirror of school life and culture, but also an effective commentator on it. Under the pitiless glare of "The Tettenhallian," few members of the school dared give any less than their best. This was as much the case for staff as it was for pupils, and whilst many might have considered this a breach of discipline, the opinions of the magazine were tolerated because it was easy to see that the publication formed a useful forum for feedback, as well as a vital "safety valve" that allowed both staff and boys alike to air any problems without the risk of permanent damage to relations. A good case in point is the occasion when the College had hired some professional cricket coaches. The Tettenhallian said of one that: "if he did little harm, he certainly did no good." After this, the cricket coaches were removed and replaced with ones that eventually pleased "The Tettenhallian."

Scathing reports in "The Tettenhallian" were commonplace, but only when warranted. "Cricket Characters" for 1889, for example, describe one cricketer as "a flukey bat and weak field," and another as "a very nervous bat; bowls well now and then, should keep his eyes open in the field more." Likewise, poorly organised or otherwise unsuccessful outings were criticised, as was the perennial issue of the quality of school food – or rather, the lack of quality. One supposes that "The Tettenhallian" allowed these issues to be properly addressed without the all too frequent recourse of sweeping them under the carpet, and it is likely that this is one of the many reasons why the College survives to this day.

The school magazine was not just a parochial version of "Punch" though. It also served as a vehicle for boys to recount much-loved stories of their life at the College, many of which would long since be lost if not for "The Tettenhallian." H, F. Straker tells us of many incidents of "derring-do" that took place at the school. "I remember one winter we had a long spell of cold weather, and skating lasted for six weeks," recounts Straker. "When on several days boys fell through the ice, Mr. Young announced that the next one to do it would have to go straight to bed for the rest of the day. After that, immersions became a daily occurrence among a certain set of biggish boys in the second and third forms. One afternoon skating on a pond near the College, the ice was so good that I stayed until the very last moment. I noticed a group of these Lower School boys retire behind some bushes and skated up to see what they were doing. I found that they were breaking the ice on an old hole that had been lightly frozen over, after which they lowered into it up to his armpits, the boy who claimed that it was his turn. As I was not then a monitor, I did not interfere. Soon afterwards Mr. Young

THE BANTOCK ERA BEGINS

gave out that the next boy to fall in would receive a caning or a thousand lines and NOT be sent to bed. No further accidents occurred after the announcement."

There is no doubt that many of these lovingly related tales were the result of the memorable and profound effect that College life was having on the boys of the day. Up until Mr. Young's last year, there were many recorded incidents of Old Tettenhallians returning to their old school to try and recapture some of the flavour of their youth, and, one supposes, to try to gain some comfort from memories of a less complicated phase of their lives. Eventually, this practice reached the stage where the Headmaster had to order Matron to prepare permanent quarters for returning Old Boys so that they would at least still feel part of the "family". It is no surprise therefore that in Mr. Young's final years, continued pressure from "The Tettenhallian", in the form of reports of the progress of Old Tettenhallians, eventually resulted in the formation of The Old Tettenhallian's Club. This was no doubt an obvious progression in the eyes of those involved, but one that was later to prove a tremendously significant factor in the College's continued survival. As will later be seen, it was the continued awareness of the College's fates on the part of the Old Boys that often allowed them to step in and help wherever they could. Without The Old Tettenhallians Club, the school may well have capitulated long ago. Of course, the College's Old Boys had met informally long before the O.T.s Club was officially recognised, but one can see 1888 as the year when efforts became properly focused.

It followed then that The Old Tettenhallians (often abbreviated to O.Ts) Club decided to produce its own magazine, called, not surprisingly, "The Old Tettenhallian", which took a lot of pressure off "The Tettenhallian" when reporting the achievements of the ever-growing number of the school's Old Boys. In Mr. Young's last years there had been a steady flow of news – of university successes and within the professions. We hear of W.M. Stevens winning the University College, London's gold medals for Physiology and Anatomy, and of equal distinction being won by Arthur Harden and the Reverend R.F. Horton. There's F.W. Simon, the architect of the Edinburgh Exhibition, and J. Lloyd-Morgan elected Liberal M.P. for West Carmarthenshire in 1889, and later to become a County Court Judge. We hear too, of E.E. Shaw and Dr. H. Taylor, missionaries in Africa and China respectively. And there are sporting achievements too, County Caps for rugger, a "Blue" for lacrosse won by L.W. Grenville at Cambridge, and a number of skating records broken by C.G. Tebbut. There is no doubt that hearing of the successes of one's peers drove Old Tettenhallians on to further successes and this helped maintain the College's atmosphere of "friendly competition" long after pupils had left to take up positions in society.

The year 1889 saw the first of the O.T. Dinners, which have been held annually ever since. Growing numbers have often forced the event to be held off the school premises, but in those early days, there was ample room in the Dining Hall. However, that first menu was indeed a sumptuous affair and consisted of an appetiser of oysters followed by a choice of either clear oxtail or tomato soup. Then came the fish course, again with a choice between salmon and hollandaise sauce, or turbot with lobster sauce. The entrees consisted of sweetbread and mushrooms, or pigeons and truffles, with the "remove" course as a choice between roast lamb, braised beef or spring chicken and asparagus. There then followed a wide choice of extravagant sweets comprising the rather cryptically named "ice" pudding, clear jelly (obviously for those with little room left), orange cream, or Swiss pastry. All of this was washed down with several wines including Champagne, still hock and claret. Finally the feast was rounded off with caviar, cheese soufflé, coffee and the inevitable cigars – no doubt with a choice of liqueur or Cognac. One almost senses that the sumptuousness of this feast was at least a subconscious reaction to the poor standard of College food that those early Tettenhallians must have endured.

Clearly the College's Old Boys thought enough about their old school to lavish such a feast in the College's honour. It was, no doubt, a throwback to the sumptuous leaving dinners held up until only a year before, and a testament to the continued support the Old Boys have given the College over the years. Old Boys' dinners are no less lavish today than they were in Victorian times, and whilst much of the richness of the food has now been toned down in the interests of modern health awareness, the flavour of these events remains no less pungent.

But times were soon to change. Two years later in April 1891, Mr. Young announced his retirement as Headmaster and whilst he was still (even by the standards of the day) relatively young at fifty-five, he had served twenty-one years at Tettenhall, and undoubtedly these years had taken their toll. During this time, the number of boys had peaked at 108, although by 1891, this had slipped to 70. As has previously been mentioned, society of the day was undergoing rapid change following the technological leaps precipitated by the Industrial Revolution, and it must have become clear to Mr. Young that the school needed new blood that was, perhaps, more in tune with ever-changing times. This does not detract in any way from Mr. Young's marvellous achievements as Headmaster though. The good state the school was in by 1889 is ample testament to the wonderful job he did of quite literally putting Tettenhall College on the map. The school was well established financially, and in the year of Mr. Young's retirement, the College paid the sixth, and as it turned out to be, the last, of its dividends to the Shareholders.

In his last term, G.E. Hodgson won his Open Scholarship to St. Catharine's College, Cambridge – an event that is representative of the great academic successes enjoyed during Mr. Young's time. The confidence of directors in Mr. Young is proven by the way in which, as the years went by, they had increasingly left matters to him. Accounts of his Headmastership were legion, and throughout most of them, there is ample evidence that this "giant of a man" enjoyed genuine affection from all those around him, staff and boys alike. Many boys remember his heavy tread through the dormitories late at night to check on his charges, whilst many members of staff remember his genuine concern that they were getting fulfilment from their jobs by ensuring their skills were utilised to the full.

But what impressed Mr. Young's pupils, his Directors, and all who came in contact with him, was his powerful desire to do good. This factor is more than adequately expressed in an address given by Samuel Dickinson (then chairman of the Directors) in the former Headmaster's honour some years after his retirement. This address spoke of "…the enthusiasm and interest with which you invested subjects often made very dry, by moral tone of your government, and by the manly spirit which you infused into the whole life of the school, it was raised into a high position and you have trained and inspired large numbers of men, who, we believe, are exerting a strong influence on righteousness in their various walks of life in different parts of the world."

Mr. Dickinson went on to say that Mr. Young had successfully lived up to the school's creed of "providing an education to provide boys with the skills to live in the world of the present" by broadening the curriculum to encompass the newer and increasingly important disciplines of science; and perhaps more importantly, he had created a school where Old Boys "…look back to your influence with reverence and thankfulness." Indeed, a fitting accolade for a Headmaster that had steered the College out of very troubled waters into a new era of strength.

From Tettenhall College, Mr. Young retired to Edinburgh where, after twenty-four years of retirement, he died on Saturday, 23rd January 1915. He was, says Rev. Charles Salmond, "…a scholar, but he carried his attainments and acquisitions as lightly as a flower."

CHAPTER 5

THE "NINETIES"

Headmaster: J.H. Haydon, Esq.

Apersonal letter by one of the Directors of 1891 to a friend spoke of the "large hiatus" left behind for Mr. Young's successor to fill. True indeed, but clearly the Board felt that there was a man out there capable of doing this. The outgoing Headmaster had asked to assist in the choice of his successor, and one would like to think that it was in no small part down to Mr. Young's wisdom that the Board unanimously chose John Hampton Haydon as the next Headmaster of Tettenhall College.

It is with more than a hint of historical coincidence that Mr. Haydon was born in the year the College was founded, and this happenstance is further compounded by the fact that Mr. Haydon's name lives on with the College right up to the present day with the founding of Haydon House in this Headmaster's honour, many years after his departure. This means that on the day that Mr. Haydon first came striding purposefully through what is now known as the Quadrangle, he was just twenty-eight years old and the youngest Headmaster appointed at the College to date.

By all accounts, Mr. Haydon was a venerable scholar. Educated at St. Paul's, he went on from there to King's College, Cambridge; and there in part one of the Classical Tripos, he not only secured First Class Honours, but headed the division with one other candidate. Upon arrival at Tettenhall, he showed no less drive, discipline and energy than his predecessor. Judging from letters written about him, mostly by boys from this period, he displayed a "dignity of his bearing" and it seems that boys had "a very wholesome respect" for him. It is likely that this is mostly down to the fact that he enjoyed a firm reputation for justice, and all accounts are unanimous in the view that he was a wonderful teacher. Some eye trouble prevented him from taking Part Two of the Classical Tripos, but on moving to London University he won a gold medal for Classics, before taking his M.A. there. Subsequently he took his M.A. again, this time in Modern Languages (French and German). From London he went, as Senior Classics Master, to the Leys School in Cambridge.

A keen athlete, cricketer and hockey player, he claimed in his letter of application to

John Hampden Haydon Esq., M.A. (Headmaster 1891-1905)

Tettenhall College that during five years at the Leys School he had not missed a day's work through illness – a factor that he put down to his athletic prowess. That letter of application also tells of his offer to join the Congregational Church – he said, "I am a Wesleyan [and] the great majority of the boys at the College are of Congregational origin, [so] I should regard it as my duty to join that church in order to be of the same persuasion as those committed to my charge."

There is no doubt that Mr. Haydon's predecessor had left on a high note, so Mr. Haydon inherited the Headmastership during what many describe as a "Golden Age". However, as time progressed, the school's Board of Directors suffered from periodic bouts of non-attendance, down largely to the fact that many Board members were playing an active part in the Local Government of Wolverhampton, and it is likely that many of them gave these duties priority over the College. By this time also, many of the school's original founders had moved on or died, and the perfunctory nature of Board minutes for this late nineteenth century period suggests that the College badly missed the drive and enthusiasm of these men. Of course, there were many new supporters of the school, but the lack of any kind of financial endowment made sure that this support was in spirit more than in sound financial backing. All of this meant that the College needed to maintain a large number of boys to remain solvent; and during the times when numbers dwindled, there was no financial backup to compensate for the shortfall in income. This, in turn, led to an accumulation of debt, which forced the Directors to impose budgetary cutbacks. This is all set against the backdrop of greater government expenditure on State Secondary Education, which of course left Tettenhall College, as a completely independent entity, struggling to compete.

However, in their report of 1893, the Board indicated their pleasure in Mr. Haydon's abilities as a Headmaster. By this time, Mr. Haydon had settled into the Headmaster's chair very well, and the Board recognised this by saying: "…we are much gratified… to state that the change made has been a great advantage to the school. Mr. Haydon has thrown great energy into the management of the institution, and his great ability and tact have brought the school into a most efficient state." Whilst many would see this as an implied slur on the achievements of Mr. Young, it must be remembered that the Board were concerned less about praising past achievements and more about convincing the shareholders that their money was being used wisely and in a way that might yield long-term benefits. This notwithstanding though, numbers did fall to 70 in 1891 and 55 in 1893, and this may have been down to a fall in confidence in the wake of Mr. Young's departure, but it is more likely to be due to what the directors dubbed a "general depression in trade". At this time, the College drew its numbers from the new business classes mostly in the West Midlands, and when this sector of society suffered a depression, then so too did Tettenhall College. All this meant that despite Mr. Haydon's best efforts, the fall in numbers led to the College's first financial deficit for many years. This caused considerable panic among Board members, although the actual loss of £48 on the year's working would have been seen as a success by earlier Boards.

All kinds of ideas to bolster up the College's overstretched finances were mooted, and many were attempted. Earlier proposals to repair the chimneys were scrapped, as was the plan to carry out remedial work to the main building's leaky roof. Attempts to reduce the College's tax liability proved unsuccessful, as did those to raise money by charitable donations. Despite this though, as Mr. Young became more of a distant memory, the numbers began to rise. There were 55 boys in 1893 and a high of 120 in 1897 – a figure not surpassed until as late as 1918.

There is little doubt that much of this increase in numbers owed much to the hard work of the newly appointed Mr. Haydon, although mention must also be made of the new Secretary to the Directors – Rev. A. Thompson – who, according to Board minutes, travelled the length and breadth of the country to find new pupils. These trips often proved expensive to the College, but the long-term results speak for themselves. In each town, the Secretary would try to get in touch with the resident Congregational and Baptist minister to enlist their support. To our eyes, this really just seems like a perfectly justifiable attempt to market the College, but to Victorian morals, many considered this idea of "touting for business" as "just not the way decent businesses were run." However, the times were rapidly changing and to the new post-mercantile middle classes, the practice of raising awareness of a service such as Tettenhall College offered was seen by many Non-conformists as a godsend, since there were precious few schools where they could send their sons in the assurance that the letter of their spiritual needs were catered for.

These efforts eventually yielded fruit by easing the College's somewhat viscous cash-flow, and this was also due to the Board's continued determination to keep costs down by driving hard bargains with suppliers. This latter measure, however, didn't prove too popular with Matron and other support staff. Every contract was sent out to tender, including even haircutting! A tender for coal was accepted when the supplier's offer of a fifteen per cent discount for quarterly settlement was improved to twenty-five per cent for monthly settlement. An estimate for match-boarding the Red Corridor was considered too high at £10 4s, and the carpenter had to reduce it to £9 18s 6d so as to get the job. When new blankets were needed, the Secretary was told to send a sample blanket to a number of firms and accept the lowest tender. Very often, these tenders would be decided on as little a quarter of a percent difference, on the assumption, obviously, that every little saving helps.

The Secretary on one occasion delayed paying the Headmaster's gas bill on the grounds that it was twenty-five per cent higher than the previous year. All of these domestic cuts fell more heavily on the supply staff though. Matron was always being taken to task if there was ever anything more than a slight increase in costs over the previous years. The Board insisted on scrutinising all non-essential outgoings. However, all orders needed to be in writing and countersigned by either the secretary, the Headmaster, or by Matron.

All this meant a lowering in the quality of meals at the College, not that it was particularly high in the first place. Firsthand accounts describe the food as "rough," although there were some that, surprisingly, said that there just wasn't enough to go round. "The porridge was usually lumpy," writes one boy. "I remember, and the eggs were not edible, and certainly not new laid." All this meant that the boys were forced to supplement their diet in various ways. The practice of "cogging" or "bagging" scraps of toast from the masters' table was one such foraging method, as was scrumping fruit from various trees in the area, much to the chagrin of local residents. These raids were described in detail by many boys of the day, and accounts of foraging parties raiding neighbour's gardens for gooseberries, apples and pears were the most popular. Needless to say that those caught or forced to own up to such activities were punished with the ubiquitous "six of the best."

Those boys with the resources could afford to take advantage of the baker's shop in the village. It seems that the buns and pork pies were the most popular fare from this establishment, although many speak highly of the cakes and fresh bread. Some boys claimed that these dietary supplements enabled them to achieve better academic and sporting achievements, although the veracity of these claims is often doubtful. However, there is little doubt that the long hikes to country pubs for "chops and steaks, tomato sauce, omelette, etc." during half-term breaks was an event to be looked forward to, as was the once-a-term dormitory feast that usually featured such items as condensed milk, sardines in tomato sauce, biscuits and chestnuts roasted over gas mantles. Naturally, all of this was washed down with soda pop. Such activities were a constant source of amusement for the boys and it is likely that even if the school food had been worthy of the best London restaurant, these activities would still have taken place. This notwithstanding though, it is clear that in the light of the stringent economies made on catering, the food was not of the best standard possible, and complaints from boys recorded in personal letters and journals are legion. Sometimes this insurrection bubbled over into physical protests, with one master being mobbed after a particularly awful tea.

On occasion, even the Board complained about the food, despite the fact that it was their insistence on economies that had often led to the poor quality of meals in the first place. During this period, the food served to Board members, Headmaster and staff was different to that served to the boys, and was clearly of better quality. One can only imagine what standard the boys' food was when directors often complained! Parents of boys had insisted that fresh vegetables be provided on a daily basis, and whilst the Board struggled to provide the funding for this, it was always the Matron that had to deal with the consequences of the practical issues of delivering the goods. No wonder many considered her difficult to get on with!

However, these measures, despite being unpopular with many, not least with the boys, all helped the College to get its financial house in order. The middle period of Mr. Haydon's Headmastership was relatively free from financial worries, and although the Board paid no dividends to its shareholders and built no more new facilities, the College was able to do much to improve the amenities of the buildings it already possessed. Among these improvements were a new and more efficient heating system, along with new steel joists and glass sheeting for the swimming pool roof. There were new closable doors to replace the open archways to classrooms in the Red Corridor, and new and improved fire escapes were installed on Main School, incorporating canvas chutes, which made fire drills (and even recreational use) much more pleasurable for the boys than before. In addition, there was a new engineering workshop to cater for the increasing demand for increasing demand for mechanical engineering; and all this was rounded off by a new forty-foot flagpole erected on the main tower in honour of Queen Victoria's Jubilee.

Mr. Haydon's appointment saw no slackening of the school discipline established by Mr. Young. There are various mentions in "The Tettenhallian" of how many, staff and boys alike, regarded Mr. Haydon as something of a slave-driver. Whilst afternoons were set aside for extra-curricular activities, this was more than made up for in the evening, when boys had to endure at least three hours extra class work. Mornings were no different either, and the practice of early morning prep was maintained and morning school began at 9.15am, rather than 10.00am. Whilst there was no Lower School in those days, the foundations for this institution were set in place by the introduction of a "junior department" to prepare younger boys for senior work. The idea of working during the "holidays" was encouraged by the Headmaster, and many remember him for his generous granting of a whole day off during term time for those boys whose holiday work was outstanding.

A cloud drifted over the face of the sun in 1897, when an unsatisfactory Educational Examiner's report caused anxiety with the Board. However, the Headmaster managed to discredit the report's criticisms by pointing out that the examiners had not inspected the two top forms. After much discussion, the Board then decided that the report was "too sweeping and did not represent a fair comment on the work done during the year." Whilst many would consider this to be an act of subjective disregard on the part of the Board, the fact that the Education Examiner's report had been scrutinised so deeply by Headmaster and Board alike was evidence of how seriously they all took their jobs. There is ample evidence to support the fact that Mr. Haydon was a Headmaster of drive and zeal, and this is exemplified by the hours he was prepared to spend on individual tuition, and the frequency with which the boys were tested on their work. E.C. Kendall says that after sixty years he can still remember Mr. Haydon's practice of making all his fifth form boys learn four lines of verse from *Palgrave's Golden Treasury*[1], which had to be recited to him before the day's Latin lesson began.

---

1. A popular anthology of English poetry, originally selected for publication by Francis Turner Palgrave in 1861. It was considerably revised, with input from Tennyson, about three decades later. Palgrave excluded all poems by poets then still alive. The book is still published today, but in updated form.

It seems that to be anything less than word perfect was a punishable offence, as was falling short of the high standards expected in any other test.

So far, a lot of emphasis has been placed on the abilities and exemplary qualities of the Headmaster. Mention must also be made of the growing body of equally talented support staff, without whom the College would probably not have been able to achieve the high standards that it did. The Second Master, A.T. Simmonds, was well-liked by the boys, often due to his penchant for cracking a wry joke or two. Despite this, Mr. Simmonds was a firm disciplinarian who was firm as well as fair. One boy recounts being seen by Mr. Simmonds after lights out, and felt obliged to confess to this crime since both the master and the boy knew the offence had been committed and Mr. Simmonds was waiting for the boy to show the strength of character to confess. That boy recounts of Mr. Simmonds forgoing the usual punishment in favour of a warning because the boy had "learned the lesson of owning up." Two other members of staff who were popular were "Cherry" Orchard, a most able Science teacher, and Dick Grenville, who founded a choir, and did a great deal to make a success of the Sunday evening entertainments.

It is, of course, always difficult to judge how effective the teaching was, at any rate where the rank and file were concerned, but the achievement of A.D. Dallow in securing first place in the country in the Oxford and Cambridge examination, and the Open Scholarships won to Cambridge by W.C. Bottomley (later Sir Cecil Bottomley, K.C. M.C. C.B. O.B.E.) Under Secretary of State for the Colonies) in 1896 and N.F. Berry in 1898, in which year there were five Old Tettenhallians up at Cambridge, are at any rate convincing evidence that the abler boys, at least, were well taught.

Whilst Mr. Haydon was a much-respected scholar and a brilliant teacher, he also did a tremendous amount for games at the College. It is clear from the evidence he left behind him that the Headmaster believed strongly in the positive influence of competitive sport on the minds of growing boys. In these final decades of the nineteenth century, the British Empire was a dominant force in global economics and the need to foster a team spirit was seen as essential to carry out into the fiercely competitive new age that was a by-product of the Industrial Revolution. Not only this, but the same economic forces were being felt in microcosm in more parochial areas such as the West Midlands, and the need to educate "team player" mentality was becoming more and more a necessity in educational establishments. There is little doubt that other schools clinging on to the former wisdom of pushing the three "R"s to the exclusion of virtually all else did manage to survive due to sheer volume of academic achievement, but Tettenhall College was, and still is, about much more than this. There is little doubt that Mr. Haydon's desire to promote sport was borne, probably in no small part, by his desire to further the College's fundamental aim of providing and education to allow its students to thrive in a modern environment.

So, one can image one of the youngest Headmasters the College has known, embarking upon investing all his youthful drive and energy into sport. He began by introducing hockey and lacrosse to those excused playing compulsory rugby, and the rugger teams soon took on board these sports as an alternative way of reinforcing team bonding and keeping fit. Over the years these sports took on a life of their own and, by 1898, H. Foster was playing hockey for Staffordshire and later for Midland Counties. More national sporting achievements followed with J. Ambler playing for Yorkshire and J.H. Thompson being invited to play for England and Wales.

After Mr. Haydon's first year at Tettenhall, the College Rugby first XV scored 195 points, with only 27 scored against it. E.E. Bottomley, played full back for Yorkshire in 1899, and by 1904 Harry Lee had obtained his rugger blue at Cambridge. No doubt the Headmaster had much to do with these successes. There were of course times when teams didn't live up to his own high standards, as the following extract from "The Tettenhallian" makes clear: "Regular practice… has put the team in fairly good condition, though a more rigid abstention from the good things of this world would still rather improve matters."

One area in which the Headmaster did definitely "improve matters" was in the area of cricket. A batsman of many fine strokes, he frequently took part in the matches that the school team played against club sides, and usually emerged with a higher batting average than anyone else. And, being the consummate teacher, he was keen to pass on the secrets of these successes to his boys. At this time, there were often long lines of boys in the playground armed with broomsticks copying the way in which the Headmaster demonstrated his cricket strokes. That his coaching was necessary is indicated by Mr. Haydon's comment upon a player soon after he came to Tettenhall. Following its tradition of calling a spade a spade, "The Tettenhallian" described one who shall be nameless as an "ugly batsman with cramped action, very sleepy in the field, but of some value as a change bowler." No doubt the threat of these acerbic prods made by "The Tettenhallian" helped to spur on the boys to the considerable cricketing achievement mostly established during Mr. Haydon's time.

Among these notable achievements were C.R. Bantock, who scored 83 in 1892, and H. Lee, who got five fifties in 1901. Earlier on in 1894, The College defeated the Grammar School second eleven for nine runs, but perhaps one of the best College victories over the Grammar School occurred in 1903 where there were three centuries scored in just one afternoon. In Mr. Haydon's final year, H.J. Stinson had a tremendous season, scoring six half centuries, four in consecutive matches, and 106 not out against the Wolverhampton Cricket Club.

The College's cricketing achievements also spilled out into the Old Tettenhallian's Club, who set up a touring team called the Nomads. During the course of a tour, the Nomads played a strong Cheshire side known as Broughton Hall, a side that in its last match had scored over four hundred runs against one of the best Liverpool clubs. However, the Nomads bowled and fielded so well that they had nine wickets down for 79 runs. "The Tettenhallian" continues the story: "The eleventh man was not forthcoming so we adjourned for tea, and their innings was closed. Just as the home side was taking the field after tea their eleventh man turned up. We thought we could afford to be generous so we let them go in again. The last wicket added 107 runs." Match drawn!

With the spotlight mostly on rugger and cricket, athletics was far from neglected at the College during Mr. Haydon's time. The most notable event here was Billy Stokes' long-standing long-jump record achieved in 1904. It was the best jump made in all the English Public Schools during that year, and caused many competitors to consider that their athletics training methods should be modified to include a diet of "pop" and cream buns, and of course the cold showers that followed all games, winter and summer alike in those days.

Sport certainly played a large part in the life of the College, but there were plenty of other things to do, and Mr. Haydon gave boys every opportunity and encouragement to do them. The more intellectually minded could listen to their Headmaster lecturing at Tettenhall Wood and elsewhere on aspects of English History. There was an active Discussion Group that, in 1900, during the South African War, was debating "Has England attained the zenith of its development and power?" Then there were countless visits to places of local interest including the annual outing to Sutton Park. In 1893 the boys went by train instead of horse-drawn brakes "so missing that charming and delightful drive through Willenhall." "The cocoa nuts were well hit" on this occasion, says "The Tettenhallian," but one sixth former had to spend the night at a hotel after turning a canoe over. At this time, some of the boys made a series of canoes in the carpentry shop, and D. V. Hotchkiss, later to become marine architect of note, rather bravely tried out the first of these craft on the murky waters of the College Swimming Pool. Whether or not this test was successful is not recorded, but the fact that Hotchkiss clearly survived the experiment and went on to make a career out of designing boats must speak for itself.

This is just one example of how encouraging extracurricular activities of a vocational nature can greatly augment all the theory that is absorbed in the classroom. Mr. Haydon believed in the idea that learning put to practical use could only be a good thing. This is a notion that thrives at the College to this day, and later Headmasters have all followed Mr. Haydon's example of encouraging hobbies in whatever way they could. At one time, the Headmaster even set aside a room in his house where boys could keep pets. Rats, mice, owls, jackdaws and ferrets all found a home there. "The Tettenhallian" tells us that at one time there was a craze for keeping caterpillars; "some fellows have herds of them, browsing in biscuit tins." This practice of keeping pets and encouraging an interest in nature thrives at the College today, with current Groundsman Alex Poile's nature walks and pet zoo being famous in the local area, and on at least one occasion featured on national TV.

Back in the last decade of the nineteenth century, there was of course, no TV. This meant that Saturday evening entertainment was very much a homespun affair and a very much looked forward to one at that. There was a great deal of singing around the piano with solos by the staff including the Headmaster, and many a rousing chorus from the boys. Many Old Tettenhallians at the College during this period speak enthusiastically of dramatic sketches and the visits from local entertainers. Gerry Parkyn writes well about such an entertainer, who was skilful at spinning plates both with his fingers, and at the end of a wand. It seems that this idea of spinning things so captivated the imaginations of the boys that the practice of spinning the porcelain "jerries" at use in the dormitories during this period became something of a craze. Unfortunately this had to be stopped due to the large amount of breakages that resulted.

Many of the Saturday concerts were put on for local charities. In 1895 there were concerts in aid of the Tettenhall Distress Relief Fund, and for the Wolverhampton Orphanage to which the boys made considerable contributions. Other concerts were put on for Indian Famine Relief, and for the victims of the South African War. Music was the staple of these shows, and it is certainly a reflection of how music was then and still is a large part of College life. Dick Grenville formed a Glee club, and in G.H. Cox the School had a music master that enjoyed a more than local reputation. His oratorio, "Christus" won him some fame as did his "King's Thanksgiving March," which was played both by Dan Godfrey's Bournemouth orchestra (now the Bournemouth Symphony Orchestra) and the famous band of J.P. Sousa. Among the boys, J.C. Parsons and W.A. Stokes both made great contributions to the music of the College. The former has written feelingly of the tribulations of those who endeavoured to become proficient upon the Chapel organ, not least of which was the positioning of the control tap of the hydraulic system down in the boys' washroom. It was a favourite trick to slip into this washroom and turn off the tap just at the moment when the artist up aloft was reaching the climax of his piece, and then to flee in haste before the furious victim thundered down the Chapel stairs in vain pursuit.

The achievements of Old Tettenhallians reported in the pages of the school magazine became more and more numerous. During Mr. Haydon's time, C.E. Shaw became M.P. for Stafford who sat for Stafford while S.T. Mander and G.R. Thorne both became Mayors of Wolverhampton – at different times, of course. However, many of these achievements were eclipsed to a degree by the outbreak of the second Boer War in 1899, which was followed by the boys with great interest. National rejoicing at the relief of Mafeking in 1900 meant all the more to the boys because an Old Tettenhallian, J. Pearson, had endured the siege, which had lasted six months.

Even sporting victories reported in the school magazine were robbed of their usual victorious zeal whenever an opposing side had lost players to the ongoing war in South

Africa. Also reported in "The Tettenhallian" are the half-holidays that were granted in honour of war victories. There was one such holiday for the relief of Ladysmith, and another for that of Mafeking. Also worthy of note is the return from the conflict of Captain Cozens, one of the College's most distinguished participants in the war.

Meanwhile, Colonel Thorneycroft, by now a firm friend and supporter of the College, was also interested in the war. Anxious to educate the boys in the events of the conflict, the Colonel gave the boys a rifle and the use of a racquet court on which to practise with it. He also gave a number of "lantern lectures" in the Towers Theatre upon various aspects of the war. His son, Colonel Alexander Thorneycroft, was one of the heroes of the Boer War, and no doubt the famous incident on Spion Kop when he came upon some of his men on the point of surrendering to the Boers, and having stopped their surrender, stood with his back to the fusillade of bullets from the enemy lines while he lectured his men, was widely told at the College.

The year 1897 saw Queen Victoria's Diamond Jubilee, and this was occasion for great celebration at the College. There was a whole day's holiday for this, in the course of which boys assisted in the lighting of a great bonfire on the ridge near the Mount, one of a chain of bonfires across the country. Four years later a noontime service in Chapel commemorated the great Queen's passing.

Sad to say, the enthusiastic contributions by Colonel Thorneycroft to the life of the College were also soon to come to an end. This stalwart friend to the school had been troubled by ill health for some time, and in 1903, the same year as Queen Victoria, he died. It is strange to note that in 1863, the year of the College's founding, the Colonel had taken legal advice in an attempt to prevent the College opening, whilst just years before his death, his rising to speak at successive Speech Days was always the cue for rapturous applause. It was one of the Colonel's dying wishes that the College should attend his funeral, and so everyone, staff and boys, joined the great procession down to the Parish Church.

For many years after his death, boys at the College remembered Colonel Thorneycroft with great fondness. Benjy Williams remembers many an illicit exploration into the Colonel's grounds, and on one of those being caught sailing one of the Colonel's boats on his swimming pool down in the wood. Fortunately, the Thorneycroft Groundsman was somewhat overweight and unable to catch Williams as he made his escape back on to College territory. Despite these incidents though, the Colonel remained a stalwart supporter of the College until his death.

During this time, there was a definite air of hi-jinks about College life. Whilst Mr. Haydon's firm discipline remained unwavering, the boys often lightened the load by numerous escapades that often must have been observed in true Nelsonian tradition, by the Headmaster's blind eye. One such thing was the practice at the end of term to observe U.B.O.

day, or more fully, UnButton One day. This took place on the fourth Sunday before the end of term, and on this day, each boy went about with the bottom button of his waistcoat undone, and woe betide the boy who forgot to observe the custom. The next Sunday was UnButton Two day, and the last but one Sunday was C.H., or Cocked Hat day, at which time every boy had to wear his cap on the side of his head. The last Sunday of all was K.D. day – Kick Door day. The unoffending door was that leading into the gallery at Queen Street Chapel in Wolverhampton. What the congregation seated below thought of this custom as each boy kicked at the door on his way into the gallery where the boys always sat, is not recorded, which is perhaps just as well.

Very often though, these practices got out of hand. One such event was Pay Day, in which monitors went around armed with rubber tyres meting out "payback" to boys who had caused them trouble during the term. This particular incidence of organised bullying was soon curtailed by the Headmaster who rightly felt that punishment should be dealt out only by those with the maturity to judge when it was required. In the days when bullying was more tolerated as way of life than it is today, this was a particularly progressive attitude. Another seemingly intolerable act of bullying that was rapidly nipped in the bud was the way in which new boys were forced to tell a story or be forced to endure a piece of soap in their mouth. It must be remembered here that soap in those days was far more unpleasantly astringent than modern soap, and even the thought of having a piece of carbolic soap in one's mouth even for a few seconds forces the eyes to water.

Fighting in the school playground has always been a part of school life, and despite efforts to curb it, still remains to this day. At Tettenhall College in the late portion of the nineteenth century though, when boys quarrelled, a fight was often arranged. A notice would be posted in Big School giving details of the fight, and naming Seconds. The boys fought in the playground in the midst of a circle of onlookers, and the fight finished when one of the boys drew blood. Afterwards, it was the unwritten, but undeviating tradition of the College that the boys shook hands at the end of the fight.

CHAPTER 6

THE NEED FOR A TRUST

Headmaster: J.H. Haydon, Esq.

By 1897, the College's future looked rosy. All of the College's staff and its 120 pupils had enjoyed Queen Victoria's Diamond Jubilee year with its attendant parties, and so it seems fitting that a letter to the Board of Directors effectively became the first of several clouds that would later appear on the horizon.

The letter was an answer to enquiries made by the College's Directors about Council Grants to Secondary Schools. At this time, the increased public interest in education had led to Local Government ceding funds to established educational institutions, and the College had hoped to benefit from this. However, the Council's letter told the Board in no uncertain terms that since Tettenhall College was a constituted as a company owned by shareholders, it did not qualify for any such grant. The other main reason why the College didn't qualify for a grant was that it didn't impose a conscience clause allowing boys the right to waive religious instruction if their conscience, or that of their legal guardians, required it. According to Board minutes, the inclusion of such a clause into contracts would not have presented any practical problems, but it did receive opposition from those members that had strong Non-conformist convictions. They pointed out, quite rightly, that the inclusion of such a clause would undermine the intentions of the College's founding fathers, in that it would effectively cease to become a school intended exclusively for Non-conformists.

But this was a small issue compared to the notion of re-structuring the College's financial foundations. The point is put succinctly in a memorandum that the Directors were to send later on to the shareholders: "In the academic world we are scarcely recognised as educationalists, but are regarded as traders who seek to make a profit out of education."

Those members of the Board that had opposed the inclusion of a conscience clause were suitably chastened by those who pointed out that the College wasn't receiving any acknowledgement or assistance from the religious organisations whose doctrines it sought to install in its pupils. In 1892 the Congregational Union had published a report, from its own denomination's point of view, of Secondary School education, and had failed to mention the

College in it, nor had any representative of the College been invited to sit upon the committee that drew up this report. The College did protest about this, but all it received in return was a terse and "unsatisfactory" reply. The bleak conclusion is reported in a Board memorandum as follows: "We are not looked upon as a Public School by Public Bodies. Under our present constitution we are debarred from receiving aid from the County Council and other public bodies in the way of scholarships and grants for the teaching of science, and we shall certainly be excluded from the benefits of any future scheme for promoting Secondary Education."

It seems clear therefore, that this single letter from Staffordshire County Council proved to be a wake-up call to the College either to move with rapidly changing times, or face the threat of ruin. In an increasingly competitive education market, the College needed to provide services in keeping with the times, and it was clear that unless it received support from outside, it would not be able to do this. Board minutes of the day record an ever-growing realisation that the College would have to cease being a Joint Stock Company so that it would then be perceived as a non-profit making organisation and would therefore qualify for various grants and other assistance on offer to such organisations. During 1897, this fact became increasingly clear in the many Board debates on the subject. What wasn't clear, however, was how to change the College's financial constitution, or even what it should be changed to.

The solution to the problem came in a timely fashion during 1897 (some did say due to the "College's ever-present guardian angel") when one shareholder called Whittaker offered his shares back to the College with a call for others to do the same. It then became clear that if the College could recover all of its shares, it could declare a cessation as a Joint Stock Company, and immediately re-constitute itself as being governed by a Trust. This sounds simple, but the process was to prove much harder than it sounded. Looking at the situation from a modern perspective though, this proposed change of constitution proved to be a strong factor in the College's continued survival. As it turned out, the process of converting the College to a Trust, from its preliminary mooting in April 1897 to its eventual re-constitution in 1916, took nineteen long years complete. Not only was it a lengthy process, but it also proved extremely hazardous in that the Board's dogged determination to complete the Trust Scheme often led to it neglecting the day-to-day running of the school.

The first of many obstacles came in the realisation that it was actually illegal for the College to buy its own shares. This meant that unless Shareholders were willing to give their shares up voluntarily, it would be necessary persuade individuals to act as trustees and buy the shares on the College's behalf with only the vague possibility of being reimbursed at a later date. Not surprisingly, there were very few volunteers.

The second difficulty concerned the ownership of those shares not yet given in or bought out. The Board had previously deemed that Non-conformists only should hold such shares, since in other hands the original character of the school might be endangered. Thus a great row blew up, which led to both parties taking legal advice, when the Board refused to allow a parent who had five boys at the School to purchase shares in it. The parent was an Anglican, and although the College solicitors felt that the Board would have difficulty in law in denying its shares to anyone, the gentleman eventually gave up his claim, and brokers were instructed in future to sell only to Non-conformists.

However, the first major step towards becoming a Trust-funded school came in 1899 when Arthur Nicholson of Leek, a name later to be of great importance to the College, offered his shares to the School, and the Board decided to appoint Trustees to receive them. These Trustees were J. Highfield-Jones, A. B. Bantock and W. Hall-Jones. This was the first step in the long journey of financial transformation, and by 1901, the Board realised that it would have to obtain at least three-quarters of the shares if the Trust Scheme could ever become a reality. In addition to this, no Director could hold more than twenty shares, so this meant appointing new Trustees outside the Board. The process wasn't made any easier by the apparent difficulty the Board was having in reaching quorum at meetings, and this was largely due to factors outside the College's control, such as commitments to the war effort in South Africa and various other outside commitments of Board members. When the Board did meet, its minutes indicate that it did little except discuss the Trust Scheme, and indeed, as suggested earlier, it is easy to see that all this came at the expense of the day-to-day running of the school.

Despite this, the Board must be praised for showing dogged determination to achieve their goal, since the majority saw this as the only way to look after the College's long-term future. A memorandum issued by the Board in 1902 began as follows: "Tettenhall College was founded by Independents nearly forty years ago, not as a business speculation, but solely with the desire to provide in a Non-conformist atmosphere, a sound education equal to that given by any Public School of England." In goes on to point out that "ever widening demands for more thorough and extended training" have restricted dividends," and indeed states: "your Directors cannot see any prospect of dividends being paid in the future." Having listed the disadvantages of the old system quoted above, the memorandum continues that it is the intention of the board to dissolve the company and invest the property in a new corporation, registered with liability limited by guarantee, and on a non-profit-making basis; any surplus made on the year's working would be ploughed back into the school.

The aims were to remain as before: "a sound and liberal education, both professional and commercial, in connection with a religious training in accordance with principles held by Congregational Independent Churches." Later, when the approval of both the Congregational and Baptist churches had been sought, these aims were revised slightly to read "in accordance with the spirit of the Congregational Churches whether Independent or

Baptist. A conscience clause will give complete freedom to any parents who do not wish their boys to receive religious instruction." The controversial conscience clause eventually adopted was: "The parent or guardian of any scholar may claim by notice in writing to the headmaster the exemption of such scholar from prayers or religious services or any lesson on a religious subject. Such exemption shall be no prejudice in any way to the scholar concerned whether from a pecuniary point of view or educational point of view."

Members of the newly founded Trust were to be known as Governors, and qualified either as shareholders, former pupils graduated at a university, former pupils contributing five guineas to the College's funds, those who contributed 10 guineas to the College's finds, and co-opted members. A governing body was made responsible for the management of the College, and this was to consist of 24 members at least, of whom half at least should be elected by the governors from among their number. The co-opted members of the Governing body were to be representatives of the various branches of the Congregational and Baptist Unions before agreement was reached on the composition of this body. It is significant that that the Board took great pains to keep the Old Tettenhallians well informed of what was happening, and on many occasions, asked for their assistance.

This all looked full of positive purpose, but the Board could be chastised for failing to spot the clear harbingers of impending crisis. This is probably down to poor attendance at meetings, although it is difficult to say this with any degree of certainty since Board minutes for this period are perfunctory at best. The first of these harbingers came in the form of dwindling numbers, which, it will be remembered peaked at 120 in 1897. However, the numbers dropped rapidly to 102 in 1898, and then to 77 in 1905. In September 1904, it was decided that "in view of the serious financial position of the College" a full meeting of the Board should be held to deal with the situation. The problem, of course, was the College's dwindling revenue caused by diminishing numbers, and the Board dealt with the situation in the following December by drastically reducing the fees (thereby bringing them into line with those of other schools) in order to attract more boys.

Other incidents that fanned the flames of dwindling numbers include a bitter argument between the Board and the Secretary, who ended up handing in his notice. Then there was the damaging incident of a complaint brought by an assistant master against the Headmaster. This complaint was given to the Board in writing and it came up for discussion in December, but a policy for settling the complaint wasn't reached until two days later when the Board heard the Headmaster's explanation, and passed a resolution to the effect that there was no truth in the charges against the Headmaster. Unfortunately, the details of this complaint are lost, but it is not hard to see that many people could have believed that there was no smoke without fire.

On the positive side, the Board received a Christmas present in the shape of an offer by the Birmingham and District Bank to lend the School £1,550 by way of overdraft at 5% in return for a debenture for that amount upon the school property. In January, the new Secretary, the Rev. L.K. Fletcher entered upon his duties, and in February the Board was able to sign a large number of cheques. So delighted was the Board with its newfound affluence that it voted a guinea for the purchase of some armorial standards for the College.

But these were really side issues that were relatively easily solved compared to the fundamental state of the school's revenue. Despite the reduction of fees, in July 1905, forecasts showed an expected expenditure of £2,577 against an income of only £1,855. In September, the College was actually £1,572 overdrawn at the Bank with outstanding debts of £950. All of this underlined quite clearly that the College needed outside help, and everyone knew that this was not likely to be forthcoming in the immediate future, since the transition to becoming a Trust funded school was still eleven years in the future.

The Board held several meetings to work the problem, but it was clear that there was no real solution other than simply to cut overheads. This meant that the newly appointed Secretary was instructed to give notice to all the company's servants that unless financial help was forthcoming within the next few weeks, it would be necessary to dispense with their services at the end of the term. It isn't clear whether this move was in preparation towards the end of winding up the school, but it is clear that it was certainly a drastic cost-cutting move.

The crisis deepened when in October the number of boys had dropped to 74, and the Board was left with no choice other than to beg help from outside. Mrs. Rylands, the widow of the great Manchester cotton spinner, was approached, and so too were the Old Tettenhallians, such as Old Tettenhallian nephews of the founder of Unilever Ltd., Sir W.H. Lever, to see if they could secure the assistance of their incredibly wealthy uncle. Another possible source of donation was the Congregational Union, who suggested amalgamation with another Congregational School, Silcoates in Yorkshire, a school that was also going through something of a crisis. The headmaster of Silcoates and several members of its Board seemed interested and agreed to inspect the College.

Desperate times they were, and these desperate measures are a good measure of the College's indomitable spirit. Despite this though, it seems that the Headmaster had had enough, and late in 1905, he tendered his resignation to the board "to leave the Directors a free hand in dealing with the finances of the College… It will only be with deep regret that I shall be severing my connection with the College and its governing body," he wrote. The Directors accepted the Headmaster's resignation with reluctance, since many Tettenhallians praised his scholarship and humanity. Despite this, the demoralising effects of dwindling numbers, and the constant struggle to re-constitute the school must have had a strong bearing on the Headmaster's fortitude, and whilst he is clearly not responsible for the College's fundamental funding difficulties, the rapidly diminishing numbers must speak for themselves. The Jubilee issue of "The Tettenhallian" asserts that because of financial difficulties of the later years the Headmaster "could not command assistants of the calibre of his early days." The increasing lack of interest in the Headmaster's work indicated by the decay of the once active board sub-committee, and the repeated failure of Board meetings to produce a quorum, together with the almost total diversion of the Board's interest in the direction of the Trust Scheme, must also have played their parts.

And so "Bill" Haydon – "Danger Bill" – left the College to spend some time as an Inspector of Schools. After this, he became Chief Classics Master at Mill Hill. Despite the tragic death of his only son in the First World War, his interest in the College remained undiminished until the day of his death. Of Mr. Haydon, Dr. W.A. Stokes has written: "In the midst of all this stood John Hampden Haydon, scholar, rare teacher, sportsman, disciplinarian; whom all respected and feared; whom all who truly knew him loved. Many of us owe our careers to him and to the Tettenhall of his best days."

Mr. Haydon died in September 1936 at the age of 73.

CHAPTER 7

CRISIS MANAGEMENT

Headmaster: R. L. Ager, Esq.

Despite everything else that was happening, Mr. Haydon's resignation came as blow to the College. With its revenue in a poor state and its whole financial foundation in a state of flux, the Board were undecided as to whether a new Headmaster should be appointed at all. Indeed, what perfunctory minutes there are show that there was a strong element that favoured throwing in the towel rather than attempt to surmount what seemed like insurmountable difficulties. The Board's desperate attempts to beg money from wealthy philanthropists were all met with sympathetic but tactfully firm refusals. Mrs. Rylands understood the College's plight but regretted to say she was heavily committed elsewhere. Sir W. Wills, of tobacco fame, was no less sympathetic but no less heavily committed in supporting both Mill Hill and Taunton Schools – two other Free Church Schools much in need of help. W.H. Lever proved a little more hopeful, and asked for further details. Silcoates, having sent people to inspect the College, had, after careful consideration, decided not to amalgamate.

So it was with all these refusals ringing in their ears that the Board decided to continue nonetheless, and to do this they needed to raise a fund of £2,000. Mr. Bantock stepped in with a donation of £250, as did Mr. Thompson (of Banks's Beer fame). Both of these donations were given on condition that fees should be raised to their former level and that a new Headmaster should be appointed as soon as possible – and certainly before Christmas. They also insisted that the Board should be consulted about the appointment of junior masters. With no other possible options, the Board was forced to agree since the only alternative was capitulation.

The first task was to appoint a new Headmaster, and with this in mind, the Board sought the advice of J.L. Paton, the distinguished High Master of Manchester Grammar School, about the choice of a new Headmaster. The Board also let Silcoates know that it had decided not to close the School despite their refusal to amalgamate. It seems that following from this, the Headmaster of Silcoates applied for the vacant Headmastership of Tettenhall, although clearly he did not get the job, and it is not hard to see at least one of the reasons why.

Richard Lester Ager Esq., M.A. (Headmaster 1906-1912)

With the appointment of a new Headmaster in hand, the Board then turned to the problem of how to secure the support of the Free Churches. The College Board knew that as far as these religious organisations were concerned, Tettenhall College would have to discard its seemingly "profiteering" image, and they needed to know whether their transformation from Joint Stock Company to Trust would change attitudes towards them. With this in mind, the Board decided to question prominent members of the Free Churches with a view to finding out what the College needed to do to secure their financial support and endorsement.

As far as other outside donations were concerned, the College was given a small nugget of hope in the form of a loan of £1,000 from W.H. Lever, who promised to consider lending more at a later date. This slender lifeline gave the Board the fortitude to turn down another offer of amalgamation with Silcoates, which was further encouraged by the positive sounds that the College was getting from prominent Free Church members. Sir George White, the Reverend T. Law, the Reverend J.H. Shakespeare, Mr. M. Marnham, the Reverend C. Silvester Horne, Mr A.J. Shepheard, and Dr. Fairbairn – some of the most eminent men of the Free Church world – all agreed to sit with members of the Board at a meeting in London to appoint a new Headmaster for Tettenhall.

After much deliberation the committee chose Richard Lester Ager. Born in 1878, Mr. Ager was educated at Rugby, and then at Oxford, winning an open scholarship in Classics to Corpus Christi College. After a most successful university career, and with a good degree in Classics, Mr. Ager went in 1901 to Bishop's Stortford, and four years later, when Mr. Haydon resigned from Tettenhall, had become a House Master and a Sixth Form Classics master. At 27, he is one of the youngest Headmasters to be appointed at Tettenhall, and possibly at any school of a similar type at that time. It is clear from various correspondences that the Board hoped that a young Headmaster would be better able to cope with rapidly changing times and would be less influenced by "any fossilised system of education." This move is evidently a clear indication of the College's ongoing desire to keep up with the times – which is a policy that has continued strong and clear to the present day.

From his very first day at Tettenhall, Mr. Ager set about justifying the Board's high hopes for him. Despite his relative lack of experience, he went on to steer the College through many severe crises in the coming years. Certainly, no one can doubt his popularity – both with his colleagues, and with those whom he taught. Many accounts praise his kindness, and the great gifts he enjoyed as a teacher. "Dick Ager," said one who knew him well "was both a scholar and a gentleman."

At this time, society was beginning to throw off what many perceived as the shackles of autocracy, and an indication of Mr. Ager's youthful grasp of this changing world is the fact that one of the first things he did after arriving at Tettenhall was to remove the practice of having better food served at the Top Table than the boys were eating. Mr. Ager instructed that henceforth the Headmaster's table should always receive the same food as the boys.

Even though some feared that Mr. Ager's youthful lack of experience would be a hindrance, he silenced many of these doubters by gathering around him some highly talented staff. Three of these were R. Lobb, W.A. Holland and G.P. Furneaux. The latter, who went on to become Headmaster of Aylesbury Grammar School for over twenty years, did much to reorganise the science teaching at the College, and as one of the "Tettenhallians" records, "raised the subject of chemistry from the position of the most disreputable of subjects at the school to that of one of the most important." When he eventually left Tettenhall, Mr. Furneaux wrote as follows: "I have always been grateful to Mr. Ager… for giving me a free hand to work out my own salvation, find my feet, and to try and engender in the boys my own enthusiasm for my subjects. I loved every minute of my time at Tettenhall because of the friendly atmosphere and the feeling that the College stood for something worthwhile to staff and boys alike."

Many would say that Mr. Ager's best appointment was Horace Pearson. H.P., as he later became known, would go on to achieve great things for Tettenhall, but everything in its place – suffice it to say for the present that despite his apparent youth, Mr. Ager certainly was a good judge of character and ability. "The Tettenhallian" – noticeably more critical of the staff at this time – said: "We will admit that his intelligence is quite beyond the ordinary as was to be expected from a member of the staff." Grudging admiration for a man who gave encouragement for all to work hard. However, one small change introduced by Mr. Ager that produced a spirited opposition from "The Tettenhallian" was the move to make the school an examination centre for the Oxford Locals. Previously, boys had gone down into Wolverhampton town centre to sit these exams and were in the habit of storing up strength for the examination by consuming large quantities of pop and ice cream. Now that the examinations were to be held on the College premises, this popular method of fortification would have to end.

Despite this minor niggle, pupils at the College found Mr. Ager a source of inspiration. One such pupil was Dr. W.A. Stokes, who was one of six Old Tettenhallians at Cambridge in 1908. By 1912, there were five Old Tettenhallians at Oxford, and in 1910 H.R. Howard won an Open Mathematical Scholarship to Selwyn College, Cambridge. In the following year L.R. Horne, a most distinguished maritime engineer, won the Boyd Scholarship for Mathematics and Science at Liverpool University. During Mr. Ager's time, good results were also achieved in the Oxford Local Examinations, the principal external examinations for which boys at the School entered at that time.

It must not be forgotten though that Richard Ager came to Tettenhall in the middle of several crises, which meant that the problems facing him were difficult indeed. The goal of becoming a Trust was still as ever elusive, and numbers were continuing to fall. All this came at a time when many of the more influential Board members were unable to devote their usual quota of time to the College due to commitments elsewhere. Most notable of these was Baldwin Bantock, who was beginning his first term of office as Mayor of Wolverhampton. In addition to this, he was also Governor of the Royal Hospital and the Women's Hospital; and was an active member of the Governing Board of the Eye Infirmary, eventually becoming its Chairman from 1910-1936. Another busy member of the College Board was George Thorne, who in 1908, was elected Member of Parliament for Wolverhampton East. These and several others were conspicuous by their absence at meetings, especially as this was certainly a time when the College needed their various talents (not to mention their money) very badly indeed.

Just after Mr. Ager's appointment, the Board set up a sub-committee to appoint and assess junior masters in consultation with the Headmaster. One supposes that this was the direct result of the complaint levelled at Mr. Haydon by a junior master shortly before, but this is just supposition. One thing is clear though, and that is that the Board wanted more control over the appointment of academic staff. One stroke of good fortune the Board had at this time was the timely loan of £1,000 from J.W. Goddard, of the famous Leicester polish firm. The Board rewarded Mr. Goddard by appointing him a Director.

However, despite all the academic achievements and hard scholarly work, the numbers continued to fall, and by January of 1906 were down to 67. Efforts to secure financial help from W.P. Hartley of Hartley's Jam failed, and the Board was forced to admit to a loss of £954. Running true to form, the Board reacted to the loss by introducing severe cutbacks, and afterwards claimed to have saved £120 in 1906. A lot of this was down to the blessed intervention of the Secretary's wife, who introduced a comprehensive reorganisation of the domestic side, which involved firing virtually all the existing staff and replacing them with new. The academic staff didn't get off lightly either since the new Headmaster dismissed all of his staff and re-engaged them on different terms – where all but the Housemasters would be paid a flat rate of £110 per annum. After this, the College had to struggle on with only four masters, until (probably very reluctantly) the Board were forced to engage a fifth.

Whilst such economies did help to ease the problem, they didn't really attack the heart of it. What the school badly needed to achieve a fundamental resolution of its difficulties was a tremendous amount of financial help from outside, coupled with a great deal more boys. In a spirit of determined optimism, approaches were made to Carnegie and J. Compton Rickett, W.H. Lever and several Free Church businessmen, all of which achieved precisely nothing, despite the invitation extended to Lever to present prizes on Speech Day. It is not known whether these generous philanthropists genuinely believed that the College was a lost cause, or whether they simply had their resources devoted to other projects, although this experience does indicate a constant trend in the history of Tettenhall College, and that is the school's apparent bad fortune in obtaining *endowments* from its various backers. It must be noted that at this time as well as in later years, the College's competitors (such as the Grammar School) were suitably fortified by endowments, and this meant that in comparative terms, Tettenhall was at a distinct financial disadvantage.

At this time though, *any* kind of cash injection from *any* source would have been welcome. Liabilities approached £8,000 by the end of 1906, and Chairman W. Hall-Jones (another Wolverhampton Councillor) was making his way once more to the bank with a request for a further overdraft. Efforts to win recruits by advertising in the national press produced no results whatsoever, and no appreciable benefit was derived from circulars sent to Congregational and Baptist Ministers informing them of the discounts in fees available for the sons of such Ministers.

Some minor gifts did come trickling in though. One Old Tettenhallian offered to have all the studies decorated and another donated a flag. In addition, the school was pleased to receive from the Edwards brothers three handsome shields adorned with the College colours, of which two still survive with other trophies in the Dining Hall. Old Boys had reason to be grateful to Mr. Ager, for he made them welcome at the College, as no Headmaster before him had done. There was in fact an open invitation to Old boys to visit the College, and even to spend the weekend there. As will be seen later, this attention to the College's Old Boys turned out to be one of the Headmaster's major triumphs, since in the years to come, the school was to have great need of the support of the Old Tettenhallians.

It must be mentioned that by this time, the number of Old Tettenhallians had grown during the College's forty some years of life, and many of these former pupils were achieving substantial successes. Three of them represented the Liberal Party in Parliament: G.R. Thorne (East Wolverhampton), C.E. Shaw (Staffordshire) and J. Lloyd Morgan (Carmarthenshire). The latter was made Recorder of Swansea, and eventually a County Court Judge. A number of Old Tettenhallians became magistrates and F. W. Simon, an architect of some note, won a prize of £2,000 for his work in connection with the Manitoba Parliament House. This meant that many OTs carried a great deal of influence, not to mention wealth.

Nevertheless, in the early part of Mr. Ager's Headmastership, Tettenhall College desperately needed extra income over that earned by dwindling fees to help it out of its immediate problems. Indeed, revenue for the Christmas term of 1906 was £939, and expenditure £1,260 of which £623 was owed to tradesmen. Despite this though, the Board still continued its policy of helping out where they could when parents were suffering from genuine hardship.

By 1907 there was still no let up and by then the College's finances were all but hanging from a single thread. More desperate approaches were made to prominent representatives of the Free Church, but it seems that these rivers of income had all dried up. The same was true of several efforts to obtain loans from wealthy Non-conformists in the Wolverhampton area. In August of this year, a special meeting was called when the liabilities were revealed as being £9,842, of which a huge £1,812 was owing to tradesmen.

All Old Tettenhallians and parents were circularised to try to secure more boys, and an offer from the Tettenhall Urban District Council to purchase the College's smallholding in Henwood Lane was rejected. The feeling here was that the College would not be able to move on if it allowed itself to be carved up. A glimmer of hope came when three of the Directors offered to raise a thousand pounds to endow the College – provided other parties made a similar response, but nobody else followed their lead, so the offer was withdrawn. Looking back over the history of the college, it seems that on the rare occasions when the Holy Grail of endowment is even tentatively teased, it is always snatched away again. One can never say that the College's guardian angel could ever be accused of slacking, but it seemed to draw the line at providing financial endowment.

In January 1908 another helpful venture failed when Colonel Pilkington of the Warrington glass firm, after some correspondence, finally decided against helping the College. "My feeling," he wrote, "is that we pay quite enough. While it was all right to provide schools in times past, there is now no reason for it." He was referring of course to the passing of the Balfour Act of 1902, which allowed Local Education Authorities to set up Secondary Schools – a step that led to the rapid development of "free" Secondary Education in this country, and which, by its very "free" nature, increased the difficulties faced by Tettenhall College.

Reading through Board minutes from this period leaves one wondering how the College survived these extremely troubled times. There was reduced attendance at these gatherings to the point where several of them lacked sufficient quorum, and at this time, the College Secretary could probably have papered the fives court wall with all the red-inked "Final Demands" on his desk. While all this was happening, numbers continued to diminish, and the Board's morale sank lower and lower. It is ominous that attempts were made to value all the College's assets, presumably with a view to liquidating them, and whilst the realisation of actual value would have allowed the College to walk away from its troubles, it is a testament to the determination of the Board in the light of poor morale that no one decided to go down this route.

Despite repeated appeals, even the Old Tettenhallians remained ominously silent and while the odd donation did trickle in, nothing was of the calibre needed. Even O.T.s were seeing the financial advantage of sending their sons (and daughters) to the newly founded State Schools and since these were still in their "novelty" stage, the long-term disadvantages experienced by later generations (such as overcrowding, largely as a result of a post-war baby boom) were not yet apparent to the people of this time.

And so, the numbers at the College diminished even more, and it is gratifying and certainly amazing to see that sport actually flourished during these years. The pre-breakfast dip in the murky waters of the swimming pool was introduced at this time, and strangely enough, the small numbers actually acted as a stimulus to sporting competition. L.R. Horne recalls: "The athletic side gained as much as it lost by the decline in numbers for it meant that none was left out of games, and talent that in a larger school might have remained hidden was soon spotted." Even boys who were no good at games felt that they must play a part, too. "It never occurred to us that if we were wanted for the Dormitory or Second teams, our incompetence gave us the right to avoid the task. I think it all made for a strong *esprit de corps*. For inter-school matches, though there was no roll-call, my recollection is that practically no one failed to turn up and cheer."

And, despite the small numbers, there was quite a lot to cheer about. Cricket flourished with H.J. Stinson beginning with 106 not out against the Wolverhampton Club's first team. In 1907 C.R. Ridgway (who later acted as Manager to the South African Test team) scored 135 not out, and in the following year the College dismissed the Grammar School for 13 runs, scoring 101 in reply. Two years later Ridgway scored 139 not out against Queen Mary's, Walsall, and 105 not out against the Grammar School. It wasn't often that the College beat the Grammar School in the annual cross country race, but it did so in 1907 when Noel Whitfield came in first by some half a mile.

The Headmaster was also a keen supporter of the College rugby teams, and regularly played at wing three-quarter when the school played club sides. There were some good rugger sides, but seasons tended to be uneven because with the very small numbers at the College, a good rugger side might disappear entirely at the end of the season, leaving the next year's fixtures in the hands of a very young and inexperienced team. This happened in 1911 when in the course of a poor season, the College lost to Warwick School by 78 points to nil. Yet in the previous season the College had enjoyed a glorious season, losing only one school match (and that by only one point) to Denstone College, and beating Aston Grammar School by 90 points to nil.

Whilst the boys were enjoying these successes (as well as plenty of hard work), the situation in the Boardroom was getting worse. By May 1908, losses exceeded £10,000, yet still the Board refused to allow Big School to be hired for a political meeting. But the Board did put up a spirited fight with the telegraph company, whose wires crossed the Headmaster's garden (now garden to the Old House). The College demanded £1 a year rental for this privilege, and when this was refused, ordered that the wires be removed. The College later settled for half a crown a year. From these seemingly minor incidents we can still see more than a glimmer of Tettenhall's indomitable spirit. At a time when Messrs Bantock and Thompson were pressing for an £8,000 mortgage in order to absorb the other mortgages, the butcher was pressing for his account. While salaries were going unpaid and lawyers were being instructed, the Board still spent money upon cosmetic repairs, no doubt due to Bantock's insistence on "keeping up appearances, no matter what."

The Headmaster had turned out to be a man who was good at getting things done at little cost, including a complete re-fit of the Gymnasium at no expense to the College. He also contrived to find more "money efficient" ways of stretching his meagre budget, such as buying second hand books rather than new ones.

Probably as a result of having its budget slashed, "The Tettenhallian" was now published once a term. It is obvious from the pages of the magazine that the boys were encouraged to develop their own interests, and this led to many flourishing societies. A Natural History Society was well patronised and boys were allowed to keep pets. At one time there were three rabbits, six pigeons and one ferret. This latter proved most effective in dealing with College rats. At this time, there was a craze for "Diabolo" – a game played with a top, spun on a stretched cord. "Broken windows and black eyes speak eloquently for the Diabolo craze," reported "The Tettenhallian."

The Headmaster regularly took parties of boys to the theatre. Indeed, Drama at the College was very much encouraged, with Saturday night revues just as popular as they had ever been. There was an active Photographic Society, and a Discussion Society, which, among other topics in 1910, was debating the pros and cons of the House of Lords, the Suffragette movement, and the "Yellow Press." Some boys went riding, and "The Tettenhallian" has an amusing story of a member of staff who joined them on one occasion but who subsequently showed a distinct disinclination to sit down, and even called for a cushion during the course of a lesson.

No doubt the Directors all felt like they deserved a good caning, since in September 1908, they learned that there had been no success in finding a mortgage, despite substantial efforts and expense to publicise the College. A letter was sent to 882 Congregational and Baptist ministers in Wales, and these letters eventually produced the names of 128 potential parents that might be interested in the school. It is not recorded whether any of these people actually ended up sending their boys to the College, but it is clear that every effort was made to persuade them. Sir George White and W.H. Lever said that they would join with the others in finding the money to save the school, and once again Bantock and Thompson rose to the challenge, the former offering £500 and the latter £250, provided others chipped in to help them establish a fund of £3,000. However, just like the last time, there were no takers, and all this at a time when the College creditors were pressing harder and harder for settlement of their accounts, the cumulative total of which far exceeded the school's ability to pay.

Up until this point, the College's bankers had been United Counties. The Chairman of the College Board had made repeated efforts to secure an overdraft from them, but without success, so Mr. Bantock stepped in and used his influence to persuade Lloyds Bank to take on the school's account instead. There is no doubt that Lloyds were reluctant to do this, and in a letter to the Board, they pointed out in no uncertain terms that had it not been for Mr. Bantock's substantial clout, they would certainly have turned the College down as a bad risk. They also made a proviso that should the account get out of hand, Mr. Bantock's attention should be "called to the position." However, despite being admonished in such a blunt manner, the College did receive additional overdraft facilities of £1,000, which it immediately spent – half on salaries and the other half paying off some of its other creditors.

Whilst the introduction of new bankers provided a much-needed breathing space for the Board, it still had not been successful in securing a financial endowment for the College. It had already made several approaches to W.F. Hartley and R.W. Hudson, but at this point nothing had been forthcoming. Sir E. Holden, a College Director, was another wealthy gentleman who had declined to make any sort of donation, and when his term of office came to an end, the Board declined to renew his appointment. However, when he later made a loan of £200, the Board hastily re-appointed him.

Reading through Board minutes from here onwards, it is clear that there was certainly a more business-like approach to making policy and one supposes that this was down to the appointment of a new Secretary. A committee was set up to take charge of the College advertising – J. Thompson had offered £25 a year for three years for this purpose – but the first results of the advertising were not encouraging. By January 1909, the College's overdraft had crept up to £2,440, although this was ameliorated a little by a loan of £250 from J.H. Jones. W.H. Lever suggested, too, that his nephew might be willing to help, but when this Old Tettenhallian was approached, he offered £25, which was better than nothing, but nowhere near the sort of sum the College needed. It therefore sent out a deputation to visit this Old Boy to see if he could be persuaded to do better, but this effort proved a vain one.

All these valiant efforts to obtain a suitably large cash-cow mostly came to nothing. True, there had been a number of small donations; E.H. Carver had paid to have the dormitories re-decorated and another Old Boy had donated a piano, but there was little to stop the College's overdraft rising to £2,500. When Mr. Bantock was made aware of this (no doubt by a very panic-stricken manager of Lloyd's Bank), he made an immediate donation of £500 to take off a little of the pressure. He also chastised the Board for allowing things to get so badly out of hand, and a measure was promptly passed that clearly stated that in future the overdraft should never exceed £1,800. However, despite this bold resolution, it became clear to Mr. Bantock that the College would be unable to keep to its word for very long and he made a further "loan" of £500, although this time he stipulated that if the College's finances ever improved substantially, his money should be used to provide scholarships. A vain hope, and one can imagine Mr. Bantock's sigh as he stoically waved goodbye to his money.

No doubt Mr. Bantock's seemingly unbridled optimism rubbed off on the Board, since they immediately invested some of their newfound money on a number of "small-leaved ivy creepers" to adorn the College's buildings. An amazing gesture of defiance against all the seemingly insurmountable financial difficulties the College was facing at that time. No doubt this move acted as a catalyst to stir up redoubled activity in advertising the College. At this time, there had been several requests from shareholders that the company should be wound up, but all of these were turned down and a brand new prospectus was prepared (including testimonials from parents) and circulated in large numbers. A full-page advertisement was taken in "The Sunday Strand," and the editor even wrote a good article about the school, which was perhaps inspired in no small part by the College's promise to buy 500 copies of that issue. No doubt the standard of toilet paper at least improved at the College for a brief period, if nothing else.

Whilst all of these heartening measures were designed to protect the College's future, they did little to ease the immediate problem of an overdraft of over £1,000 and debts of a further £1,600. At this point, the school's financial situation had only been significantly improved by the £1,000 given by Mr. Bantock, and everyone was aware that whilst Mr. Bantock was a stalwart supporter of the College, his generosity could not be relied upon indefinitely. With no other philanthropists to call upon, it seems that the Board threw all their last hopes into securing support from the Church.

And so it was in the summer of 1910 – the same year that H.R. Howard won an open scholarship to Cambridge – that the Board sent W.H. Jones and J. Thompson to inform the Congregational Union that it was intending to close the College in December of that year, and that the Board did not wish to do so without first giving the Union the opportunity of giving its assistance in preventing this. Whether closing the school was the true intent of the Directors, or whether it was a bluff is unclear, although the memorandum to the Congregational Union is quite explicit: "In order to carry on the School, the minimum required is £2,500 to pay off all existing liabilities, and £1,500 for working capital, making a total of £4,500. The Board are quite prepared to retire, if desired, and hand over to the appointees of the Free Churches the entire management of the School: or to receive into their ranks a number of members to be appointed by the Free Churches. They have kept the school alive solely for the sake of Free Churches, and are prepared to render any and every assistance to that end."

This effectively placed the College's fate in the hands of the Congregational Union, and one cannot help seeing the problem from their point of view. On one hand, Tettenhall College was producing extremely good academic results, all of which were achieved in an atmosphere of harmony and cooperation; it also enjoyed a good academic reputation throughout the West Midlands, and it employed some excellent staff. On the other hand, the

College lacked sufficient boys to make it financially viable, and it had fallen seriously into debt. Hindsight tells us that this lack of boys may have been down to the marked reluctance for Non-conformists to send their children to Free Church schools such as Tettenhall, and it is significant that from this time onwards the proportion of Non-conformist children in the Free Church Schools steadily declined – something not confined to Tettenhall, as Horace Pearson pointed out in an analysis of sectarian views in Free Church Schools in 1932. This analysis indicated the way in which latter-day Non-conformists failed to support their schools in the way that other denominations, such as the Quakers, did.

The Congregational Union was also aware that Tettenhall wasn't the only school in difficulties. In 1910, Caterham was desperately trying to pay off a debt of £8,000, and several other schools owed more than this. Most of them were seeking help from the Union in one form or another, and clearly there was only a limited amount it could do. A lot of Free Church schools, including Tettenhall, were suffering from declining numbers, and this in itself precipitated a vicious spiral downward, since parents were reluctant to send their sons to a school with dwindling numbers. One parent who decided to send his sons elsewhere said, when taking his boys away, that he did so because the small number of boys at the College provided insufficient competition for each other. We have seen that this was in fact not the case, but parents could at least be forgiven a little for supposing that it was.

The situation wasn't helped much by the fact that in 1905, the Board had passed a resolution prohibiting any more Day Boys. The reasoning here was that Day Boys enter "so little into the life of a school… rarely play the games; joining only to a limited extent the full school life, [they are] deprived of a most important part of the training that a Public School has to offer, and the *esprit de corps* of the school also suffers." This was a brave resolution since the non-admittance of Day Boys only served to diminish numbers more, and whilst Day Boys may not have received the full benefit of life at Tettenhall, their presence would certainly have boosted the school's income and provided more encouragement for other parents to send their sons to the College.

So, in a spirit of grim determination, a deputation went from Tettenhall to visit the Congregational Union in July of 1910. The Board minutes discussing this meeting describe the Union as being "sympathetic," a fact that is reflected in the promise to launch an appeal to raise £500 to help the College to continue. The Union also promised to review its relationship with its schools. It seems though that these bold words actually produced no results, and in September the Secretary wrote to the Union informing it that the College would close the following Easter.

CHAPTER 8

CRISIS? WHAT CRISIS?

Headmaster: R. L. Ager, Esq.

To anyone not privy to the events transpiring in the Boardroom, the Tettenhall College of this "Ager" period seemed idyllic. One Old Tettenhallian, A.J.P. Andrews, writes: "I loved the freedom we had to go long walks or cycle rides in the beautiful countryside on half-holidays. I learned to row on the Severn at Bridgnorth, and to skate on a lake near a burnt out mansion. I loved the swimming pool – once I had got over my early fear of it. I loved the Chapel, and especially when I played the organ for services… and the walks to the services in Wolverhampton. I learnt to like rugger after a time, but not cricket.

"I remember games of 'last to the top' when the playground was thick with fog; of chasing 'roosters,' the bluebells in our wood; of climbing trees – till the younger Milward fell out of one and nearly died. And of being often cold; I was thin and probably underclad, and the wind can howl around the dormitories."

L.R. Horne says: "No comment on the College in the 1910 era would be faithful that did not include the religious side. Most boys came of good homes and accepted naturally the Sunday morning parade to Queen Street and the Heads of my day invariably managed to make Evening Chapel inspiring. The Queen Street ministers – I remember particularly Mr. Carter and Mr. Thompson – took a very friendly interest in us and were held in respect. We, or most of us, left school with a firm philosophy, and that was perhaps the most valuable thing [that] we acquired from Tettenhall."

Andrew Horne had this to say: "I believe the College to have been a good school during those years; it was a happy school, and as was even more the fashion in boarding schools then than now, emphasis was laid on character building more than on academic achievement. For this reason, the quality of the teaching staff was all-important, and I think myself lucky to have enjoyed the benefits of the example and precepts of the staff in my time."

A.J.P Andrews makes two other interesting comments; one is that the small numbers enabled the brighter boys to have much more individual attention than they would have obtained in a larger school. He then makes a defence of the practice of "fagging," which he thought worked well at Tettenhall. "I once saw a huge Scottish boy heating something over a gas flame, and was astounded to be told that he was fagging for a tiny boy not half his size. People who criticise this forget that there will always be fagging, and without some recognised system, it will just depend on the size and pugnacity of the two boys concerned, [therefore] leading to endless abuses. They also forget how much the older boys do for the younger ones in organising games and the school life generally."

Dwindling numbers at the school did, it seem, have a positive side, but by 1910, the financial drawbacks of fewer boys had caused the College to make the hard decision to close its gates permanently. Despite more advertisements, more circulars to parents, ministers and Old Boys, the malaise continued, and numbers fell steadily from 57 in 1910 to 48 in 1913. While income was falling, expenditure remained about the same (including a pay rise of £10 for Matron) and the College fell deeper into debt. Of course, the supporters of the College did what they could. The Headmaster lent to the school a complete new set of desks, and there were a few small donations from Old Boys, but nothing of significance. By December 1910, the Congregational Union had managed to raise only £65 5s of the hoped for £500 despite over 200 appeals. It seemed that the proposal to close the College at Easter 1911 would have to go ahead as planned.

At this point, the Headmaster made a formal request that the official closing date be deferred from Easter to the end of the summer term so that the boys could sit their examinations and the staff would have more time to find alternative employment. Despite the extra expense involved with keeping the College open that small time longer, the Board agreed, and as it turned out, this gave a valuable breathing space for those who wished the College to continue.

The trouble was that no one knew how to bail it out of the serious dilemma it had managed to find itself in. By February of 1911, the College owed £1,650 with numbers set to fall again with twelve boys leaving and only nine starting in that year. Notification had been sent to the Congregational Union of the College's intent to close in July, and those people who wanted this not to happen were working hard to make good use of the extra time they had been given. One desperate measure was the notion that that the College could continue if it amalgamated with Caterham School. However, as there were huge practical issues that could not be resolved, this idea was dismissed before it even reached the debate stage. The Baptist Union was approached to see whether they wanted to take over the school, but they politely declined, saying that they were over-committed elsewhere. All of this was being done against a backdrop of industrious preparation to wind up the College. The Board took legal advice as to what should happen to all the shares when the school ceased trading, and approaches were made to Staffordshire County Council to see if they wanted to buy the premises for a Teacher Training College. However, no one seemed interested in the College premises, so preparations were made to place them on the open market. The die-hards then made several appeals to the Congregational and Baptist Unions, but were politely but firmly turned down. It seemed that all avenues of escape were now closed and a special Board meeting in April was summoned to close the school officially.

And so, after 48 years of varying fortunes, Tettenhall College prepared to go quietly into the night. It would not have been alone in this, since at this time, there were many other schools that had sprung up, flourished and then disappeared. Many Board members, in letters to colleagues, supposed that it wouldn't be the last.

But the Tettenhall College indomitable spirit refused to die. The Board summoned up a tremendous reserve of verve and energy, and met in March rather than April as originally planned. All Directors were present at this meeting and the minutes reflect an air of "never say die!" In a vast sweep of flagrant defiance, the Board rejected the idea of considering the possibility of receiving a Board of Education grant to save the school. It must be said that there were those that favoured taking such a grant, but to do so would undoubtedly have taken away the College's independent status. Those people argued at the March meeting that it surely was better to have a Tettenhall College in existence without its state independence than not have a Tettenhall College at all. Despite these arguments, the Board decided to follow the example of Silcoates, who when rejecting the possibility of a state grant, their Board declared: "We do not propose to accept Governmental aid, and in this respect, as our school at Tettenhall is doing, show the country that as Congregationalists we value the privilege of educating the sons of our ministers and laymen in a school where our Free Church principles will not be neglected, but continued with the highest moral, literary and physical training as at Mill Hill, Caterham, Tettenhall, and other Congregational schools."

In much the same spirit, the Directors of Tettenhall College vowed to go on, despite the protestations from accountants and bankers who pointed out the almost certain financial folly of doing so. Sweeping these objections aside, the Board made three resolutions:

1. That the fees of Boarders should be raised by three guineas a term and those of Day Boarders two guineas.
2. That the Old Tettenhallians should be appealed to, to provide a substantial sum now, and to guarantee an annual contribution over the next five years.
3. That the Congregational Union should be asked to forward any sums collected on behalf of the College.

The spirit of this meeting is related and referred to in correspondence from many of those present. It seems that Mr. Bantock's firebrand presence provided the impetus for all of this fervent determination. It is likely that he didn't want to see his old school fade away like so many others had done, and whilst it would be pleasant to think that this desire was born from a love of the school and a yearning to continue carrying his father's "education at all costs" torch, it is likely that he was also motivated by the desire to ensure that his business credibility was not tarnished by the fact that he had been educated at (and been instrumental in managing) a school that had been forced to close due to insolvency.

But Bantock wasn't the only benefactor of the College present at the meeting. The Reverend T.F. Kinloch, and Messrs. Hall-Jones, Dickinson, Goddard and Stockburn were also present, and no doubt they had no desire to see the sums of money they had invested in the College over its 48-year life disappear into the hands of receivers and liquidators. Three of these immediately guaranteed yearly contributions – Stockburn offered £5, Hall-Jones £10 and Bantock £20 over the next five years. With this, the meeting was adjourned.

Whilst the Directors had drummed up a lot of renewed enthusiasm for the College at their meeting, many left fully aware that unless the parents and Old Tettenhallians were infected with this new fervour, it would all be for nothing. Unless the parents agreed to the new fees and the Old Boys rallied round in sufficient numbers to keep the College going until income picked up, then the College would be back at square one.

It seems that the Board's renewed enthusiasm proved to be infectious after all. At a meeting in April, the Headmaster reported that only one parent had objected to the new fees. Other Directors reported that Old Tettenhallians had indeed rallied round and provided a guaranteed £111 a year and £44 in cash up front. Even the prosaic nature of the minutes reflects the jubilation of the Board when its desire to keep the College going had been vindicated. All this meant that the Board could pass a unanimous resolution that the College should continue – providing the reactions from the remaining parents and OTs was favourable. In addition to this, the Directors renewed their determination to put an end to the company that was Tettenhall College and set up a Trust to run the school.

The College was not out of the woods yet though. After going through the accounts with a fine toothcomb, the Board realised that stringent economies and efforts to produce extra income would also be needed. They decided to rent out the field on Henwood Road for £9 10s per annum and then to lease the Headmaster's house for £65 per annum. This meant, of course, that the Headmaster would have to move into the school, and in addition, the typically generous Mr. Ager offered to accept a reduced salary of £300. However, the Congregational Union, when asked for the sum collected on behalf of the School, replied by saying that following the announcement to close the College, they had returned the £65 5s already collected. Not to be outdone, the Board asked for the names and addresses of those that had contributed with a view to recovering the money.

But the efforts of the Directors to cope with the crisis had clearly overtaxed their strength, and no quorums could be found for two meetings called in May, and others in July and September. By October, however, the financial prospects looked more encouraging. £225 per annum had now been promised, and £149 given in cash. Moreover, all the parents were now paying the new fees and no boys had been withdrawn because of them. This meant that the Board was able to announce: "It is resolved to continue the school in the hopes that under these revised conditions, the company may pay its way and enter on a period of prosperity."

The £225 per annum promised by Old Boys represented two things to the College – firstly a sum of over one thousand pounds spread over the five years, quite independent of the amount raised in fees, and secondly, and possibly more important, an expression of faith in the school from its Old Boys for which it can never be sufficiently grateful.

But all of this was nearly for nothing. In 1911, the College picked itself up only to face another tremendous financial hurdle. There was a mortgage on the College property of £4,000 held by a man called Perks. In September, the College was informed by lawyers that Mr. Perks had died and that his executors were calling in said mortgage. This meant that the Board had either to find £4,000 out of fresh air, or find someone else willing to take on the mortgage. As if this weren't enough, the College's other financial liabilities had risen as high as £2,100 by the end of 1911, although income had picked up, and if it hadn't been for the business of the mortgage, the College could easily have managed this deficit. The Old Tettenhallian annual contribution had now reached £308, and the College had also received a £500 bequest from Joseph Smalle. Under normal circumstances, this would have been a tremendous boon to the school, but put up against the urgent need to raise £4,000, it was relatively small.

So what was to be done? The Board began by asking two financial houses to take the mortgage on board, but both efforts proved fruitless. Many letters were sent out appealing for help, but few were even replied to. Even Mr. Bantock was either unwilling or unable to raise such a sum, and it seemed that the only way out was to sell the College's premises to raise the money. However, the Board did manage to obtain extra time to pay the mortgage, although this was at the expense of higher interest rates – they now had until September to pay.

While every effort was made to try and raise the funds, there is a certain air of "burying one's head in the sand" to the events leading up to the September deadline. Tuck Shop funds were used to pay for new troughs and hot water for the baths. A new Secretary was appointed at £75 per annum with a 5% bonus for all fees exceeding the 1910 figures. One of the first things he had to cope with was a request from the bank to make an annual reduction in the overdraft of £100. It is not clear how he coped with this, if at all, since he also couldn't even do anything about an unpaid meat bill of £150, or one of £75 for printing.

In spite of all this financial difficulty, the College was actually doing very well academically, with A.J.P. Andrews winning an open scholarship to New College, Oxford, and many other achieving excellent exam results. But despite this tremendously brave face, the September deadline was getting ever closer.

September came, and not surprisingly, the College still hadn't obtained the £4,000 needed to pay off the mortgage. The Perks executors were pressing for their money and had informed the College that bailiffs would soon be instructed unless a cheque was forthcoming. The Board held an emergency meeting and spirits were further dampened by the Secretary's report that there were many unpaid accounts requiring action. After much discussion, the Board could only say that: "nothing could be done at the moment." On a very rough estimate, they went on, "we shall lose from £300 to £400 this year, which will bring the total of our outstanding debts to some £2,600. We now require a year's credit from our trades people." Yet in the previous month the Board remitted a term's fees to a parent whose boy had been ill and in consequence withdrawn – although admitting full liability to pay. As far as the mortgage was concerned, in a spirit of unbridled optimism, the Board decided that all it could do at the moment was ask for even more time, during which a fund could be set up to pay this monstrous liability and even leave money left for improvements to the College!

After this had been decided, the Board then turned to the pressing matter of the impending fiftieth Jubilee celebrations and how they should be commemorated. At no point whatsoever did anyone consider even the vague possibility that once the bailiffs had arrived, there probably would be no College left to celebrate by the time 1913 came around.

But, as ever, the College was not fighting its battles alone. Just as bailiffs were being instructed to liquidate the College's assets to pay off the money owing to the Perks estate, H. Whiston, the president of the Old Tettenhallians, had a meeting with Sir Arthur Nicholson, a prominent Leek businessman in the textiles industry and former College shareholder. It is not known what the agenda of this meeting was, but Mr. Whiston managed to persuade Sir Arthur to take on the College's £4,000 mortgage. Just as bailiffs were preparing to tear the College apart, Sir Arthur's cheque immediately took the wind from their sails and sent them away empty handed.

Whilst some Board members balked at paying 5% interest instead of the 4¼% it had been paying previously, the College showed its appreciation of Sir Arthur's generosity by naming a school House after him. Probably not wishing to be outshone by Sir Arthur's generosity, Mr. Bantock promptly made another "loan" to the College of £500 to reduce other liabilities. All this generosity in the face of such adversity is really a testament to how well the school was doing academically, in that people thought it worth keeping it alive, seemingly for this reason alone. Certainly, this sense of loyalty is no less strong today than it was in these earlier days, and one cannot help wondering what other indefinable quality other than academic achievement could inspire such devotion. From all accounts, the College had (and still has) a definite "family" feel to it that certainly lived on in its Old Boys and encouraged them to keep this feeling alive by giving their loyalty and devotion.

There can be little doubt that Mr. Ager's work at the College did a lot to inspire the same loyalty and devotion, and possibly the financial roller-coaster ride of his relatively short time as Headmaster had taken its toll, since at the same meeting that Mr. Bantock offered his loan, the Headmaster offered his resignation. He had, he told the Board, been offered a post at Manchester Grammar School by his old Headmaster, Mr. J.L. Paton, the famous Head of that much renowned school. The Board agreed to release him at the end of the present term, and Mr. Bantock made a point of expressing "the Board's high appreciation of the work Mr. Ager had done at the College, especially in training the character of the boys." This is characteristic of Bantock – the training of character was the great test he applied to schools and schoolmasters, and he was not the sort of man to have praised Mr. Ager in this regard if he had not meant it most sincerely.

In a typically modest and self-deprecating letter to the Directors, the outgoing Headmaster wrote: "Whatever my mistakes have been – and I doubt not that they have been many – I have tried to do my best, and I venture to think that, neither from the educational point of view, nor as regards the moral training of the boys, had my work been altogether without result." But what had his mistakes been? Some have suggested that discipline was weaker at this time than previously, and that the Headmaster's lack of experience had been something of a handicap. It is true of course that the Headmaster was only 27 when he was appointed to Tettenhall, and his extreme youth must certainly have presented problems, but two impressions clearly emerge from the recollections of Old Tettenhallians and the pages of the school magazine. The first is that bullying was far less rife in the school than it had been, and the second is that it was a happy school with a friendly atmosphere between teachers and taught. Whilst Mr. Ager maintained an adequate level of discipline, he had had to achieve a fine balance between this and a relaxed friendly atmosphere to achieve the deep feeling of belonging that has subsisted at the College to the present day. It certainly seems that later Headmasters have learned well from this shining example.

It must be said that Mr. Ager's achievements are even more remarkable when one considers the appalling financial situations the College endured during his time as Headmaster. At no time during his Headmastership was the possibility of bankruptcy and the closing down of the School ever far away. There was no time when he could plan ahead and make long-term policies with any hope of these ever coming to fruition. As previously mentioned, the Board often neglected the day-to-day running of the school since the "higher" matters of the Trust Scheme, various financial crises and their various civic duties often preoccupied them in ways that did not allow them to give their Headmaster the full support he needed and deserved. It is a testament to Mr. Ager's achievements that the Old

Tettenhallians and parents alike all rallied around the College in its time of need, since if the College hadn't been delivering consistently good results, few of these people would have considered it worth saving.

After leaving Tettenhall, Mr. Ager went to Manchester Grammar School, where he stayed for three years. After this, he was appointed Headmaster at Batley Grammar School from 1916 to 1923 and then at Newton's School, Leicester from 1923 to 1945. He has a room in the Towers named in his honour.

PART TWO

ADOLESCENCE

Chapter 9

A Half Century

Headmaster: A.H. Angus Esq.

As had happened before, the Headmaster's sudden resignation and departure left the Tettenhall College Board in quandary. There was no time to appoint a new Headmaster, and the College needed to show a solid footing in the eyes of its numerous stakeholders – to have done otherwise would have undermined the faith that so many people had shown in the College in the time of its greatest need. The College desperately needed a new Headmaster, so the Board invited the Second Master Horace Pearson to stand in as acting Head. Mr. Pearson was much respected and admired and he was, at least, a face familiar to all those concerned. It is likely that some Board members favoured appointing Mr. Pearson as Headmaster, but as some Directors pointed out, he was very young and had no degree. Nevertheless, H.P., as he later became affectionately known, rose to the challenge and accepted this temporary position with a fortitude that certainly foreshadowed his later achievements at the College.

At this point, one may wonder why the role of Headmaster was never filled from the ranks of existing staff. If Horace Pearson was the best man for the job, why not let him get on with it? Appointing a figurehead or C.E.O has never been an easy issue, but one thing is clear and that is it is not wise to appoint from the ranks. This is because existing staff have had time to develop unique relationships among one another and to promote one to C.E.O. would undermine those relationships and possibly disrupt the "power-base" beyond repair. Not only this, but it would also create rivalries among possible contenders that might also endanger the efficient working of the corporate machine. This is why the Directors (and later Governors) of Tettenhall College have always chosen to appoint a "fresh face" as Headmaster, if only on the assumption that "a new broom always sweeps clean."

After the decision to appoint a new Headmaster while H.P. "watched the shop" had been settled, the Secretary to the Tettenhall College Board then wrote to the Headmasters of Free Church Schools asking them to recommend suitable candidates. The advertisement said that the successful candidate would be paid a salary of £300 to live in and £450 to live out; he

Alfred H. Angus Esq., BSc. F.R.G.S. (Headmaster 1913-1925)

should be a Free Churchman, a university graduate, and an experienced teacher. Fifty men applied for the position, and this was reduced to a shortlist of five. Eventually, Mr. Ager and Reverend T.F. Kinloch decided upon Alfred H. Angus. In a characteristic tactic of negotiation, Mr. Angus then withdrew his application on the grounds that the salary was too low, whereupon the Board increased the salary by £100 per annum and Mr. Angus accepted.

The new Headmaster was forty years old when he came to Tettenhall in 1913, having been born in Yorkshire in 1873. He was educated at Sir Joseph Pease's School before going to Liverpool University and from there to Leeds Teacher's Training Centre, where he lectured in History, English and Mathematics. After a year there he became Resident House Master at Harrogate College, and in 1901 went to the Central Secondary School in Birmingham, soon afterwards becoming Second Master there. In 1906 he was appointed Headmaster of George Dixon's, Birmingham, and from which he came to Tettenhall. He was the author of two books: *A Preliminary Course in Differential and Integral Calculus*, and in a very different field, *Ideals in Sunday-School Teaching*. Closely connected with the latter publication was his great interest in the Boys Brigade Movement. A most active man, he had captained his university soccer team, and was a renowned crack shot, cricketer and golfer.

While the process of appointing a new Headmaster was going on, Horace Pearson took up his duties as acting Headmaster – a post he held for just one term, during which very little of note actually happened. There had been a Board of Education inspection of the school in 1912 and the consequent report had not been very good at all. True, it had commended Mr. Pearson's teaching, but the wording of this seems very grudging. In their report, the Board of Education made a formal complaint about the standard of gas fittings at the school, so Mr. Pearson saw to it that the letter of the Governors' demands was met. After this, the Board of Education offered their assistance with rebuilding the College and whilst the Directors could not deny that the College needed help in this direction, they firmly but politely declined the offer since they felt that to have accepted it would have been the first fall down the greasy pole to full State ownership.

At this time, the College decided to install one of those "new fangled" telephones, and Lloyds Bank wrote to the Board suggesting it pay off the overdraft with money from the Jubilee fund that it had set up to celebrate the College's first fifty years of life. The Board, presided over by Mr. Bantock, agreed to this and also supported Mr. Pearson when he refused to accept a boy back into school after a parent withdrew him for a weekend without permission. In April 1913, Mr. Bantock paid £500 into the College's current account as his contribution to the Jubilee Fund, and the Board allowed a particular parent an allowance of one guinea a term "in consideration of his profession as a schoolmaster." The Board also paid £94 to equip the new washroom in the Front Quad, and under advice from Mr. Baker, the florist, cleared the shrubbery from the Quad and gravelled it.

When Mr. Angus finally took up office he made a number of changes. Honours boards were set up in Big School (now School House Library), and in the Chapel the pews were turned around to face the organ, the pulpit being moved from where it was at the back of the Chapel to the front. The Chapel lighting was greatly improved at the same time and the floors were laid with linoleum and the windows received new curtains.

Despite these improvements, the College finances were still a source of major anxiety to the Board. On the day that Mr. Angus entered the College gates for the first time, there were only 55 boys in attendance. Even allowing for Mr. Bantock's generous gift of £500, the Secretary could only pay off minor bills. When the school butcher died in 1914, his executors claimed that the school owed a grand total of £659 7s. 8d. and needed the bill paid in full. Eventually, the College negotiated a monthly payment scheme with the butcher's son, which must have taken a very long time to pay off in full.

But what of the new Headmaster? Board minutes do not record the motives of those who chose him, although there is a broad range of opinion about him. As has already been mentioned, in 1913 school numbers were at an all time low, and it seems that the Board needed a man who had the charisma and popular appeal to entice more parents to send their sons to Tettenhall. Coupled with this, they needed a man that displayed a strong commercial awareness together with a desire to do good for the College. It is likely, but by no means certain that the Board were even prepared to give these qualities priority over strong academic achievement and ability.

Those who disliked Mr. Angus pointed out that he was no outstanding scholar like several of his predecessors had been. Many said in retrospect that his achievements at the College were more down to luck than good management, and that he would have been better suited to being a commercial traveller than a teacher. It is argued that the College had already been saved when Mr. Angus became Headmaster, and that the outbreak of the First World War, which so greatly increased the demand for boarding school places, came most fortuitously to his assistance. It is true that the outbreak of war helped increase the numbers, but it was only one factor among many that improved the school's fortunes, and one of the major factors here is Mr. Angus' formidable marketing, administrative and people skills. It is true that Mr. Angus was certainly a charming man who was blessed with what many today would refer to as the "gift of the gab," and he frequently exercised this gift from the pulpit, and enjoyed a glowing reputation as a preacher of renown throughout the country. He was, and never claimed to be, an expert in any one subject, but this is not to say that he was not a good teacher. It's true that he didn't do much teaching during his time at the College, but he did greatly impress those who heard him when he did – including many of his detractors. This is probably why many Old Tettenhallians hold him in real affection, and look back upon him as a great influence on their lives.

As has already been mentioned, Mr. Angus was an accomplished preacher and orator. As such people came from all over the country to hear his sermons, and it is certain that this greatly influenced parents in their decision as to where to send their sons to school. One Old Tettenhallian comments: "My father was a strong Non-conformist, and in 1922 I was at a School with an Anglican Headmaster. Mr. Angus came to preach in my home area, and father heard him. After that there was only one school for me."

But it wasn't only Mr. Angus' gifts as a preacher that captivated so many of the boys whom he taught, or the parents and friends of the College with whom he came into contact. There was also the famous "Angus charm." Many people felt that with his athletic physique, dark moustache over a beaming smile, he had a gift of making those with whom he talked feel that, however insignificant they might be, they really mattered to him. Not surprisingly, women especially admired him; one said that any woman talking to him was always made to feel that she was THE woman. One supposes that it was the monogrammed cigarettes, the college tie, the embossed cufflinks, the smart suits and immaculate grooming that served to enhance what was already a very charismatic man.

So, Mr. Angus could provide the charm and administrative skills to get more desperately needed boys to the College, but what of the desire to further the interests of the College? Evidence of this can be found in the book of press cuttings that was kept in the visitor's waiting room, which was clearly there to impress to visitors the newsworthiness and therefore the importance of Tettenhall College and also of its Headmaster. This is clearly an indication that Mr. Angus was very well aware of the power of the media in exerting influence and the obvious benefits of having good publicity and public relations. Of course, there were critics of the press cuttings book, but however much one accuses it of being "ostentatious and vulgar," none can deny the power it had in influencing the decision of parents in sending their sons to the College. Indeed, Mr. Angus regularly fed the press with College news and his ability to pen sparkling press releases was certainly an asset here. One such case in point was a school trip to London when Mr Angus took a number of boys to sample the "high life" at a London Hotel – an event that was reported on most enthusiastically in many papers and journals.

After the tragic loss of Robert Scott and his fellow adventurers on their ill-fated journey to the South Pole, Mr. Angus enthusiastically invited the leader of another proposed Antarctic trip to give a lecture at the College. Of course, the event was well reported in the press, especially since the Headmaster presented the explorer with the gift of a tent, which would be used in the trip to Antarctica complete with Tettenhall College pennant. Sadly, the expedition never really got off the ground due to lack of funding, although one gets the impression that Mr. Angus would have given College funds to sponsor the trip if any had been available.

All of this added up to the first time in its history that Tettenhall College actually had a waiting list of parents anxious to send their sons there. The Board received this with a modicum of mixed feelings since the increased numbers would eventually necessitate developing the existing school premises to accommodate the extra boys. No one could doubt, though, that the increased fee income was just what the College needed at that time.

The famous "Angus charm" wasn't something just reserved for parents, Directors or representatives of the press – it was also lavished on the boys. Yes, the Headmaster could be a strict disciplinarian when the occasion demanded it, but he also took an active interest in the lives of all his charges – one of which admired the Headmaster so much he confesses to even imitating Mr. Angus' handwriting.

Then there was the Tettenhall College Jubilee commemorating the school's fifty years of life, which was held in the summer of 1913, just a few months after Mr. Angus took up his post as Headmaster. As has been mentioned previously, the Board had set up a Jubilee find to finance the various celebrations, and whilst some of it had been used to ease the pressure on the overdraft, there was clearly sufficient left to pay for the festivities. Visitors began to arrive on Saturday July 26th and there were services in Chapel on the Sunday, and on the Monday. Mr. Angus's famous oratorical skill were in evidence on both occasions, and it is highly likely that many church-goers present made a note in their diaries to look out for this man's sermons in future.

There were cricket and swimming matches against the Old Tettenhallians, and a formidable Old Boy's team defeated the Wolverhampton and Walsall clubs on the two succeeding days. The Bantocks gave a garden party on the Wednesday afternoon, and this was followed by the Club dinner in the evening. Speech Day followed on the Thursday. From beginning to end, the sun shone gloriously, and the weather matched the mood of the College. Even Mr. Bantock said in his speech that the dark times were passing away, and that there was a bright future in store for the College. Others commented upon the "spirit of progress in the air," and "the realisation that a new dawn had come for the school that they loved." J.P. Shaw, one of the first fifteen boys with whom the school had begun fifty years before, spoke at the dinner, and there was a great deal of talk about the new Trust Scheme. It was announced that although the difficulty of discovering the whereabouts of many of the Shareholders had caused difficulty, the Board now had the necessary three quarters of the shares, and could go ahead with implementing the New Scheme. Indeed, once the Jubilee celebrations were over, the task of doing so was handed over to the College solicitors.

It seems that Mr. Angus was in his element in hosting the Jubilee, and he was certainly the right man to host such a sumptuous occasion. His ability to put people at their ease, to get the best out of them, his good manners, and of course the famous Angus charm, undoubtedly made a powerful contribution to the success of the Jubilee, and made it seem inconceivable that the College could fail to flourish in the years that lay ahead.

But the festivities were soon over and the Board realised that it was now time to pay for it all. Not only this, but the College still had a lot of debts that needed to be repaid and this was the subject of much discussion over the summer months and into the autumn term. The Headmaster, who already seemed to hold a great deal of influence with the Board, decided to grasp the nettle firmly and write to several of the school's creditors asking if they would convert the loans they had made to the College into gifts. James Thompson, to whom the College owed £525, Sir E. Holden (£200) and B. Highfield-Jones (£250) all agreed to this rather unusual request, but J.W. Goddard who had lent the School £1,500 declined at this time to convert his loan into a gift, probably due to the fact that his loan was a considerably larger sum of money than the others. However, it must be said that Mr. Goddard never made any formal attempts to recover his money – at this time the question of whether or not to sell the College premises to pay outstanding debt was still looming large over the Board, and if this actually happened, then Mr. Goddard was probably expecting to recover his money then. In any event, this audacious move on the part of the Headmaster resulted in a £975 reduction of the College's debt, and even those who hated Mr. Angus had to do so through tightly clenched teeth.

It is a testament to the faith the Board had in their Headmaster's commercial acumen that they allowed him to approach some of the College's other creditors in the same way. No doubt those who had favoured his appointment felt that their choice had been royally vindicated. Indeed, the Headmaster seemed to hold so much influence with the Board that in reply to a question about what the directors were like, Mr. Angus said: "My dear fellow, I am the Directors!"

As the College entered the autumn term of 1913, it became clear that there was a growing need for more staff. With this in mind, the Headmaster and his Board appointed a new member of staff – a man, as it turned out, who was to have a profound effect on the future of the College. The new man was R.E. Pond, and one Old Tettenhallian wrote of him: "He came to the College as a junior assistant when I was no longer a junior boy, and he had to earn my respect. This he did very quickly, and we became, and still are, friends. What he brought was a breeze from a more academic world, and though he did not have much of a success with me, he did open my eyes to the fact that such a world existed, that it was an exciting world, and that entry to it was by hard work." This is only one of several missives praising Mr. Pond, and space does not allow them all to be recorded, but suffice to say that more will be said of this new master later.

Meanwhile, the Headmaster was coaxing even more generous gifts from Old Tettenhallians. Seven fire grates and four blackboards were donated. One Old Tettenhallian paid to have fixed washbasins at the end of each dormitory, thereby replacing the old portable washbowls in each cubicle. As well as these gifts, the solid silver cup for swimming that still adorns the trophy board was given to the school at this time by Mrs. W. Hall-Jones. The College acquired many more books as a result of the Headmaster's initiative, together with several anonymous cash donations. It seemed that the fabled Angus charm was reaping dividends! Evidently pleased with their new Headmaster, the Board authorised him to secure the services of a part-time secretary at a salary not to exceed £25 per annum.

As 1914 arrived, everything seemed to be going smoothly – the final term of 1913 had not seen even one visit from the College doctor, and all looked well for the coming year. Whilst the Board were still beset with financial woes, everyone was confident that these could be managed.

And then, world affairs took a hand in the fate of Tettenhall College when war broke out in the summer of 1914, and things would never be the same again.

CHAPTER 10

THE COLLEGE GOES TO WAR

Headmaster: A.H. Angus Esq.

On the 28th June 1914, the assassination of Archduke Franz Ferdinand, heir to the Austro-Hungarian throne, by Gavrilo Princip, a Bosnian Serb citizen of Austria-Hungary and member of the Black Hand Pan-Slavist nationalist secret society, was the incident that precipitated the First World War. The retaliation by Austria-Hungary against the Kingdom of Serbia activated a series of alliances that, in turn, set off a chain reaction of war declarations. Within a month, much of Europe, including Great Britain, was in a state of open warfare.

Most of Britain's able-bodied men either volunteered or were conscripted to fight. This meant that Tettenhall College lost most of its staff, and the Headmaster with Mr. Pearson the Second Master, finding themselves the only staff at the College for several long periods. The same was true of many other schools at this time, and the net result was a strain on those members of staff remaining. As far as Messrs. Angus and Pearson were concerned, the demands made on them during this period resulted in bouts of ill health in years to come, but everything in its turn.

In spite of the disruption though, the College flourished as a direct result of what came to be known as the Great War. With most of the men fighting at the Front and most of the mothers engaged in war work, the need to send children to boarding schools was inevitable. When the Great War began in 1914 there were 62 boys at the College, and when it came to an end in 1918 the number had risen to 134 – the highest total ever in the history of the school so far. There was even a waiting list for entry to the College, and so great was the demand for space, that boys were sleeping in the Headmaster's House, and in the small dormitory that had previously been used as a Physics Laboratory. The Board even contemplated asking the lady teachers who were resident to move out of the College so that their rooms could be used for yet more boys.

Whilst the First World War brought good fortune for Tettenhall College, the same cannot be said for many of its Old Boys. Twenty-four Old Tettenhallians, and one member of the teaching staff died while serving in the forces during the Great War. The (then) future Deputy Chairman of the Governing Body, S.F. Snape was one of the many who were badly wounded, and others such as E.W Pidduck, a senior member of the College Board, endured long years of imprisonment at the hands of the enemy. These individuals are still honoured by a plaque in the College chapel to this day and their names, together with those who lost their lives in the Second World War, are recited every Armistice Day.

It was in 1916, when the war was at its height, that the College Board finally succeeded in its long and arduous task of changing the school's financial constitution from Joint Stock Company to Trust. This meant that the Midland Counties Preparatory School (the name of the College's holding company) ceased to exist and Tettenhall College Incorporated was born. The new regime meant that the College no longer had Shareholders or Directors – instead, it was to be managed by a Council (or Board) of Governors who would preside over the Trust and ensure that all profits were re-invested back into the College. "Bluntly speaking," wrote the Headmaster, "instead of being regarded as a Public School in courtesy… only, we shall be a Public School absolutely and solely, and in unsentimental legal fact." Bold words indeed, but not entirely accurate, since the *official* designation of "Public School" was actually not conferred on Tettenhall College until almost fifty years later.

However, in 1916, the journey to becoming a Trust had been over twenty years in the making and the achievement of this goal meant that the College's non-profit-making status would gain it more respectability with the various religious organisations. As such, the College's newly acquired Trust status might lead to more in the way of grants and charitable donations from organisations who previously did not want their money to go into shareholders' pockets in the way of dividends. All this meant that the Board, not to mention the Headmaster, would have to re-double their efforts to get these cash donations.

With school numbers rising and the prospect of fresh monetary injections, those at the College felt they had good cause to celebrate. So, on 17th June 1916, the school enjoyed a day's holiday. Mr. Hall-Jones, then Chairman of the Governing Body, began the day by giving each boy in the school a shilling, and then everyone amused themselves until dinner that evening. After dinner, most of the boys went, in two specially chartered charabancs, to the cinema in Wolverhampton. On their return they enjoyed "a thumping supper" of ham, tongue and salad, followed by fruit and jelly. After this, in true Tettenhallian fashion, they rounded off the evening with a concert.

It seems strange to consider that while all this merrymaking was taking place, so many lives were being lost on mainland Europe. An issue of "The Tettenhallian" that records the celebrations of the 17th June lists four Old Boys as dead, one missing and five wounded. In the same issue, F.E. Lefevre, after a long spell in the trenches, writes: "I found one or two warm spots in the trenches. What the 'Daily Mail' refers to as the 'Hose of Death,' a machine gun to wit, is a most unpleasant thing when you happen to be two hundred yards from the wrong end of it. Still, things might be much worse. I am glad to hear that the College is doing better at cricket. Talking of cricket, how do you fancy me as a bomber? But still, there it is! I assure you I am most deadly. So far, I haven't put one in the wrong trench, from our point of view, as I did with my cricket!" There are many such letters to "The Tettenhallian" during the war years, and most of them are characterised by the same determined cheerfulness, with now and again a touch of wistfulness and, not surprisingly, even a touch of fear creeping in. This is, perhaps a good example of how "The Tettenhallian" helped to draw the school together and engender a sense of oneness among Tettenhallians and Old Tettenhallians alike during this extremely troubled and violent time.

Later on that year, two of the College's most valuable teachers, Mr. Pond and Mr. Cooper, had received their conscription papers, but had objected on conscientious grounds to serving in their county's forces. When the authorities turned down their appeals, they both elected to suffer terms of imprisonment rather than compromise their beliefs. This, at a time when public opinion was so against conscientious objectors, must have taken a lot of courage. Clearly the Council of Governors shared this opinion since they unanimously voted not to re-employ either man upon their release from prison.

With most able-bodied men away fighting the war, the Headmaster and his newly created Council of Governors had a great deal of difficulty in recruiting and keeping male teachers. With numbers steadily rising, so was the need for more teachers. At the beginning of 1918 there was just the Headmaster, Mr. Pearson, one part-resident master and four lady teachers with four occasional visiting teachers. Although Mr. Angus was in his forties, even he was called up in that final year of the Great War, although with the full backing of the Governors, he appealed to the Tettenhall Tribunal and to the Ministry of Education. No doubt the famous Angus gift with words paid off handsomely when he personally conducted his case and was duly awarded a deferment of his conscription for six months.

The shortage of men teachers, besides the other difficulties that it caused, had a considerable effect upon the running of the College games. Sports Day vanished for the duration of the war, and so did most of the hockey fixtures – as few schools played the game, most of the school fixtures were with men's clubs, and most of these, of course, had also been suspended or wound up. There were some matches with the Girl's High School, however. Rugger also suffered when the authorities commandeered the College rugby field for use as allotments.

In spite of all the hardship brought about by the war, life at the College was never dull. There were organised snowball fights in the woods and skating in the winter months. Many of the College's clubs and societies flourished under the guidance of various masters. There was the Discussion Society, which under the guidance of Mr. Pond, not only held many exciting debates, but also took to going on bicycle outings.

Everyone at the College followed the war with avid interest. It is not surprising therefore that the Training Corps organised by Mr. Pearson proved to be very popular. The Corps held frequent drills as well as outdoor exercises at Rindleford and Penn Common. Another war-related club was the First Aid Group, which came about largely as the result of the College's official status as a First Aid Centre as part of the war effort.

Despite the war, the College still maintained its Saturday evening concerts, many of which were attended by wounded soldiers convalescing at the Towers next door. Mock trials were popular with the Headmaster acting as judge, as were mock Parliaments. Many might think that the school was making light of the war, although this was definitely not the case. During the holidays, boys were encouraged to work on the land and even in munitions factories; and in term time, boys made splints and often held fund-raising events to assist Prisoners of War and for Old Tettenhallians who were at the Front. The fact that many men were actively aiding the war effort meant that there was a shortage of support staff at the College, so the boys often had to carry out this work themselves. Some of them helped to clean out the Swimming Pool; others cut timber in the wood, and did a spot of coal heaving. "Such is their spirit of devotion" says "The Tettenhallian," "that they have been known to forgo the joys of lessons and prep that their fellows might not be obliged to bathe in cold water." All during this, Christmas festivities were not neglected. At this time, the boys used to gather in the darkened Dining Hall, and listen to a choir from the Girls High School singing carols in the Headmaster's garden.

A Zeppelin raid on the Midlands resulted in the College having to undergo regular blackouts – for some time the boys went to bed in the dark. Rigorous drills were also in place to practice evacuations of the buildings. "Dormy" time for the evacuation of the entire Boarding House to the cellars was two minutes. Speech Days were put on hold and, at the suggestion of the boys, diplomas replaced books as prizes.

As the College began to grow, so it started to evolve. In 1917, the School Houses were re-structured – Cambridge, Non-Cambridge and Junior House were replaced by School, Bantock, Nicholson and New houses. The latter was designated a "New House not yet named," and, as often happens to temporary names, popular usage caused it to stick. One other change that took place during the war concerned Prefectorial headgear. The "black bowler" replaced the old "speckled straw". Not everyone approved the change, and "The Tettenhallian" made its usually acerbic comment: "If one member of this august assembly could be prevailed upon to place the hat at the correct angle instead of latching it upon the very back of his head, one would be less tempted to approach and inquire the odds on the next horse." The inference here is that the prefects in their new black bowlers looked not unlike racing touts.

By this time, the College was in a much-improved financial position, and only the heavy expenses of instigating the Trust Scheme prevented it from making a profit. In 1918, it actually did make a profit of £174. Later on in the year, when the School numbers reached the record total of 121, everyone (especially Mr. Bantock and the Headmaster) had good reason to be pleased. Contributing factors to this pleasant state of affairs included a gift of £250 from H.N. Bickerton, and W.H. Lever's agreement to waive the payment of both interest and capital upon his loan of £1,250 to the College. After some negotiation it was also agreed that J.W. Goddard would give up the interest due to him upon his loan to the College, provided that interest was paid in the future. Sir Arthur Nicholson, however, caused some anxiety by pointing out that he had been shouldering the burden of the £4,000 mortgage since before the war, and suggested that seven other Governors should each take up £500 of the mortgage. This idea was not popular though, and eventually, at Mr. Bantock's suggestion, the College bankers took over the mortgage, using the school property as security.

All throughout the war years the Headmaster took the College to new heights, and very often his sheer energy and dedication proved an inspiration to many. He conducted and preached most of the services in the College Chapel during the war and enthusiasm and inventiveness in coming up with new and interesting entertainments for the boys was talked about for many years to come. However, there is a price to pay for everything, and it seems that Mr. Angus' health deteriorated badly just after the war and Mr. Pearson had to step into his place while he recovered.

It is still unclear how many Tettenhallians fought in the Great War or even how many were injured or lost their lives. Previous accounts of this period say that there were over 200 Old Tettenhallians involved in the war, at least twenty-four of whom lost their lives, or were wounded in action.

Here, so far as it is known, is the full list of those who died:

R.H. Colbourne	T.E. Graham	E. Ridgway
J.A. Cooksey	D.B.H. Haydon	G.M. Rimmer
V.J. Cooper	S. Hirst	H.L. Shaw
A.P. Deverell	C.H. Lloyd	G.H. Shelton
T.A. Dickinson	S.D. Page	J.P. Thorne
H.T. Dreschfield	D.J. Pickard	W.H. Webb
A.W. Eld		
J. Field	I.L. Pinson	A.D. Whittaker
R.W. Fox	C.H. Pragneu	M.J. Williams

Little more than names are known about the careers of many of the former pupils on this list, although A.P. Deverell, had been Head Prefect in his last year in 1913. From Tettenhall College, he went to Bristol University after failing his army medical due to poor eyesight. At this time, the development of gas warfare on the Front had given rise to the need for specialist chemists and biologists to go to the Front to analyse what the enemy was doing. Deverell volunteered for this and was sent to the Front in spite of his poor eyesight. Within months of arriving in France he was killed in action.

Eric Graham was a good athlete when at Tettenhall College, and enlisted at only seventeen. He won the Military Cross within only weeks of going to the Front. He earned this posthumous award after he covered the retreat of many men over a bridge, refused to withdraw for medical treatment following a wound on his arm, although he was later killed by a shot in the head.

We also know that Sidney Hirst was one of the last to die, shot down while going to the aid of a fellow pilot.

A total of twelve Old Tettenhallians won the Military Cross. Three of these were the Muras brothers. N.W.R. Mawle served, like a number of his schoolmates, in the Royal Flying Corps, and was awarded the Royal Flying Cross. Records say that this award was won following the shooting down of nine enemy aircraft. Most Old Tettenhallians held commissions; one who didn't and achieved distinction from the ranks was A.J.P. Andrews. As a motorcycle despatch rider, he won the Distinguished Conduct Medal for, on several occasions, carrying important despatches through barrages of gas and shrapnel. "The Times" published a number of his letters home. In one of them he describes meeting his old Maths master, R. Lobb. It was in the aftermath of a big attack. "I met someone I knew on a stretcher. He told me that Lobb was there wounded among the crowd inside. I rushed in, feeling awful. I searched for about a quarter of an hour, and finally found him under a blanket. He was deathly white and still. I stayed for a while, feeling rotten and wondering if he would die, when he opened his eyes and talked to me." Mr. Lobb recovered, but another teacher, F.J. Thorns was not so lucky. On the Sunday following the news of his death, two of the hymns he had composed while at Tettenhall were sung in the College Chapel.

There is no doubt whatsoever that those at the College felt very strongly for The Tettenhallians who gave so much to the war effort. The poem published in "The Tettenhallian" sums up this feeling most succinctly:

TO THOSE WHO HAVE GONE
FROM THOSE WHO ARE LEFT

Sons of the same dear mother, to you the call has come,
You heard the music sounding, the beating of the drum;
The life you and I had known was shattered in a trice, at the blast of war,
You gave yourselves to your country, and thought of your ease no more.

And we who are left in classrooms, the rooms that you knew of old,
We think of you out in the darkness, the mud, the rain, and the cold,
And to you in dirt and danger, and to us in comfort still,
There comes the self-same message from the School on the windy hill.

Sons who are still on my bosom, sons who have left my side,
Remember the School that bore you, do justice now to my pride;
England has need of your service – 'tis a chance which you all can take –
To live your life, or to give it, not for self, but for other's sake.

And then the voice is silent, but with the strength it's bought
We turn again to the same old work, feeling it's not for nought.
Then we think again of you others, and our shout is changed to a prayer,
Now Coll., play up well, you fellows! – God keep you all in his care!

And so, the Great War came to an end and those at the College vigorously joined in the rejoicing. Again, "The Tettenhallian" sums up the spirit of the occasion very well:

What is this sound that throbs in my ear,
With its volume outswelling like cheer upon cheer?
'Tis borne by the breezes from far, far away,
'Tis the echo of joy caused by Victory Day.

It is sung by the brooks, it is told by the sea,
It is caught by the breezes and carried to me –
But what do the streams; winds and sea seem to say?
They seem to be murmuring "Victory Day."

Chapter 11

Aftermath

Headmaster: A.H. Angus Esq.

After the Great War, things were never the same at Tettenhall College. It seems that with 134 boys and even a waiting list for entry into the College, the days of overstretched finances and the constant threat of bankruptcy were finally over. The year 1918 saw a profit of over £1,000 and the newly formed Governing Body were pleased to note that the new Trust Scheme was working much better than anyone had predicted.

The Governors had every confidence in their Headmaster, although there is some doubt that Mr. Bantock fully shared the same level of confidence as his fellow Governors. Despite this though, Mr. Angus led the school into what many thought would be a new age of prosperity. The Prime Minister of the day, David Lloyd George, had promised "a land fit for heroes to live in," and in a spirit of optimism there were few at the College who doubted that this would not be the case.

There were four organised celebratory events at the College. Many thought that the highlight of these was the Sports Supper with 150 candles twinkling on the tables. There were also some exciting addresses from those who had fought in the war, and the visits to the War Relics Exhibition, and the Flying Display at Dunstall Park. Sergeant's return brought the return of constant supplies of hot water, a small thing perhaps, but one that brought increased comfort to many.

All of this improved morale considerably, which is just as well since fortunes were about to take a turn for the worse. The years immediately following the Great War had brought with them a considerable amount of unemployment and this was to have a detrimental effect on the fortune of the College since its own financial well-being was closely geared to the fortunes of the West Midlands, which is where much of the country's unemployment was.

The first unfortunate turn in the College's affairs came from a most unexpected direction though. The new Matron appointed in 1918 suffered badly from ill health, causing great unrest in the domestic staff. This was closely followed by the widespread outbreak at the

College of Spanish flu that was sweeping through Europe, reputedly killing more people than the war had.

No doubt fortified by its recent good fortune, the Governors took immediate action by hiring more medical staff and reorganising the domestic staff so that Matron's duties were shared by the main Matron and the House Matron. The former was to be responsible for the health of the boys, and the care of their clothes, while the latter saw to the housekeeping side. Pleased with its efforts, the Board recorded in its minutes that despite "the extraordinary state of the labour market, never has greater efficiency prevailed nor have the boys ever been better fed and looked after."

As has been mentioned, the lack of male teachers during the war had necessitated more female teachers, and gradually, these were replaced by men, namely A.F. Hall, R.S. Morley. F.B. Whalley, L.J. Cheyney and R.A. Theobald. All were well qualified, and as the Board was quick to point out, all had served in the forces during the war. Mr. Cheyney was the author of the most popular of the three school songs that have flourished during the College's history; Mr. Whalley was destined to become Second Master, but the most notable of these men was Mr. Theobald, who taught modern languages at the College from 1919 to 1950. During this time, accounts say that he was determined to make his students work very hard to achieve high goals, and his passion for his subject was only equalled, it seems, by his love of cricket.

So far, the Governors had succeeded in weathering the first storms quite successfully. However, the next major blow came when the Second Master, Mr. Pearson handed in his resignation. The war had placed a great strain on everybody, and Mr. Pearson was no exception. He had already in 1919 taken a term's sabbatical during which he agreed to accept half his normal salary with the balance being paid to those who had to make up the shortfall of work. Everyone hoped that this time off would help him to recover from the strain he had been put under, but it seems that this was not sufficient and Mr. Pearson decided that he had to leave. It is possible that he may have had other reasons for wanting to go, the most likely of which could have been the clash of personalities between himself and the Headmaster, although this is by no means certain. It is certain though that Mr. Angus was a talented organiser, a genius at public relations with the wit and charm to match. On the other hand, Mr. Pearson believed strongly that the foundation of all education was the training of character and this should come second to nothing. The most influential member of the Council of Governors, Mr. Bantock, also believed strongly in this ideal and it is likely that this caused him to side more heavily with the Second Master rather than the Headmaster. If this were the case, then it is likely that Mr. Pearson must have been in an intolerable clash of views. There is no documentary evidence to support this contention, but it is possible to see the details of the situation with a historian's benefit of hindsight.

So, in 1919, H.P. left Tettenhall to go to Eltham College, where he had a profound effect on the shaping of that school – no less so than he did at Tettenhall. "The Tettenhallian" wrote: "We have greatly missed a sympathetic friend to whom we could carry our little troubles." Words that express the high esteem that Mr. Pearson was held in the eyes of Tettenhallians.

In 1920, the Board recognised the Headmaster's valuable contribution to the success of the College by raising his salary. This was soon followed by a Board of Education inspection, which praised the College at length, saying: "We consider that you have to thank your Headmaster for this happy state of affairs. The whole establishment has been run with great care throughout a very difficult time, and your Headmaster has managed things not only with skill but [also] with great efficiency… Altogether it is a good school and in our opinion very little fault can be found with it. The boys are quite nice boys. They are clearly well treated, very happy, very well cared for and the discipline is excellent." However, the Inspectors recommended the provision of more equipment in the laboratories and workshops, and more books in the Library. They also recommended changes in the lavatories and modifications to the changing rooms. It was at this time that the College decided to give up the Oxford Locals as the school's principal external examiners and switch to the Northern Universities.

By the following year, increasing ill health had forced Mr. Bantock to tender his resignation from the Council of Governors. He made it clear that this was a reluctant move, although he made it quite clear that he felt the College was in good hands and "should have a bright future." The Board asked if Mr. Bantock was prepared to change his mind, and when told that the decision was final, it placed on record their "admiration and gratitude for his magnificent and timely generosity."

Up until this point, the College had been forced to rent fields in and around Tettenhall for the playing of sport and it was decided that it was high time to purchase grounds dedicated to that purpose. With this in mind, the College bought some grounds at Newbridge adjacent to the canal. There were twelve and a quarter acres in total and it all cost £6,267, of which the Old Tettenhallians Club paid £1,600 and the College raised a mortgage to cover the rest. Whilst the fields were actually not that close to the College, they did provide more than adequate sports facilities for many years. Mainly owing to the sports field's proximity to the canal, a Boat Club was soon formed where boys could row or sail on the canal.

The Board's treasurer reported that 1921 was the best financial year the College had ever experienced. So pleased was the Board with the Headmaster, that when he expressed his wish to attend the World conference of Workers Among Boys, being held in Austria, the Board insisted upon paying his expenses, and insisted upon giving him another honorarium of 100 guineas in appreciation of the "excellent balance sheet of 1921, the efficient state of the school, and the extraordinary heavy expenses to which the Headmaster has been put through [due to] illness in his family." In the following year another large profit was made – some £1,618, and two years later in 1924 there was once more a waiting list for entry to the College.

It wasn't just the College finances that were showing promise. Examination results for 1924 were good and the number of matriculations obtained was well above the national average. The Board gave generous credit to the Headmaster, who in turn praised his teaching staff. In conclusion, the Board said that: "from the educational, moral and social point of view, the School is exceptionally sound. The staff is adequate in numbers, thoroughly well qualified and delightfully keen."

All of this meant that money could be spent on improving the College buildings. The first task carried out was to reinforce the ceiling of the Dining Hall with the steel joists that are still there today. In the same year, the Headmaster showed his versatility by designing some strengthening members to reinforce the Main School first and second floors, which were displaying rather alarming signs of wear and tear. In the following year, the College had electric lighting installed to replace the gas lighting that had been there previously. This was also the time when the Tuck Shop was officially opened and proved not only popular, but also quite profitable, so much so that the shop was able to finance the purchase of a new clock and lawn mower. In later years, the Tuck Shop also funded a new boathouse and a pair of gates.

Mr. Angus will always be remembered for the encouragement he gave to boys to donate to charities. Around about this time, the Headmaster set up a "School Charity Fund," to organise the donation of money to several worthy causes. Unfortunately there is now only scanty information concerning the causes that the fund donated to, but it is known that money was paid to the Wolverhampton Fund for the Unemployed and to the Disabled Soldier's Institute.

As has been noted several times earlier, successive Headmasters had always encouraged extra-curricular activities, and Mr. Angus was no exception. A lot of the clubs and societies that had been abandoned during the Great War were revived, including the Chess Club, which set up an annual tournament with the Grammar School. There were frequent visits to the Wolverhampton Grand Theatre and there were occasional visits to the College by dramatic artists. The Headmaster also introduced dance classes for the boys, which proved to be highly popular. There was an active Cycling Club, and frequent visits were made to Edgbaston and other sporting centres to see top class games of various sorts. It was around this time when Saturday afternoon classes were abandoned in favour of allowing the boys to enjoy recreational activities, and this also had the benefit of lessening the pressure on the staff.

While the College was proud to boast that it had a telephone, another step into the world of high technology was made with the acquisition of a radio set in 1922. This meant that boys could listen to broadcasts from London and Manchester, and later on this device became part of the Armistice Day Memorial celebrations, with the boys listening to the National Service being broadcast from London. At this time, Armistice Day began with the observance of the two minutes silence in Big School at eleven o'clock, and Communion followed a service in the Chapel. In the evening there was a bonfire and firework display in the playground, and after this, a celebratory supper, concluded by the Second Master asking the Head for an extra hour in bed the following morning. This was never refused.

In spite of the sad loss of several Old Tettenhallians in the Great War, the Old Tettenhallians Club continued to thrive and "The Tettenhallian" records the achievements of many OTs. C.H. Crookshank, K.C., who had been at the College from 1871 to 1876, had become a barrister of great repute, and H.G. Stevenson, who had left the School in 1887, had sprinted for England in a match against the United States. Lt. Col G.L. Chambers, one of the first fifteen boys to attend the School when it opened in 1863, had enjoyed a distinguished military career, and Gladstone Mayall, one of eight brothers to attend the College, was also a highly renowned veterinary surgeon. H. R. Howard had become Professor of Mathematics in the Xavier University of Nova Scotia, and Claude Bantock had a highly successful career with the Royal Comic Opera Company. Claude de Ville acquired some note as a concert pianist, and no less than seventeen members of the Wolverhampton Rugby Club were Old Tettenhallians. E.H. Edwards played rugby several times for the North Midlands, playing full back in the 1922 County Championship final, and Harry Wilkinson, who later won an international cap, played full back for Yorkshire against the New Zealand All Blacks.

Meanwhile, the boys at the College had discovered the game of water polo, and frequent matches were held in what were by then the far less murky waters of the College swimming pool. This was around the time that the Headmaster introduced a "tackling bar" for rugby and no one was allowed his colours until he had first obtained this. The leading games players had their own table in the dining hall at this time and this was distinguished from all the others by its bright yellow chairs. Other privileges enjoyed by leading games players included an extra hour in bed on Sunday mornings.

In 1923, the Headmaster took a party of fourteen boys on a trip to London. For three days, the Headmaster and his charges stayed at London's Metropole Hotel and experienced much of the city's high life. On the Tuesday, they watched a Royal procession to Westminster Abbey, visited the offices of "The Daily Mail," and then had tea at Lyons Corner House. After this, they had dinner at the Coliseum and toured Piccadilly Circus before going to bed. Over the next two days, they visited the Tower, St. Paul's Cathedral, watched an appeal case in the House of Lords, visited Madame Tussauds and rounded it all off with tea at the National Liberal Club. In those days, these sort of trips were largely unheard of, and since several local papers reported on the trip, it was a good publicity stunt for the College, as well as clearly being an enjoyable venture for all those concerned.

As has been mentioned before, Mr. Angus was very good at selling the school to prospective customers. With this in mind, he introduced collections of crockery bearing the College arms along with Tettenhall College cufflinks, napkin rings and cutlery. It was also at this time when an embroidered cap replaced the prefects bowler, and the prefect's tie was introduced.

Another event that received extensive local press coverage at this time was the visit of Princess Helena Victoria, the granddaughter of Queen Victoria. The Princess was in Wolverhampton to help raise funds for the Y.M.C.A. – an organisation that was also supported by Mr. Angus, and he actually accompanied her for much of her visit. At Wolverhampton Town Hall, the Head Prefect and one of the youngest boys presented purses containing money contributed by the School, and when the Princess' car stopped at Upper Green in Tettenhall, she was presented with a large box of chocolates as a gift from Tettenhall College, with all members present to give a rousing cheer.

But the College's good fortune was to be short-lived. The economic depression that was sweeping the nation, and indeed much of the world, began to bite down hard and numbers at the College began to fall. As has been mentioned before, in those days, the fate Tettenhall College was very closely geared to the health of the local economy, and also to a lesser degree, to the national economy. As soon as unemployment rose and money became scarce, private education was one of the first things to suffer, which meant that other similar schools were experiencing the same malaise. At Tettenhall though, while numbers peaked at 134 in 1922, they steadily slipped away to 115 in 1925 – not a tremendous fall, one might think, but certainly a harbinger of worse times to come. Things weren't made any better by the departure in the previous year of two highly influential members of the Governing Body, namely James Thompson and James Highfield-Jones. However, Professor Tillyard of Birmingham University joined the Board in this year.

There is no doubt that the Great War had taken a heavy toll on the health of many of the staff. The strain of overwork and the obvious stresses of wartime society had debilitated the health of both Mr. Angus and Mr. R.S. Morley, the latter of whom was mostly suffering from war wounds. It was largely due to increasing mental ill health that eventually led to the Headmaster offering his resignation. The Board was told that he "was suffering from a serious nervous breakdown brought about by the overwork and strain of the past twelve years, and that his doctor had told him very definitely that he would require six months complete rest in order to recover completely."

The tremendous achievements made in Mr. Angus' time as Headmaster were described by some as "miraculous." While the Board did make several attempts to persuade him to return after a sabbatical, Mr. Angus declined these, clearly believing it was time for new blood. The Board accepted his resignation with regret – not only had the numbers increased from 42 to 134, but the School's finances had been restored from "a state of chaos into one of soundness and hope." Not only this, but the College's good reputation had grown enormously, due down to both the increased numbers and to the famous Angus charm. A member of staff wrote on the Headmaster's departure that "he has spurred us on through mundane subjects to the more spiritual and lasting, urging that in the formation of character, Christian manhood was essential to the well being of any community, and that selfishness and self-seeking are among the poisons that corrode and destroy the moral springs not only of individuals, but of nations. Boys have thereby been made to feel their own responsibility to their homes, their school, and to the world at large."

It should also be noted that the College's good reputation was also furthered by Mr. Angus' policy of turning out a self-reliant, confident type of boy, with a strong self-respect and an intense pride in his school. His boys neither expected nor received any molly coddling, and given the choice of "six of the best" or of detention in punishment for a misdemeanour, rarely hesitated in their choice. No doubt these good results spoke for themselves to many.

Mr. Angus was only 52 when he resigned from the Headmastership, and after a period of convalescence, he switched careers and went into the advertising business. Not surprisingly, he distinguished himself there until his retirement.

He died in Bournemouth on January 11th, 1957 at the age of 83.

CHAPTER 12

HARD TIMES APPROACHING

Headmaster: P.W. Day Esq.

In 1925, the Tettenhall College Governors were faced with the extremely challenging task of finding someone to succeed Mr. Angus. Many commented that the outgoing Headmaster would be a tough act to follow, and this indeed proved to be the case. It must be remembered that the Governing Body had rewarded Mr. Angus' achievements with a substantial rise in salary – much more than many other headmasters were getting. It seems therefore that upon his departure, they felt that offering a more competitive salary made better financial sense, since the position was offered at only £450 a year, plus the usual house, rates, services and capitation fee of £1 a term for Boarders and ten shillings for Day Boarders in excess of 70.

It must also be remembered that these were times of economic hardship and many other schools had been closed down at this time, giving rise to more teachers on the employment market. This gave rise to over 150 enquiries and forty actual applications for the position. The Board had decided that the new Headmaster would not also be Board Secretary like Mr. Angus had been, and had recently appointed Rev. J.L. Chown as Secretary. It was Mr. Chown and Professor Tillyard that eventually drew up the shortlist from the forty applications.

It is clear from many letters though that several of the Board, especially Mr. Bantock, favoured inviting Horace Pearson back to become Headmaster. However, it was Mr. Pearson's lack of a degree that was really the only thing at this time standing between him and a unanimous vote to offer him the position of Headmaster.

The Board wanted the new Headmaster to be a Free Churchman, and two applicants were offered the position following interview – the Rev. Frank Lenwood of London, and H.L. Price of Christ's Hospital, who both eventually declined. Further interviews were held with the remaining five candidates on the shortlist, and it is interesting to note that all interviewees had to answer extensive questions about education, classical, modern and technical, about spiritual and religious instruction with special reference to the College services. They were also asked about their attitude to sport, including the playing of games on a Sunday, and

Percy. W. Day Esq., M.A. (Headmaster 1925-1927)

told that war service would be taken into account. In the end "it was generally felt" that Percy W. Day was the strongest candidate, and he was therefore offered the post together with an extra £100 for bursarial work. It seems that Mr. Day was the only candidate who, once the members of the Board stopped firing questions at him, took over the questioning and asked them in turn a great many questions about the College. This must have impressed the Board considerably.

After attending Bishop Stortford College, Mr. Day went to King's College, London, where he read Modern History and was awarded the Gladstone Prize. Two years research on "colonisation into the West Indies" followed, which won him his M.A., and membership of the Royal Historical Society. From London, Mr. Day went in 1916 to teach at Taunton School, where he soon became House Master of the School House, and Sixth Form master. Those who supported his candidature for the post at Tettenhall – and they were all important people in Free Church circles – spoke enthusiastically of his work at Taunton and elsewhere.

Mr. Day arrived at Tettenhall in 1925 to begin what was to be the shortest term as Headmaster in the College's history. He turned out to be an enthusiastic hard working man who made every effort to give his boys the widest possible education. He was keen on visiting lecturers to give differing perspectives on many subjects and encouraged many theatre and concert visits. An enthusiastic games player, Mr. Day did much to build up strong rugger sides. In this and in many other ways he did much to win the support of the Old Tettenhallians Club.

However, he lacked the charisma of his predecessor, and while his academic achievements were legion, he was not the consummate marketer that Mr. Angus had been. This at a time when the country's economic fortunes were forcing College numbers down, it really needed Mr. Angus' charm. Not only this, but Mr. Day was not the disciplinarian that many of his predecessors had been, and boys were given pretty much a free a hand to do as they pleased. This meant that the standard of discipline declined along with numbers.

Eyewitness accounts tell of Mr. Day's reluctance to punish boys, especially if that punishment involved a physical element. To modern eyes, this is probably not seen as much of a failing, but in those days of the early twentieth century, it was still firmly believed that "six of the best" was indeed the best way to run a tight ship. Not only this, but Mr. Day's regime was noticeably more tolerant of remarks made about staff in "The Tettenhallian," that certainly would not have been tolerated in earlier years. It is true that discipline had slipped a notch towards the end of Mr. Angus' time (largely due to staff health problems, including the Headmaster's own), but it seems that Mr. Day was either not willing or did not know how to rectify this decline.

All this meant that Mr. Day was liked, but not necessarily respected in a way that a Headmaster of a Public School needed to be. He was certainly not revered in the same way that his predecessors had been. He was also taking office during some very hard economic times, and as has been mentioned earlier, he lacked sufficient commercial acumen to tackle many of the problems the College faced.

One of the first tasks facing Mr. Day when he arrived at Tettenhall was the appointment of a new Second Master. It is clear in this instance that he did have sound judgement when it came to choosing his own right hand man. For a few years now, the post of Second Master had been rather forgotten about, with other masters doubling when the need arose for one. Clearly, Mr. Day decided to put an end to this by appointing Mr. F.C. Pine – one of the College's best-remembered masters right up until his retirement in 1959. No doubt many thought that an existing master would get the job, and rumour has it that several masters were discussing who should get it when Mr. Day walked into the room and introduced Mr. Pine as the new Second Master.

Mr. Pine brought an enormous amount of enthusiasm to everything he touched – and there wasn't much that he didn't touch in the life of the College. Many will remember Mr. Pine for his Scouting activities and the many wonderful camps he organised both at home and abroad. He was a keen boxer, and had actually been the British Army's Featherweight Champion in India. There was the Air Training Corps and a thriving Gymnastics Club, all of which received the benefit of his seemingly boundless energy. One of the things that many Tettenhallians of the time recall most vividly is Mr. Pine's ability to tell a really good story, and he was always best at telling of his own misadventures. Just like Horace Pearson, Mr. Pine had no degree, and whilst his principal subject was Geography, he could turn his hand well to most of the others. Well all was said and done though he was, also like Mr. Pearson, a firm believer in the teaching of character.

During Mr. Day's short stint as Headmaster, there were some significant moves that would lay the foundations for the way the College is structured today. The first of these was the setting up of a Prep Department, or Junior School, which is the precursor to what is now known as Lower School and later on the Drive School. Up until this point, boys of all ages were taught on the same premises, and it was this segregation that allowed different teaching methods better suited for younger pupils to be used without interfering with the older boys. At first, the Prep Department was situated in other premises rented in the village, and whilst it was slow to catch on, it was firmly established by the time Mr. Day left.

It was at this time that the changing rooms that now adjoin the Swimming Pool were built. Both the new changing rooms and the Swimming Pool were fitted with steam heating, although the great Coal Strike of 1926 and the General Strike to which it led, deprived the College for a while of the fuel it needed to keep the heat going.

The Headmaster made a proposal to the Board that the College should accept weekly Boarders, but this idea was rejected since everyone felt it easier simply to issue weekend passes to Boarders that wanted one. This meant that fee concessions would not be needed. What was accepted by the Board though, was the Headmaster's suggestion that the Governors and Staff should meet for lunch on Speech Day. Also accepted was Mr. Day's suggestion that the College should offer ten bursaries for "deserving boys" together with a reduction in fees for the sons of Non-conformist Ministers.

The Governing Body had already appointed Professor Tillyard as Chairman by 1926 and everyone was pleased that Mr. Bantock had returned as a Governor, although not this time as Chairman. At all Governors' meetings at this time, the subject of declining numbers was a much-discussed topic. There were no Day Boys at the College at this time and the decline had mostly been felt in the numbers of Boarders. In October 1925, there were 98 boys in total; of these 68 were Boarders and 30 Day Boarders. In October 1927, the number of boys had fallen to 85, which was made up of 40 Boarders and 45 Day Boarders. Many parents had requested a change in status from Boarder to Day Boarder and the Governors had, in some cases, attempted to strengthen the weakening of the boarding side by refusing to grant change of status and raising the fees for Day Boarders. Despite this, the number of Boarders continued to fall and there can be little doubt that this was mostly down to financial hardship on the part of the parents.

Despite this, the Governors voted to pay the Headmaster a hospitality allowance of £10 a term, and there is no doubt that the Headmaster used it in strengthening the connection between the College and its Old Boys. Mr Day went down on record several times as saying how valuable to the College its Old Boys were, and this allowance certainly helped to make the bond firmer. When the Annual Dinner came around, a whole dormitory was made available to Old Tettenhallians.

By January 1926, the Governors reported a loss of £455 on the previous year's working. True to form, economies were made and plans to carry out works of repair and decoration to the College buildings were put on hold for the time being. However, Mr. Bantock intervened and insisted that the works be carried out because he felt that the College needed to at least "put a good face on things." The works were carried out and the College put on a brave face to the world. Economies were made on the domestic side that were less visible though, and numbers did rise briefly to 120 by the end of the year, but fell again to 85 the following year, which was to prove to be Mr. Day's last.

It is difficult to pin down the reasons why numbers fell in 1927, but a contributing factor may well have been 1926's poor examination results. Fifteen senior entries produced only one Matriculation, and three School Certificates, and all eleven junior entrants failed. How much of this was down to the Headmaster is unclear, but there were many that argued that the poor results could well have been down to the slackening of discipline, while others blamed the large amount of time devoted to extra-curricular activities. This particular issue is always a source of controversy in educational circles – many believe that a school's sole purpose should be to get as many public examination passes as possible to the exclusion of all else, while others argue that extra-curricular activities are essential in building character and forming well-rounded people. Such debates usually result in the conclusion that it's simply a question of balance. As has previously been mentioned, there were many extra-curricular activities at the College during Mr. Day's time, including many lectures by guest speakers. Such subjects included "Butterflies," "Florence," "Musical Appreciation," "Picture Writing of Ancient Times," "Stream Life," and "Dr. Barnardo's Home," very few of which augment directly any of the exam syllabuses of the day. There were many theatre and concert visits, only a few of which were relevant to examination subjects, and the frequent visits to sporting events certainly weren't. However, many of these events took place at weekends, which should, many would argue, be free time and such activities were certainly constructive use of it, when one considers the many other alternative activities that boys are fond of getting up to.

Sport was no less popular at the College during Mr. Day's time than it had been before. We have already seen that the Headmaster was a keen rugger player, and indeed, he did much to encourage the game at the School. He even invited W.J. Davies, and English International Rugby Player to give a talk to the boys. Indeed, it was at this time that Old Tettenhallian Harry Wilkinson was playing full back for Yorkshire, and eventually secured his England cap, and three Old Tettenhallians were in the Staffordshire team that the boys went to see playing Derbyshire. The School team was doing well too, and had won thirteen of its matches in one season, and lost only four. They also scored 450 points in a season, beating Sutton Coldfield Grammar School by 100 points to nil. In the next season, they won eighteen of twenty-four matches played. In athletics, a new departure was the presentation of a cup to the pluckiest loser, the whole School deciding who should be its holder. One Sports Day was made memorable by the breaking of the tug-o-war rope, each side sitting down heavily under the impression that it had won. The Boat Club was also active in those days, although it was a school rule that no boy could take a boat out on the canal until he had demonstrated his ability and fortitude to swim four lengths of the Swimming Pool.

At this time, motorcars were becoming more popular and many boys of this generation remember the excitement at seeing Henry Seagrave's Mystery Sunbeam car that had driven to break the world land speed record of 200 mph on March 29, 1927. The car had been on loan to the Thorneycrofts, the College's next-door neighbours. Another memorable event was 1927's total eclipse of the sun, which was seen by all those at the College – much to the consternation of those who had travelled to Wales where they had been told (mistakenly) that there would be a better view. The same year saw the unveiling of the First World War memorial tablet in the Chapel. It was also in the Chapel where another unique event took place and this was the Christening by Rev. J.L. Chown of one of the Headmaster's daughters.

But 1927 was to be Mr. Day's last year as Headmaster. It is unfortunate that there is no clear indication of what actually forced his resignation. In July of 1926, he was paid an extra £50 for "his good and sound service," with a further salary increase in December, yet in July 1927, he offered the Governors his resignation. "The Tettenhallian" reports that "the climate didn't suit his wife's health," although what this means exactly is not clear. It is true that numbers were set to fall late in 1927, with only five new boys arriving and twenty-five leaving, so one supposes this took a part in forcing Mr. Day's hand. At Speech Day, he said: "events had moved rapidly in the last six weeks, and circumstances beyond my control had arisen," all of which seems to suggest the Headmaster had other personal reasons for leaving. One can speculate that he may well have found the transition from being an assistant master to being a Headmaster a little too much, and perhaps his return to becoming an assistant master (as Senior History Master at Blyth Grammar School) speaks for itself.

However, Mr. Day was always well spoken of after his departure, and the Chairman of the Governors, Professor Tillyard spoke of his "manly and sincere character," and others spoke warmly of his "bright and cheery presence." It is always interesting to speculate what would have happened to the College had Mr. Day stayed on, but one thing is certain and that is that in 1927, the Governors were aware that they would need a very special Headmaster indeed to lead the school through the hard times that everyone could see coming.

CHAPTER 13

THE DEPRESSION

Headmaster: H. Pearson Esq.

As soon as the Governors received Mr. Day's resignation, most of them knew what had to be done. As far as they were concerned, there was only one man that could possibly be right for Tettenhall College at this time, and that man was Horace Pearson. At the same meeting Mr. Day's resignation was read out, there was a unanimous vote to appoint Mr. Pearson as the new Headmaster. One assumes that he had been approached and accepted the appointment prior to the meeting, since it was resolved to pay the new Headmaster £600 per annum. It is interesting to note that Mr. Pearson himself requested that he should not receive any capitation fees, although he did receive the usual house, services, rates, etc.

Whilst it will be noted that the Board of Governors had not usually made a policy of appointing a Headmaster from existing staff, many felt that Mr. Pearson's time away from the College would allow much "dust to settle" and the usual infighting often resulting from a "peer-promotion" would not be a problem, especially since there had been quite a large turnover of staff since Mr. Pearson last worked at the College.

It will be remembered that during the Great War during Mr. Pearson's previous tenure at the College, two masters, Mr. Cooper and Mr. Pond, were forced to leave when they were imprisoned for being conscientious objectors to the First World War. The Governors had voted then not to re-employ these men upon their release, and it is a measure of the Board's respect for Mr. Pearson that in 1927, that they agreed he could summon Mr. Pond from where he had been working in Bishop's Stortford to take charge of the Boarding House at Tettenhall. Mr. Pond, in turn, agreed to return, and remained at the College until his retirement in 1950.

It is easy to imagine the tall figure of Horace Pearson striding back through the College gates, in true Arthurian fashion, to save the school in the hour of its greatest need. Indeed, one of the first things Mr. Pearson told the Board on his return was that he felt his summons to be a call that he dare not refuse. It is interesting to note that those who had previously objected to Mr. Pearson being appointed Headmaster because he lacked a degree were silent on this issue this time. No doubt Mr. Bantock held great sway as far as this was concerned,

Horace Pearson Esq., F.R.G.S. (Headmaster 1928-1941)

and his absence due to illness in 1925 was probably the only thing that had prevented Mr. Pearson's appointment as Headmaster at that time.

Mr. Pearson met with the Governors after he had re-acquainted himself with the College by carrying out a formal inspection. He noted that things were mostly in order, although he did say that some changes would need to be made. He noted that numbers had fallen in recent years and that there was evidence of a slackening of discipline, but nothing he felt that he couldn't handle given sufficient time and resources. It will be remembered that Mr. Pearson left Tettenhall in 1920, possibly in no small part down to personality differences between himself and Mr. Angus, and whilst the memory of this man's achievements were still fresh in the minds of many, it is clear that Mr. Pearson was going to place his own personal stamp on the College by doing things his own way.

After leaving Tettenhall in 1920, Mr. Pearson had spent seven years at Eltham College, and he had wasted no time in placing his own stamp on this school, whose chronicles record that after Mr. Pearson's arrival: "Immediately things began to change. The food improved, but we were not encouraged to waste it. Prefects' tannings disappeared but the House timetable worked to the half minute. Recalitrants in Geography classes and elsewhere received "love taps" or "wrath taps"… dress regulations were modernised… rugger, interest in civil affairs, the tone of the school, all flourished. His own line was common sense, fine organisation and a remarkable readiness to accept and try out new ideas, a warm and generous affection for his charges, and the demonstration throughout his life of a sterling character."

Horace Pearson was born in 1878 and educated at Mill Hill School. The son of a Congregational Minister, he originally envisaged a medical career and embarked on a degree course at Edinburgh University, but he was unable to complete this for reasons unknown. From Edinburgh, he worked as a salesman in Canada and then returned to England where he took up teaching as a career. His specialist subject was geography and the respect of other geographers is evident in the fact that Mr. Pearson was quickly appointed a Fellow of the Royal Geographical Society. The chronicles of Eltham School describe him as: "Tall, very tall, with commanding nose and gold rimmed glasses that glittered and even, it is said, bulged when he was angry. A formidable figure and most able organiser, but he also inspired deep affection and complete trust in those who knew him."

H.P., as he quickly became known, also brought with him a new housekeeper from Eltham. During her first year, Miss Walker managed to save the College £250, much to the Board's delight.

Things started getting better rather quickly. By March 1928, discipline had much improved, although the new Headmaster did complain that the "boys still needed to learn how to work." Obviously they learned very quickly, since the examination results in the summer of 1928 showed much improvement over the previous year. Seven candidates out of eleven passed, four with Matriculation, and two with distinctions in English and Geography. One of the changes made by Mr. Pearson was a reduction in the number of subjects on offer, and no doubt this allowed the boys to concentrate their minds more fully. By the end of the year, the Headmaster reported a marked improvement in the conduct of the boys, although he did have to deal with several isolated cases, one of which involved some boys who had been buying liquor from a nearby off-licence.

But these were early days, and whilst 1928 did have its problems, the following years saw a deepening of the Depression that was already gripping the country very hard. The Great Depression of 1929 brought Britain close to bankruptcy. The Depression had devastating effects in both the industrialized countries and those that exported raw materials. International trade declined sharply, as did personal incomes, tax revenues, prices, and profits. Cities all around the world were hit hard, especially those dependent on heavy industry, such as those cities making up the West Midlands. Unemployment soared and businesses collapsed causing severe hardship to all, and inevitably the College suffered too. As has been mentioned previously, at this time, the fortunes of Tettenhall College were strongly geared to the amount of prosperity in the West Midlands and the country as a whole. Clearly, in these sort of hard times, buying a private education was seen as a low priority compared to keeping food on the table. At this time, parents were aware that there had been a phenomenal growth in the State Education System, and many free State-run schools had popped up in the West Midlands, offering a free alternative to Tettenhall. Some of those parents who were feeling the Depression took their boys away from Tettenhall and this caused numbers to fall. When H.P. took over as Headmaster in 1928, there were 86 boys at the College and this number dropped quickly to 74 in 1929.

While this was happening, the Tettenhall College Governors reacted to falling numbers by introducing a new publicity campaign. Previously, the College had advertised only in religious journals and the rise in secular beliefs had, over the years, robbed these commercials of their efficacy. It was clearly time for the College to move into the growing world of multimedia where radio was commonplace and television was just around the corner. However, the Board realised that advertising in local and national newspapers was the best option for the College at this time, and it placed several adverts in "The Manchester Guardian" and "The Yorkshire Post." Attempts were made to encourage the boys to stay longer at the College by offering bursaries, but this only created fresh expense. In 1928 the College made a loss of £2,000 on the year's working, and in the following year, £1,570. Despite these grim figures, the Board refused to make some economies though. It was suggested that the smaller numbers made it not worth paying pew rent to Queen Street Church, although this idea was overturned, mainly due to generosity of the Church in waiving overdue pew rent in the past. The Board also refused to save money by cutting down the amounts spent upon repairs and decoration, no doubt at the instigation of Mr. Bantock, whose stubborn resolve to keep up appearances was well known to everyone.

So now, the College once again faced a rising tide of debt that threatened to drown it as surely as the many other independent schools killed by the Depression. With the incidence of increasing numbers of bankruptcies and bad debts, credit was becoming increasingly scarce among the College's suppliers and some even demanded payments up front, all of which prevented the school from "resting on credit" as it had done in years gone by. This meant that cash flow became much more sluggish, and there was growing need to keep more cash in hand. Lloyd's, the College's bankers, were not very helpful since they were too busy pursuing bad debts from other customers deluged by the Depression. Increasing numbers of parents were defaulting on their fees, although the Board were very magnanimous in giving what assistance they could by way of instalment payments, even though they could not really afford to do this.

As the College began to stumble and falter, its ever-constant companion – the love and generosity of its family – carried it through the hard times once again. One extremely strong factor that had always been on the school's side since the early days was the love and devotion of Tettenhallians and Old Tettenhallians alike, and whilst it is difficult to place a finger on where this unswerving enthusiasm and generosity was engendered, it is probably in no small part down to the good choice of staff who had developed a well thought out regime that provided a fun but disciplined family atmosphere. All of this added up to gratitude of loyalty from most of the Tettenhall College family, and like in all times of difficulty, the family pulled together.

Mr. Pearson and Mr. Pond managed to find a full set of new desks, some prints of famous paintings for the walls and even a radio set. The Old Tettenhallians Club paid to have the Chapel redecorated, the Swimming Pool refurbished and even found enough money left over to re-equip the Gymnasium. And, of course, there was Mr. Bantock. Thought of by many as the College's constant guardian angel, he took out his much-used cheque book once again and made a "loan" of £500 in July of 1928 and a further £500 in March 1929. This was followed up by £800 in May 1929 and £400 in October. Whilst these were officially classified as loans, they amounted to gifts since repayment was never demanded and, indeed, never made. It would be gratifying to think that these generous donations were made out of pure unadulterated love for Tettenhall, but a careful examination of Mr. Bantock's other business ventures at this time suggests that there may have been certain financial advantages to be gained by "loaning" these sums. However, let this not detract from the fact that the College received a much-needed substantial cash injection that certainly saved it from closing its door permanently, good exam results or not.

All of this boosted morale at the College at a time when suicide rates on both sides of the Atlantic had gone through the roof. Mr. Pearson commented at a Board meeting that all the generous help had been "the greatest honour" he had received. He then went on to say that he would do his utmost to justify this faith shown in him by his Board, his staff and his Old Boys. This precipitated a further gift of £550 in late 1930, and at a time when many other schools were falling like flies, Tettenhall continued to build on the solid ground that successive Headmasters had so assiduously laid down. However, a shadow fell over the College when Professor Tillyard resigned as Chairman of the Governing Body, but the Board resolutely determined to find a replacement from the world of academia up to the challenge of taking the Professor's place. Sure enough, the Governors soon appointed Professor Powicke as Chairman, and no one even broke step in their determination to prevail.

Despite the cash injections and the hard work, numbers still fell – so much so that in 1929, the Headmaster was forced to reduce the number of School Houses to two – Nicholson and Bantock. This caused at least one parent to question the "educational efficacy" of the school, since only two Houses would result in reduced competition. The Headmaster proved to be more than up to the task of soothing any doubters by pointing out that all boys were now actively involved in school life in a way that probably couldn't be achieved with larger numbers. This meant that no parents managed to wriggle out of paying fees by complaining! However, behind closed doors, the Headmaster did admit to the Board in May 1931 that if the school could just get twenty more boys, then the financial situation would be greatly improved since the balance sheet for that year showed a loss of £1,713.

To the Board's credit, it determined not simply to paper over the College's financial cracks, but to get to the heart of what was causing the decline in numbers and what they could do to alleviate this. Granted, there was the Great Depression looming large in everyone's lives, and money was short. And there was nothing the College could do about this. Next, the rise of State Education was eating away at the College's integrity with growing fervour. Nothing much it could do about that either. Lastly, the Board determined that there had been a dramatic decline in the moneyed classes (where the College drew most of its pupils from), largely due to the fall in birth rate and the increase in death rate during the Great War. This factor had also given rise to a marked fall in children between the ages of 12 to 14, which everyone thought would last for another three or four years at least. Whilst the Great War had brought substantial short-term benefits to the College in the way of increased numbers, it seems that in the long term, the results were hugely detrimental.

However, this was a factor that the Board could do something about though. If it couldn't recruit older boys, then it determined to set its age bar lower. Following several advertising initiatives involving bulk mailing and newspaper advertising, the Board succeeded in recruiting younger boys for the newly formed Prep Division. This was seen as a way of securing more long-term pupils for the College, and it was this type of thinking that helped to pave the way for the College's present policy of providing a "complete" education from nursery to Matriculation. Good results were achieved in obtaining more younger boys below the age of 10, many of whose parents were granted discounts on fees in the hope that this understanding would motivate them to leave their boys at the College for the long-term. Consequently, there was an increase in numbers of nine boys in 1931 despite the death by diphtheria of one boy in that year.

So things did begin to look up in 1931, despite indifferent exam results, although everyone was greatly cheered by the awarding of a Chemistry Nobel Prize to Old Tettenhallian Dr. Arthur Harden, who was at the College between 1877 and 1881. This distinguished Old Tettenhallian, who was Professor of Biochemistry at London University, eventually won a knighthood for discovering a substance active against pneumonia. Earlier, when he had been awarded the Davy medal of the Royal Society, "The Manchester Guardian" had referred to him as "one of England's greatest scientists." The award was made jointly between Mr. Harden along with Hans Karl August and Simon von Euler-Chelpin for their investigations into the fermentation of sugar and fermentative enzymes.

The College also attracted pupils by the awarding of bursaries and scholarships and in spite of the fact that this was costing £1,100 a year, everyone realised that without these, the dramatic fall in numbers would more than treble these losses by way of falling revenue. Late in 1931, the staff were forced to accept a ten per cent cut in salary, but numbers of boys rose to 90 in the following year and the Headmaster remarked that the school could now "see light through the trees."

Optimistic words, but ones that belied the fact that the College was still in dire financial straits. Another loan of £900 from Mr. Bantock buttressed things up substantially, although everyone knew that this was essentially a short-term remedy – what the College needed the most was more boys. Clearly, without the fee income, the College couldn't last long. In 1933, the Board held several meetings to address the problem of dwindling numbers. It was decided at the first of these meetings that the College needed to spend at least some of the money loaned by Mr. Bantock on another advertising campaign, and while many saw that this may well remedy the situation a little, the Board realised that they really weren't tackling the heart of the problem. It seems that whilst many Non-conformists ardently believed that there should be schools like Tettenhall, which catered specifically for their religious beliefs, a lot of parents realised that sending their sons to the more well-known Public Schools would give their sons a far greater chance of success than sending them to lesser known schools such as Tettenhall College. At this time, the vast majority of the "major" Public Schools were Anglican dominated and many parents felt that this was a small trade-off in return for guaranteed success. It was certainly true, as it is today, that to obtain indifferent results from a well-known school or university is far more beneficial than receiving outstanding results from an institution that few people have heard of. The rise of a more secular society also played its part – there were more people who had no profound religious beliefs than there had been back in 1863 when the College was founded. Events like the Russian Revolution and the rise of Nazism had served to undermine the religious bedrock of many very influential countries, and the repercussions in terms of more agnostic views were felt in many other countries including Great Britain.

In 1933 there was an Annual General Meeting of the Congregational Union in Wolverhampton. Tettenhall College accommodated sixteen delegates as guests and held a reception for at least 500 delegates in a marquee on the Playground. During the course of this, all delegates were invited to take a tour of the school, and in previous years, such an event would have certainly obtained more boys, although in 1933, there is little evidence that any increase in numbers was precipitated by this. Indeed, in this year, the Headmaster reported that over two thirds of the boys attending the College were Anglican, and this may well also have been a reason why Non-conformist parents saw fit to patronise the better-known schools – all at Tettenhall College's expense.

There was no obvious "quick-fix" solution to this problem, although the dawning realisation was that the College would have to move with the times if it were to survive. Mr. Bantock had made it clear that even he could not be relied upon to carry the College forever. Ill health had forced him to take a far less active part in school affairs and the Headmaster visited him regularly at his home in Merridale to discuss the College finances. Very often H.P. came away with a cheque in his pocket, much to the Board's relief, but everyone knew that they would need to make some changes soon, since this could not continue for much longer.

Ever since the turn of the twentieth century, there had been no Day Boys at Tettenhall. It will be recalled that many felt that these pupils didn't enter into the life of the school and that to allow Day Boys would essentially water down much of what the College stood for, and this was the "training of character" – a goal that was more than adequately achieved by the school's vast array of extra-curricular activities – most of which Day Boys would not be around to participate in. It was also feared that the admission of Day Boys would weaken the Boarding side, and this may well lead to a slipping of standards. But desperate times called for desperate measures and the Board set up a sub-committee to look into the changes that would need to be made. This committee decided that Day Boys should be admitted, although it insisted that the School was still to be "primarily" a "Boarding School" (their capitals). There was some nervousness on the Board as to how the general public would react to the change – some people feared that people would think that the College had failed in its purpose, so it was decided that the advertisements should be discretely worded. Not everyone liked the idea, of course: Dr. Lees, an Old Tettenhallian and father of Old Tettenhallians, all most loyal supporters of the College, was most active in opposition, and no doubt there are those today who would like to see the College either as a boarding school, or at any rate a boarding and day boarding school. Be that as it may, the Day Boys were introduced in the hope that this would change the financial fortunes of the College without compromising the College's basic premise too much.

As a result of an advertising campaign assisted by the Old Tettenhallians Club, the College gained nine more pupils. Greatly encouraged, the Board advertised more extensively (especially in the "Express & Star"), only this time using decidedly less discrete wording. This year too saw the last of Mr. Bantock's generous cash gifts during his lifetime. He had given £111 in 1936 and his final gift of £600 came in 1938. By this time, numbers had risen to 120, which gave the Board much cause for celebration.

However, the introduction of Day Boys only eased the College's financial problems slightly. The Great Depression had brought with it a substantial rise in the cost of living. Domestic labour was also costing more, and the Board found itself forced to spend over a thousand pounds upon improving the domestic quarters. In fact over two years (1936-37) the Board spent over two and a half thousand pounds on repairs and alterations to the buildings. All this meant that whilst on one hand the College was receiving hugely increased fee income, it was having to pay out pretty much all of that extra income on overheads, thereby negating any benefit.

Things were not helped at all by the fact that Tettenhall College had been established in an area very close to a much older, larger and very well respected Grammar School that in commercial terms put up some very stiff competition indeed. It is possible that Tettenhall College's history would have been far less of a "roller-coaster" ride if it had been established well away from any potential competition. As it stood in 1938, the College had competition from the Wolverhampton Grammar School and several nascent state run comprehensives. However, the saving factor for Tettenhall was that it was ostensibly a boarding school, and rather than concentrate only on high-achieving pupils, like the Grammar School did (and still does), it admitted pupils of mixed ability. These were certainly factors that helped the College to survive the rigours of competition coupled with the obvious hardships ushered in by the Depression.

But it wasn't an easy ride though – despite increased numbers, economies still needed to be made. In an effort to reduce labour costs, the Headmaster encouraged the boys to help out whenever they could, and orderlies were introduced in the Dining Hall and Boarders were all expected to make their own beds. It will be recalled that Mr. Angus had sought the assistance of the boys during the Great War, so this culture of "lending a hand" was nothing new.

Another big helping hand came from the Old Tettenhallians. It was the financial assistance of many OTs that helped to pay for refurbishing the domestic quarters and the modernisation of many other College buildings. A whip round in OT circles produced a generous cash donation of £400 and the Headmaster even accepted a reduction in salary of £100 a year. It was OT money that paid for cricket coaching, including the fees charged by several international players, such as S. Barnes. It was at this time also that the Headmaster donated a piano and a number of chairs.

By 1938, the Board had had enough time to assess their new Headmaster, and they liked what they saw. They not only praised Mr Pearson's success in propagating a "tight and efficient ship," but they also praised Mrs Walker, the Housekeeper who had arrived with him. Most accounts agree that it was the personality of the Headmaster that gave others the confidence to invest their money. However, this was recognised by some as not only being the College's greatest strength, but also ironically, its greatest weakness. Chairman of the Governors Professor Powicke summed up this conundrum quite succinctly: "It would be much better to make the School less dependent on the personality of the Headmaster. That personality and dependence are very precious now but he cannot live forever, and it would be disastrous if the Governors reconciled themselves to the view that the College would not outlive him." Wise words indeed, and it is clear that the Governors of the College intended to learn from their experience of having their figurehead leave at the wrong moment.

Between 1934 and 1938, the College was showing a consistent (small) profit for the first time in many years. This allowed the Board to restore five per cent of the ten per cent cut in salary some of the staff had taken, with full salaries restored by the end of 1935. During this time there was a School Inspection with yielded gratifyingly glowing praise for the College. The teaching of Geography and Chemistry were regarded as outstanding, and form room discipline was described as excellent. It was true, continued the report, that there was little work of true distinction in the College, but in the last three years, five boys had gone to Birmingham University, and four more to other places of further education. "Tettenhall College," the inspectors said, "has a pleasant and well ordered life, and the games are not overdone. Hobbies are rightly encouraged." In 1934, ten out of fourteen candidates had secured passes in the Certificate Examinations, five of them with Matriculation. In 1937, three candidates for the Higher School Certificate had all passed, and these were the first passes to be recorded at this level at Tettenhall since 1922. News of the first scholarship to be won since 1908 – to Birmingham University – was announced in this year. No wonder that the Headmaster was optimistic. "My grounds for this optimism," he said, "are that our reputation for good work generally – beginning with our education – and the fact that we are known to give all round education to the boys, and their happiness, is recognised by so many, especially in the locality."

But the words of Professor Powicke were to ring true in 1938 when Mr. Pearson offered the Board his resignation. H.P. said that as he was nearly sixty and that he felt the job of Headmaster would be better handled by a younger man. The Governors unanimously voted to ask him to stay on and it seems that none of them felt that a younger man could do any better, so Mr Pearson agreed to stay on. This unanimous vote of confidence is a wonderful tribute to the faith the Board had in their Headmaster, although it was a lesson to many that the idea of relying upon a figurehead to carry any kind of organisation has many severe pitfalls.

At this time, the Board set up yet another Endowment Fund, but this time at Mr. Bantock's request. His cash gifts to the College had been made on one condition, and that was that at least some of the money should be spent on scholarships. It was the intention that this new fund should be there ostensibly to build up a strong sixth form by the granting of scholarships and bursaries, but it would also serve as security for the College's overdraft. Unfortunately, the new fund was poorly subscribed to, with only twenty-seven replies to the thousand or so letters sent out appealing for money.

It is possible that Mr. Bantock suspected that setting up this endowment fund would be his last service to the College, since on 7th February 1938 the College's "most devoted son" passed away. There is no doubt whatsoever, that without Mr. Bantock's unrivalled generosity and his forceful personality, Tettenhall College would not have survived much longer than twenty years – if that. At the time of his death, his cash contributions to the College totalled £7,460, and if we count the value of other contributions, the figure rises to at least £15,000 – not a tremendous amount by today's reckoning, but in the late nineteenth and early twentieth centuries, it represented a figure well in excess of three million pounds by today's standards.

Mr. Bantock's death did not take away his generosity. He left in his will an immediate gift to the College of £5000 and an additional £20,000 payable on the death of his wife, which was to be used specifically for scholarships. It must be noted that Mr. Bantock died without direct heir, and it is clear from this that he regarded Tettenhall College as part of his legacy to future generations. Chairman of the Governors Professor Powicke commented on the announcement of his death: "There are two kinds of people in this world: those who snatch and those who enrich, and Mr. Bantock was known to us all as one of the latter."

Alderman Bantock is deeply honoured by all those at the school, past and present, by the naming of a School House after him. It was hoped then, as it is now, that this will ensure that the spirit of his personality and his wonderful generosity will live on as long as Tettenhall College endures.

Chapter 14

The Winds of War

Headmaster: H. Pearson Esq.

Mr. Bantock's passing was certainly a blow to all at Tettenhall College. Many had begun to take his generous cash gifts somewhat for granted, and the thought of having to manage without them proved daunting. At that time, the College had two mortgages and an overdraft, and the Bantock legacy allowed the Board to pay off just the one pertaining to the playing fields at Newbridge. Another legacy of £500 from G. Faulkner-Armitage (OT and ex Mayor of Altrincham, Cheshire) allowed a large chunk of the overdraft to be paid off, while the remainder went into the newly set up endowment fund. Some of this money was even used to help parents suffering from financial hardship. A cash gift form the Headmaster helped to re-equip the Gymnasium and a very generous gift of £2,000 from S.H. Clay went towards scholarships to Oxford. All of this made Mr. Bantock's death easier to accept, but everyone realised the foolishness of depending on these sort of once-only gifts carrying on into the future.

The Great Depression had brought misery and hardship to many in Europe, and this had caused a backlash of fascism in several countries including Germany, Italy and Spain. This resulted in some bitter power struggles, some of which resulted in all-out civil war. The financial hardships endured in the thirties spawned fascist movements in other countries including Great Britain, and this was in no small part a backlash to the surge of Union power in the workplace. The growing popularity of atheist-based political activists like Marx had propagated a new generation of people less motivated by religion – and the idea of a school specially for Non-conformist Christians began to look very dated indeed. All of this meant a potential decline in popularity for schools such as Tettenhall, and the ever-present shortage of money felt in the thirties more or less insured that the generous donations enjoyed in earlier years would certainly dry up.

Despite all this doom and gloom, life at Tettenhall went on surprisingly as normal during the thirties. During this time, there were several School Inspections and reading through the remaining reports given by the Inspectors reveals the high amount of praise accorded to the College for the attention devoted to hobbies and other extra-curricular activities. In a world where vocational degrees (as opposed to pure subjects) at universities were becoming more popular, the benefits of a well-rounded education were obvious when seen in this context. In this sense, the College was perhaps ahead of its time in that it made positive efforts to give the boys a wide breadth of experience that would better help them make the career choices that suited them best.

No doubt with this in mind, one of the first things Mr. Pearson did on his return to the College was to get rid of Saturday evening prep for younger boys with extra time being devoted to this activity during the week. This gave more time for hobbies at a time when the boys were more amenable to the benefits of such activities. Existing records show that the boys were quick to take advantage of this newfound free time – hobbies like fretwork, carpentry, art, photography and electronics became very popular. Even the Headmaster took an active interest in chess and billiards – no doubt to dispel the (then) popular belief that this latter activity was the sign of a misspent youth. Joking aside though, societies like the Discussion Society had a positive impact on the boys, in that the quality of public speaking was often commented upon in local society, and this certainly did benefit the boys by boosting confidence levels. The good it did to boys contemplating careers like the Law where public speaking is an essential prerequisite is obvious. The Discussion Society was even praised by Old Tettenhallian Dr. Robert Horton, the once president of the Oxford Union – easily one of the most famous debating societies in the world.

Whilst one may be forgiven for assuming that Dr. Horton's opinion of the Discussion Society was somewhat biased by his connections with the College, there is no doubt that the topics discussed by the Society are very interesting, not to say potentially controversial. There was extensive discussion on subjects like "The Monarchy," at a time when many countries like Spain and Russia had comparatively recently abolished their monarchies – events that had caused profound repercussions around the world. Another controversial subject was "Evolution [of the human species]," which was still causing heated debate in much higher circles ever since Charles Darwin had challenged the long established religious status quo by publishing *On The Origin Of The Species* nearly eighty years earlier in 1859. It is a testament to the College's long established ability to move with the times that such a debate could be tolerated at a school founded on such strong religious beliefs. If one recalls the opening paragraphs of this book, it is easy to see that the College was acting as a microcosm of an increasingly secular society, and was actively providing a way for its boys to live in that society by giving valuable and broad insights into the philosophies and beliefs that were evolving within it.

Just like his predecessor, Mr. Pearson was a keen supporter of having visiting lecturers visit the College to talk on a diverse range of subjects not usually covered by recognised educational curricula. Occasionally the boys' hard work would be rewarded by a half-day's holiday, which would give them an afternoon's free time, although there would always be a lecture in the evening. Notable among these was a visiting member of staff from Eltham who spoke to the boys about sex. The idea of formalised sex education in the 1930s was almost unheard of, and is a definite sign of progressive thinking on the part of Mr. Pearson and his staff.

Another subject close to the Headmaster's heart was "The Causes of War." This is not surprising since the country was still in the aftermath of the Great War and a great deal of debate was still raging as to its causes and the ways in which it might have been avoided. It seems that the Headmaster believed in the notion that the difference between a wise man and a fool is that the fool's mistakes never teach him anything. All of this led to an active branch of the League of Nations at the College. It will be remembered that the League of Nations was the international organisation of 58 member states set up after the Great War whose goals included disarmament, preventing war through collective security, settling disputes between countries through negotiation, diplomacy and improving global quality of life. The diplomatic philosophy behind the League represented a fundamental shift in thought from the preceding hundred years. The League lacked its own armed force and so depended on the Great Powers to enforce its resolutions, keep to economic sanctions that the League ordered, or provide an army, when needed, for the League to use. In these years leading up to the world's next and greatest global conflict to date, debates held by the League were of great importance to everyone. This contention is evident in the College's willingness to have many joint meetings with other rival schools to discuss and debate the issues that many could see leading to another, and this time much greater, armed conflict. Such liaisons included a film show in the College Chapel with the Girls High School on the work of the League of Nations. There were joint Scout meetings with the Royal School and even lectures from visiting women preachers.

On one occasion when Mr. Hunt, the organist, was ill, a discussion on gambling and sweepstakes took the place of the ordinary service. We have seen how the lectern, and the three carved chairs, appeared in Chapel, and it was at this time that they were augmented by the Communion table, which was a gift from Mr. and Mrs. A.J. Sapp, as a memorial to their son.

As mentioned previously, Mr. Pine proved to be the backbone of a lot of exciting activities at Tettenhall. Scouting was perhaps the most popular with its badge tests and several large-scale "Wide" games that involved large numbers of boys and one that was notable in the pages of "The Tettenhallian" was one called "Coastguards and Smugglers." In this, the boys were divided by Mr. Pine into two teams – a small team of "Coastguards" and the remainder as "Smugglers." The "Coastguards" then established a base, which became the "jail," and the "Smugglers" were given time to secrete themselves in various places. The "Coastguards" then had to catch all the "Smugglers." and place them in jail. However, once captured, "Smugglers" could be released from jail by being touched by a smuggler who is still free. The similarities between these games and modern "Paintballing" are obvious, and the opportunities for the boys to bond and develop "team" mentalities are no less relevant to those early Tettenhallians than they are to modern teams of "Widegamers" today. A similar "Hunt the Flag" exercise took place on a day trip to Church Stretton, where one group of boys fortified Caer Caradoc, a mount on the nearby Wenlock Edge, while the others attacked it in an effort to capture the defender's flag. Many of these "Widegames" involved other schools and a notable one was where a Grammar School boy disguised himself as a butcher's boy and penetrated the Colleges defences to capture the flag.

The gathering winds of war in Europe didn't prevent Mr. Pine taking frequent parties of boys on continental trips. At this time, severe economic hardships were gripping several countries and the rise of several fascist regimes was already well advanced. Despite this, Mr. Pine, with the ardent support of the Headmaster, managed to broaden the minds of the boys in ways that no classroom teaching ever could. Many boys involved in these excursions report that these trips very much helped them to understand foreign cultures and gave them a greater insight into in the conflict that was to become the Second World War. No doubt these trips also helped to inspire much courage and determination to win against the forces that these boys saw shaping.

But to return to pre-War Tettenhall, there was a fencing club and a boating club, and the organised snow fights followed by forty-a-side soccer. And the Christmas parties, when on occasion, each form made a contribution to the concert, or began with what "The Tettenhallian" calls a "properly organised general rag" followed by films of *Felix the Cat*, and *Charlie Chaplin*. Nor must one forget the activities of the dramatic societies. The more serious-minded came from Mr. Pond, and were widely praised. But Mr. Pine also produced plays with enormous casts, often written by himself. It was said that often there were more actors than spectators, and the most remarkable thing about these productions was that they regularly make large amounts of money, most of which went to fund the Headmaster's Social Service Camps.

Board meetings at this time had, to the grateful relief of the Governors, changed from crisis management meetings to routine management meetings. Numbers at the school remained stable during this time, although many were concerned at the small numbers of boys at Sixth Form level. This had resulted in poorer performances in sport against such sides as the Grammar School, whose Sixth form was thriving at this time. Clearly, the greater choice in older boys for sports like rugger, the better the possibility of obtaining a strong team; and whilst the Tettenhall College Board held many discussions on ways of solving this problem, unfortunately no clear solution emerged.

However, there was one exception to this. Hockey had been re-introduced to the College in 1929 and the teams managed to achieve some quite notable victories after this date. In 1933 the first team was unbeaten, and that of 1934 lost only one match out of ten played. The cricketers, too, more than held their own under the competent coaching of Mr. Theobald. The cross-country races with the Grammar School came to an end, but the School had its first swimming match – against Solihull – and this is an aspect of sport in which the College enjoyed great success during the 1930s. Another game that became important at the School was tennis. After enormous efforts on the part of the boys, working under Mr. Pine's direction, a tennis court was opened on the bottom field in 1931. Unfortunately, when war broke out in 1939, the tennis courts disappeared, to be replaced by air raid shelters.

Despite the weaker achievements at sport, the College was relatively stable financially while others were falling in great numbers. This was due in no small part to the escalating reputation of the College, not only locally, but in the country as a whole. There were several articles in the national papers that at least mention Tettenhall in glowing terms, and this was mainly down to the wonderful achievements of its Old Boys, some of whom had become very powerful, well-know and influential people and who had also carried the College's torch wherever they went. Notable among these distinguished OTs was Sir Cecil Bottomley, K.C. M.G.C.B. O.B.E., the Under Secretary of State for the Colonies. His Honour Arthur Bairstow, was presented at the King's Levee in 1937, while Ingleby Oddie (1879-86), a famous London Coroner, conducted the inquest on those who died in the R.101 Airship disaster. On a local level, was the Freedom of Wolverhampton bestowed upon T.W. Dickinson, and Colonel E. W. Pickering was made deputy Lord Lieutenant of the West Riding of Yorkshire. G.A. Barlow became Mayor of Chester, and there were, as usual, a host of Old Tettenhallians who represented their counties at cricket, rugger, hockey and tennis. F. Dobson and A.K. Jackson both played cricket for Warwickshire, and C.R. Ridgway captained Rhodesia at the game. Taking part in what at that time were relatively new sports were D.S. Green, who came fifth in the King's Cup Air Race, and Captain Palethorpe, who won the 100 miles Outboard Motor Race for the "Yachting World" trophy. All these men greatly publicised the College in ways that advertising could not, and this, coupled with Mr. Pearson's growing reputation, resulted in a steady flow of boys through the College gates.

However, the school was, at last moving from being a relatively new enterprise to being a part of the establishment. It was beginning to outlive many of its original pupils, who by now had grown from boys into old men. The thirties saw the death of Thomas "Owd Tom" Edwards, one of the College's original pupils when it began in 1863, who, in the course of a long life, never ceased to sing the praises of his old school. Another notable OT who died at this time was J.P. Shaw, who had sat in Parliament for the Liberals. Another Old Tettenhallian M.P. to die at this time was G.R. Thorne. Mayor of Wolverhampton in 1902/3, he had won

East Wolverhampton for the Liberals by the narrow margin of eight votes, and surviving the Liberal collapse of 1918, continued to represent Wolverhampton until his retirement in 1929. Appointed chief Whip to the party by Asquith in 1918 he had the reputation of a powerful speaker, Lloyd George saying there was none better in Parliament. Dr. Robert Horton, probably the College's most famous scholar, was another casualty of these years. Having won an Open Scholarship to Oxford from Tettenhall, he gained a double First there, and had the distinction of being the first Non-conformist to be President of the Union.

The deaths of these phenomenally successful OTs was perhaps the point at which many realised that at last Tettenhall College had come of age. It had survived its rite of passage that had been characterised by severe financial crises and it had showed the fortitude to come out at the other end much stronger than before. There were 120 boys in attendance and some money was even found to refurbish and modify the main school building in an effort to comply with modern safety regulations. The Chapel tower was shortened by a few feet, also in the interests of safety, and the old Scout room was converted into a biology laboratory.

Despite this, the big problem the College faced was that of space. There was no doubt that the Governors were confident that the number could increase even further, but there was no more space left to put the extra boys. Despite his sixty years, Mr. Pearson continued to have the full support of his Governors and his staff, and all reports show that his local reputation was second to none. The College had, for the first time, reached a point where, despite having the means to do so, it could expand no further despite the numerous advantages. The Board considered moving to other, larger, premises but there were none suitable to be found. Besides, because the College had become firmly established as *Tettenhall College*, there were few who wanted to risk the school's firm reputation by moving elsewhere. The Governors realised that the College now faced a new type of dilemma – of a kind it had never faced before, and there seemed to be no solution.

They were wrong though, because in September of 1939, widespread war broke out all over Europe, and over the coming years, the College's fortunes would change forever.

CHAPTER 15

THE COLLEGE FIGHTS ANOTHER WAR

Headmaster: H. Pearson Esq.

The Second World War was the largest and the most deadly global conflict ever known, with the death toll reaching over 70 million – much more than the entire population of Great Britain today. The War involved the majority of the world's nations, including all of the great powers, organized into two opposing military alliances: the Allies and the Axis. The war involved the mobilization of over 100 million military personnel, making it the most widespread war in history, and placed all the participants in a state of "total war," in which both military and civil resources were combined in one big "pot" to fund the war effort. The financial cost of this war has been estimated at about a trillion 1944 U.S. dollars worldwide, making it the most expensive war ever fought.

Like with the First World War, it is difficult to pin down what actually triggered the Second World War, and clearly this is a question of perspective. Some sources say the War was triggered by the Mukden Incident, some say the Marco Polo Bridge Incident and others say the attack on Pearl Harbour. From Britain's point of view, it all began when Nazi Germany under the rule of Adolf Hitler invaded Poland and this precipitated declarations of war from the United Kingdom, France and the British Dominions. There was an initial period of seeming inactivity to British citizens that was dubbed the "Phoney War," and whilst life carried on pretty much as normal, the immediate sense of normality belied the turmoil and frenzied but purposeful activities going on away from the public eye. Some of those activities took place in the Tettenhall College Boardroom, and when war broke out in 1939, the College came very close to closing its doors. The Board discussed proposals to send all the boys to the Grammar School, or to purchase a country house in Shropshire and maintain a wartime existence there. Even Horace Pearson didn't know of these proposals, since the meetings to discuss them were held off the College premises and were deemed secret discussions for Governors only. Despite these meetings, the College maintained the public stance it had declared at the time of the Munich crisis in 1938 that it would stay open no matter what happened. As if to prove this point, the Board ordered the building of air raid shelters and the issuing of gas masks to the boys and staff. Many Governors hoped that the War would have the same positive effect on the school that the First World War had, and that it might increase the number of Boarders. This, it seemed, was the light of optimism in a surrounding sea of impending darkness.

Horace Pearson – obviously demoralised at the thought that all his hard work and that of his staff and predecessors could soon be for nothing – offered the Board his resignation with the thought that the College might be better off with a younger man at the helm. The Board disagreed and refused his resignation, at the same time reaffirming its confidence in him. However, this was during the run up to war early in 1939 and some of the Board members pointed out that war might not actually break out. Again these were more seemingly optimistic voices out of an expectant silence before the storm.

But war did break out, and as has been mentioned before, it was all very anti-climactic. During this "Phoney War," there were practice descents to the Air Raid shelters on the College bottom field, and efforts were made to improve the shelters by putting in electricity and sanitary fittings. Hand pumps were put in each dormitory to deal with incendiary bombs and fire escape practices were held regularly, with boys sliding down the canvas chutes in the dormitories amid laughter and giggles all around. After one fire practice where boys had actually sneaked back into the dormitories for another ride on the chutes, the Headmaster commented dryly that if ever the school were to suffer an air raid, then "we would all be fried."

As can be seen, the "Phoney War" engendered a sense of unreality – that it was all a joke really, and that it would all be over by Christmas. With the actual conflict very much in the background, the College First Fifteen enjoyed its best season for some twelve years – largely down to the improved size of the Sixth Form. Oxford endowment funding of £2000 given by S.H. Clay allowed Keith Hartley to go to St. Peter's Hall, Oxford, and Joseph Highfield-Jones paid the College's overdraft of £200. The year's examination results were encouraging, and the only candidate at the Higher School Certificate Examination got through, as did twelve out of the thirteen School Certificate candidates.

As time wore on though, the war grew closer to home. The first feelings that this wasn't a "Phoney War" after all came when a Board meeting discussed the increasing number of boys who had given notice to leave at the end of the summer term 1940. Whilst the number of Boarders did rise slightly, the College started to lose its balance when staff members also had to leave after they had received their conscription papers. Food started to become scarcer and increased costs of suppliers caused the College's overdraft to grow. All this caused a drying up of generous donations to the College, and Board meetings were held to discuss how the College could firstly help the war effort, secondly improve its finances, and thirdly survive – all at the same time.

It is possible that the College might have benefited from quite a lot of donations from various philanthropists had the Second World War not happened, but the reality was that prudent controllers of wealth were, at this time, secreting their wealth in other parts of the world where it would be less likely to be seized by invading Axis powers.

To help the war effort, boys collected paper salvage, and dug over bottom field to plant potatoes. Boys were discouraged from moving too far from the College, and Boarders therefore stopped going to Queen Street on Sundays, and even to the playing fields at Newbridge. To compensate for the lack of exercise, the Headmaster introduced a period of twenty minutes P.T. before breakfast. Boys had to carry gas masks with them at all times, even on the sports field, and each boy had to maintain a kit of warm clothing (inspected regularly) in case of prolonged periods in the Air Raid Shelters.

Over this period the number of Boarders increased, since many Day Boys became Boarders and those whose homes were near to the College were allowed to go home at weekends. Fees for Day Boarders were reduced to allow for the fact that they were allowed to go home earlier than before. The Board set up a special War Council so that it might keep in closer touch with events, and members of this Council offered to come into the School one night a week to help the staff members, who were by now severely depleted due to the growing number of conscriptions.

Fewer staff members meant that responsibility for organising extra-curricular activities fell upon the boys themselves. This they did and proved to be very good at it. Bearing in mind that the Headmaster and Mr. Pond, the House Master, were the only resident members of the teaching staff, it is a credit to the boys that there was little slackening off of discipline.

It is interesting to note that the College did at this time employ a conscientious objector as a member of staff, and this seems a strange turnaround from its stance during the First World War. It is probable that the Governors reasoned that it was better for the boys that they should have a member of staff, since not to employ this man would certainly deprive them of much-needed teaching. There is little doubt when looking at this with the benefit of hindsight, that such a pragmatic approach was one the key factors to the College's survival during these tough times.

Whilst the village of Tettenhall received minimal bomb damage during the Second World War (the only bomb having landed near to the Towers, then still occupied by the Thorneycroft family), the College was officially notified that in the event of heavy air attacks in the West Midlands area, its premises would be requisitioned as an emergency hospital. Despite this "Sword of Damocles," the College did turn a profit in 1940 – its first for fifteen years. At this time, many OTs were distinguishing themselves in the field of combat with the award of a D.F.C. to Squadron Leader J.D. Collier. On the sporting front, K. Hartley won a hockey Blue at Oxford.

Despite the modest profit made by the College in 1940, the question was raised of whether the school should avail itself of government financial assistance. This question had been previously mooted before and had been firmly rejected on the grounds that such assistance would mean relinquishing at least some of the College's independent status. In the time since though, laws had changed and the obtaining of State funds had far fewer strings attached than it had before. At a Council of Governors meeting, the Headmaster pointed out that other Free Church schools were receiving state funds without compromising their independent status. However the Board was doubtful about the idea, fearing that accepting State assistance would be the beginning of a slide down a slippery slope ending in full State control. It must be remembered that, even in death, the hand of Baldwin Bantock still influenced many Governors, and many feared that accepting State aid would go against his wishes had he been alive. However, the idea was not thrown out and the Governors sent a letter to the County Director of Education asking for a full explanation of how State assistance worked. The letter said that: "although at the present time Tettenhall is nearly full, and is in no financial difficulty, it was felt that in view of the likelihood of big changes in the educational system as a result of the war, the question of assistance, if obtainable, from the L.E.A. should be faced now rather than later on." But, as it turned out, the County Education Authority was too busy dealing with the evacuation of its schools to deal with the College's request, and the matter was dropped.

This enquiry into State assistance, stating very confidently that the College was in no financial difficulty, was clearly tempting fate since in September 1940, an emergency Governor's meeting was called to discuss the College's seriously deteriorating finances. Despite the increase in Boarders, the numbers had fallen from 123 in September 1939 to 104 a year later. Apparently this represented a drop in income from £3,192 to £2,392. It was estimated that the College would lose £600 in the autumn term and probably £2,000 in the full year. Once again financial crisis loomed over the College and an examination of various letters suggests that many Board members who had previously scoffed at the possibility of State assistance were now beginning to see the benefits of such a move. However, many suggestions to avert the impending difficulties were thrown out. The first of these was Mr. Pearson's generous offer to retire from the Headmastership, but continue to give the school all the help he could, providing the Board covered his expenses. This would mean that the board would be saved the Headmaster's salary and it would be free to rent out the Headmaster's house. However, the notion of a school without a visible Headmaster at the helm was deemed to be an act of taking one step forward and two backwards, so the offer was refused. The staff were no less generous, and offered to accept a cut of twenty-five per cent in their salaries – a remarkable gesture of faith and loyalty. The Board also declined this offer, but Mr. Pine and Mr. Theobald were called into the Board meeting to receive, on behalf of their colleagues, the Board's thanks.

Another proposal was to sell the main school premises and keep a smaller school going in the Headmaster's house, but this idea was rejected as being far too retrograde, besides, where would the College expand to once its fortunes improved? One Governor put together a detailed proposal to move the College to a large country house in Gnosall, Staffordshire, although this idea was rejected because it would mean moving away from Tettenhall, and it was in Tettenhall that the College had built up its reputation. Besides, how could Tettenhall College be called as such when it was no longer in Tettenhall? Finally, the idea came up of sending the College's boys to the Grammar School for the "duration" (of what is unclear) and re-opening once fortunes had been restored. Again, the Governors rejected the notion on the grounds that this would be tantamount to dissolving the College completely, and once the "duration" was over, what reputation the College had previously enjoyed would then have been lost.

With the benefit of knowing the earlier history of the College, it seems strange that the Board should panic so much in the face of what was, after all, a minor crisis compared to previous events. However, in this latter part of 1940, the "Phoney War" was very much over and the threat of Hitler and his Nazis was all too apparent. Over the Channel, France was very much under the German yoke and Britain was rapidly losing allies. Despite the fact that British and Allied forces had "won" the Battle of Britain, to many this seemed only the beginning of a concerted German offensive that would eventually succeed. As has been mentioned before, the presence of Baldwin Bantock was still felt by many on the Council of Governors and this was largely down to the fact that everyone knew that the College no longer had a generous benefactor to save it in its hour of need.

Returning to the immediate problem, the Governors decided that forewarned was forearmed and informed the College staff that it might need to introduce economies during the coming year and this might include redundancies. It then turned to the matter of raising money to make up the deficit. Repeated approaches to the Staffordshire Local Education Authority enquiring about grants and other cash assistance received no replies, and, one supposes, was largely down to the fact that the Authority probably didn't have too much money to give out since by then every surplus penny was going into the war effort. Attempts to raise money on Baldwin Bantock's will yielded nothing since these monies were only payable on the death of Mr. Bantock's wife, and they could only be used for scholarships. At this point real panic began to set in.

Strangely enough, the College's knight in shining armour on this occasion turned out to be Lloyd's Bank. It will be remembered that these were the same bankers who had reluctantly taken on the school's account at the insistence of Mr. Bantock many years previously. It seemed that in their eyes, Tettenhall College had now turned from a potentially disastrous liability into a potentially profitable asset. This was probably down to the College's vastly improved reputation under the leadership of Horace Pearson, and also no doubt down to the fact that it had managed to return profits that its newly acquired non-profit-making status allowed it to re-invest without having to pay shareholders. In any event, Lloyds agreed an overdraft facility of £2,500 in 1940 and £2,000 in 1941. Naturally, this was provided that the School continued on its present form, and no doubt this last proviso was an added inducement to keep the School going at Tettenhall. The Governors also approached S.H. Clay and persuaded him to allow the £2,000 he had given for scholarships to be used as security for further loans. Perhaps not surprisingly, the Old Tettenhallians Club fell into line and agreed that funds it had donated for scholarships could be used as security too.

After securing the funds it needed, the Governors informed the staff that redundancies would no longer be necessary. It then increased the fees for Boarders by 7½%. At this point, the Governors felt they had every right to breathe out again. The Staffordshire Director of Education even made a visit to the College and encouraged the Governors to apply for a LEA Grant. Due to improved finances, the Board did not take the Director up on his advice, but many at the College agreed that this approach had indeed come better late than never. It is a measure of the Board's newly found confidence that it actually declined a legacy of £1,000, which was to be used for scholarships and was conditional on Boarders attending Congregational Sunday worship during term time. It is unclear why the Board felt that this condition was unreasonable since the College was still considered by many to be a Free Church school, but it may well be an indication that this definition of the College's ethos was changing with the times and allowing for other faiths and maybe even more secular beliefs.

And so, the College emerged from crisis once again, no doubt more than a little shaken, but certainly unstirred, with its eyes fixed firmly on a bright future – after all, the Governors asked themselves, in spite of the war, what could possibly go wrong now?

The answer to this seemingly rhetorical question came swiftly and suddenly. When the College had been considering selling or leasing its premises with a view to moving to the Headmaster's House, or to the house in Gnosall, approaches had been made to several government departments wanting to know if they wanted the buildings. It seems that rattling the government's cage at a time of war had not been a very wise thing to do, since the Ministry of Works had evidently decided that it *did* want Tettenhall College's premises and, under the compulsory acquisition rights afforded to it under emergency war legislation, it was going to take the College buildings whether the Governors wanted it or not.

After notification of their intent by telephone, a deputation from the Ministry of Supply arrived at Tettenhall College to commandeer the premises. The Governors told the deputation that it had decided it was best for the College to remain in Tettenhall, although this objection was swept aside and the Ministry announced that the premises were suitable for its purposes and that the College would get £2,000 per annum rental for it together with reasonable moving expenses and a small compensation for loss of fees. As if this weren't enough, the Ministry also "commandeered" Miss Horobin, the Headmaster's secretary and Ted Gibbins, the College Caretaker.

In the face of loud protests from various Governors, the Ministry expressed its regrets, but began to commandeer the College premises regardless. Large parties of civil servants arrived armed with clipboards and tape measures to plan how the buildings should be used and what other resources should be acquired. Board minutes for this period are understandably vague, since no one wanted to be seen to be obstructing the war effort by objecting to the commandeering of the College premises. However, there can be little doubt that the Governors must have felt very despondent to see the inevitable demise of the College after all their hard work, and that of preceding generations, to keep it alive. The Board finally resolved that: "in the event of His Majesty's Government deciding to requisition the premises of Tettenhall College, in our view it is impracticable to offer any alternative premises in a satisfactory scheme of Secondary Education, and we suggest to the Governing Body that the school be closed until after the war."

It is ironic that this was the year when the College had bolstered its reputation by achieving its best exam results ever, and had managed to secure the respect and support of its bankers, only to be faced with destruction by a force from elsewhere. As the days wore on, the Board reluctantly wrote to parents, telling them what had happened, and made arrangements to remove furniture and equipment that the Ministry didn't want. Once again, the process of winding up the College had begun, and none doubted that this time it would be forever.

But, it wasn't the end. On the day when letters informing parents of the College' intention to close were piled up to be posted, the Headmaster, in a truly inspired action, made a telephone call to Sir Geoffrey Mander – a local Wolverhampton MP, whose family had long since been supporters of the College. Sir Geoffrey then contacted the Minister of Education and persuaded him to use his power to stop the commandeering of Tettenhall College. Sir Geoffrey also won the support of other local MPs, who all added their voices imploring the Minister to give the College a stay of execution. After much consideration, the Minister came down in the College's favour and ordered that the Ministry of Works should leave the school premises immediately.

And so, to the tune of the Minister's pipe, all the civil servants that had been swarming over the College building, packed up their things and scurried away, leaving everyone at Tettenhall College breathing a heartfelt sigh of relief.

It didn't take long for the College to return to normal, or as normal as it could get in wartime. Despite the fact that his telephone call had undoubtedly saved the College, the Headmaster was beginning to feel the strain of it all. It will be remembered that he suffered a breakdown in health as a result of his efforts during the First World War, but now he found that the Second World War was proving to be even more burdensome, since the conflict was actually being experienced here at home in ways that it hadn't in the First War. Not only was there the constant threat of air raids, but there was also the severe rationing to cope with, as well as the heavy staff shortages. Not all the parents had responded to the Board's appeal to pay the additional 7½% on top of their normal fees. Twenty-six parents of Boarders did, twenty-five didn't. The increased fear of air raids in 1941 was something else with which the Headmaster had to cope. It was difficult to decide just what decisions the school could make on behalf of parents in this connection. It was thought necessary, for example, to get written permission from parents to allow their boys to help the staff in dealing with incendiary bombs. It was at this time that the Headmaster gave the Local Auxiliary Fire Service permission to use the premises as a local rest and refreshment centre in the event of large-scale raid. In return, said the Headmaster, "the local AFS were very appreciative and would regard the school as their first concern."

Soon after this on 16th May 1941, two bombs landed within a quarter of a mile of the College. Some 128 panes of glass were broken and many others weakened. Shortly before this, the Headmaster had once more offered his resignation. He was badly in need of a rest, and the Board, though it regretted the prospect of his departure, felt it could not stand in his way this time. Following the Board's acceptance of his resignation, Mr. Pearson offered to stay on until Christmas to help the Board in its task of finding a new Headmaster.

And so, one of Tettenhall College's most revered Headmasters prepared to leave, and no doubt many wondered who could possibly take his place. Strangely enough, Horace Pearson was not considered to be a scholar, as he had no university degree, and he was not a brilliant administrator as Mr. Angus had been. However, he did keep firm discipline and managed to achieve a firm common ground between academic achievement and character building extra-curricular activities. The type of boys leaving the College during Mr. Pearson's time were usually characterized by their good manners, by their sense of responsibility and by their self-confidence. Such attributes were achieved in a way that can only command admiration. Discipline was firm, but not based on fear. In this regard, the Headmaster openly opposed fagging as well as any kind of cadet force at the school. "There were," he said on one occasion, "no bayonets, no rifles, or weekly parades." These, he argued, tended to leave an "indelible militarist mark on a boy's mind." Undoubtedly, Mr. Pearson supported Baldwin Bantock's philosophy that character building was paramount in education.

What also mattered to Mr. Pearson was the attitude to life of boys at the College. He wanted them to think adventurously. One of his criticisms of the boys was that they were, to some extent, losing their spirit of adventure. This, he believed, was due to the over emphasis on Safety First.

Mr. Pearson also wanted his boys to acquire something of a social conscience, to want to do something for those less fortunately endowed. Boys were encouraged to do a great deal to help with the running of the school, but they were also encouraged to do something outside it as well. They set up weekly collections, for example, for the child refugees from Bilbao during the Spanish Civil War. Some of the boys volunteered to help a disabled ex-serviceman with the working of his allotment, but for many Old Tettenhallians, their chief memory in this connection is the Social Service Camps that the Headmaster had set up. The idea was that some twenty or thirty boys from poor homes in the West Midlands should be invited to spend the first six days of summer at Tettenhall. Sometimes they camped in the grounds; sometimes they occupied the lower two dormitories. Nine or ten of the senior boys acted as hosts, and did their best to try to give these boys a good time. It was wholly in keeping with Horace Pearson's feelings on this matter of social service that, when he died, the Old Tettenhallian Club used the money collected for a wreath upon an entertainment at the "Royal Cripples Hospital."

Looking back on the College's history, it is not hard to see that one of the factors that has helped its survival is its ability to change with the times. Horace Pearson was the embodiment of this ability not to fear change, rather to embrace it and make the best of it. A good example of this was his decision to get rid of the College's old desks in favour of new ones. He said: "As occasion permits it is my intention to get rid of the old mutilated and much carved desks that you all loved so much… and although I know you will regret it, we shall have to make room for progress, and discard some of your cherished traditions."

Mr. Pearson went on to say that a Headmaster's life "is one continual act of faith in the School, its life and spirit, and in the boys entrusted to his care… If I have been able to accomplish anything at Tettenhall College, it is because of people who have had faith in me. But I am not leaving Tettenhall with the College in my debt. I have got far more out of Tettenhall College than anything I have given." Horace Pearson retired to Birmingham, where he spent his declining years caring for disabled children. He died on 22nd February 1946 just four years after retiring from Tettenhall. Right up until his death, Mr. Pearson had never married.

And so it was that the Governors drew up a short list of candidates for the post of Headmaster. There were 62 candidates – a testament in itself to the good reputation that the school had built up – and after careful deliberation, the Board appointed Mr. F. D. Field-Hyde as the Tettenhall College's next Headmaster.

PART THREE

MATURITY

CHAPTER 16

COMING OF AGE

Headmaster: F.D. Field-Hyde Esq.

As Mr. Field-Hyde prepared to take up the Headmastership of Tettenhall College, the Second World War raged on, both at home and abroad. Whilst the U.S.A. had entered the war, so had Japan and this meant that the conflict had truly reached global proportions. Great Britain had been severely debilitated in practically every way by its efforts to fight off the Nazi onslaught, and by the time the Americans came to our aid, the country was teetering on the verge of bankruptcy. The war in the Pacific theatre was not going well, and at home the regular blackouts and severe food shortages had lowered morale considerably.

What made matters worse was that 1942 saw one of the most severe winters on record with tall snowdrifts clogging up roads, railways and even burying buildings. These were the conditions prevailing on the day that Mr. Field-Hyde first walked – or rather dug – his way, through the College gates for the first time. He was later to comment somewhat dryly that he spent most of his first term and a half clearing away snowdrifts and making repairs to burst pipes in the kitchen and boiler room. But arrive he did, and one can imagine him entering his office for the first time, stamping off the snow from his boots, hanging up his hat and coat, and thinking about the career that had eventually brought him here to Tettenhall.

Frederick Douglas Field-Hyde was born in Cambridge on 17th January 1903. He first went to Perse Preparatory School, Cambridge and after winning a Foundation Scholarship, he moved on to Perse Senior School. From there he attended St. Catharine's College, Cambridge and took his degree in French Language and Literature, and in Part II of the History Tripos. After this, he took the Teacher's Training Course and diploma at Cambridge. From there he went to Bishop's Stortford College, where he spent four years before moving to Repton in 1929, where he served under Dr. Fisher, who later became the Archbishop of Canterbury. In 1941 Mr. Field-Hyde was appointed Headmaster of Tettenhall College. A Free Church Congregationalist, he was also a keen supporter of Rugby as well as an enthusiastic and active player.

Many who remember Mr. Field-Hyde will also remember his car. F.W. Brown writes:

Frederick Douglas Field-Hyde Esq., M.A. (Headmaster 1942-1968)

"For many years Mr. Field-Hyde was the proud possessor of a very old and very dilapidated Ford car. This frightening contraption had a very bad habit: it tended to fling open its doors. This could be quite disconcerting when zooming along at breakneck speed. I recall several hair-raising experiences with Mr. Field-Hyde at the wheel. On one occasion, sitting at the back of the car with another member of staff, we came to a sharp and blind bend along the Wrottesley Road, and we were petrified to find ourselves overtaking a lorry [that had been] immediately in front of us. My colleague turned to me and whispered: "Oh God!"

Mr. Field-Hyde was a consummate musician. A keen violinist, he often organised community singing in the Dining Hall on Saturday nights, when benches would be drawn up to the grand piano, then at the top of the hall, and the Headmaster would conduct while others would play and sing. On one occasion, the Headmaster organised an informal Sunday evening concert where a number of musicians performed French and German madrigals. L.N. Chown reports that: "On the final Tuesday evening of term we had a memorable musical hour in Chapel, which included the H.M. playing his recorder (flute). This particular concert ended with "Waltzing Matilda," which I doubt if the Chapel walls, or many people in that audience, had ever heard sung with such interest and feeling. It was probably the first time the school had tasted anything which contained the flavour of a full-blown end-of-term Public School concert, a most uplifting as well as entertaining occasion as all those who have been to one well know."

Another thing that characterised the new Headmaster was his penchant for "fixing" things that were broken. A hint of a mechanical breakdown in any kind of machinery, whether it was a motor car or a floor polisher, would always bring a sudden gleam into his eye. After he had been at the College a while, there were many who would make a point never to mention any kind of mechanical breakdown for fear of taking up too much of the Headmaster's valuable time.

It seems that Mr. Field-Hyde thought that the College needed fixing too, since he began his time at Tettenhall by impressing his own personality on the school from the word "go." By the time he arrived in the spring term of 1942, the numbers at the College had increased to 121, made up of 42 Boarders, 15 Day Boarders, and 64 Day Boys. This unprecedented increase was down largely to an upswing of prosperity enjoyed by the West Midlands since a lot of the war effort and its attendant monetary investment had been concentrated there. Another influential factor was the Education Act of 1944 (also known as the Butler Act), which defined and reorganised State secondary education in Britain. This Act of Parliament made education compulsory and free for everyone between the ages of 5 to 15, and whilst it outlined the need to raise the school leaving age to 16, this did not actually happen until 1971. The Act also brought in an examination known as the 11-plus for all eleven-year-olds to sit. The results of this intelligence test would determine which sort of secondary school they would go to: technical, secondary modern, or grammar. This was known as the "tripartite" system but in most places, only the latter two types of schools existed and it was predominantly the Grammar Schools that could offer examinations (Matriculation) and possible university entrance. It is understandable, therefore, that the 11-plus was dreaded by pupils and parents alike because it determined to a large extent what sort of education and job a child would end up with. This meant that an increasing number of parents could see the benefits of sending their children to private schools that were not bound by the tripartite system. However, this Act did not come into force for some years after Mr. Field-Hyde came to Tettenhall, and it is a credit to him that he managed to maintain the steady increase in numbers until the consequences of the Act began to be felt.

However, much of the increase in numbers was down to the spreading reputation of the College whose Old Boys were by then numbered in their thousands, many of whom had gained national and international recognition for their achievements; either in their various professions or in the field of sport. The Headmaster also promoted the College in the active role he played in the Incorporated Association of Headmasters, and the Society of Headmasters of Independent Schools. A new association linking together the smaller Public Schools, has also contributed to the College becoming better known, as has the much larger number of boys proceeding to the universities. At this time, the phenomenon we now refer to as multimedia was just getting started with widespread radio broadcasts and the embryonic BBC TV giving limited broadcasts in the southeast of the country after its wartime cessation. There can be little doubt that the BBC's radio broadcast of the College's Sunday evening service on 31st January 1954 helped to spread the word all over the country.

When the new Headmaster first arrived though, the College House system had been made up of only two houses – Bantock and Nicholson. In an effort to strengthen this system, the Headmaster added two new Houses, Pearson and Haydon – both named in honour of previous Headmasters. This was done to introduce more competition among the boys, many of whom were Day Boys or Day Boarders.

The increase in numbers eased the College's financial liabilities considerably, although it did highlight the problem of where the College was going to accommodate its burgeoning population. By this time there was a large faction within the Governing Body that felt uncomfortable about this, since it meant that there was a clearly marked ceiling on the College's revenue balanced against the need to invest increasingly greater sums to make sure the school could compete with the ever-growing competition from the State schools. This meant that there was talk once again of moving to larger premises, although these propositions were dismissed when it was pointed out that the school would have to move out of Tettenhall to do this.

To resolve this situation, it was clear that the College needed to expand its facilities considerably, and this meant investment in new buildings on a hitherto unprecedented scale. This meant that more funds were needed, so working committees were set up to look into ways of doing this. The College succeeded in securing the Ministry of Education's authority to vary the trusts governing the Bantock and Clay legacies. (Besides the £2,000 given earlier for scholarships, S.H. Clay left the College on his death a much larger sum to be used for the same purpose). This meant that the College was allowed to borrow the capital sums involved to improve the College amenities, while providing annually for scholarship purposes the interest that the capital sums would have brought.

Another fresh cash injection was the grant of £12,500 from the Industrial Fund set up by a cartel of industrial companies to improve the teaching of science in schools. This allowed plans to be drawn up for new science laboratories, thereby allowing more boarding space in Main School, which is where science had been taught previously. However, one of the first building programmes embarked upon at this time was the building of the Horace Pearson Memorial Pavilion, which was financed by donations from Old Tettenhallians.

In 1942, when it was decided to embark on an extensive project of new buildings, the biggest problem was lack of space. At that time, the College had only 6½ acres of land and this certainly would not allow for much building without sacrificing the large amounts of space needed for sporting activities. Again, the possibility of relocation reared its ugly head, but as usual, the College's guardian angel had not been idle. While the Governors were scratching their heads over the problem of the lack of space, Colonel Thorneycroft's daughter and only surviving heir placed her family home on the market.

This event precipitated a lot of discussion among the Governors. There were those who declared quite openly that the College simply could not afford to buy the Towers. They argued that it was an old rambling building that would pose serious maintenance costs coupled with a potential public liability problem. However, no one could refute the obvious benefit of the Towers' 26½ acres of land, which would provide the College with almost boundless development possibilities. Not only this, but it was clear by now that the College needed its own on-campus playing fields. The existing fields at Newbridge sufficed, but the fact that the Towers enjoyed extensive fields bordering Henwood Road was seen by the Headmaster and many others as an opportunity too good to miss. Increasing levels of traffic on the Tettenhall and Henwood Roads was making travel on foot to Newbridge extremely hazardous and the need for playing fields within the College grounds was all too apparent, also as was the amount of time taken out of the school timetable to get to Newbridge. While drama at the College had always been popular, the boys had, on many occasions needed to borrow the Towers theatre, and there was a strong faction in the Governing Body that saw the acquisition of the Towers and its magnificent theatre as a massive step forward.

Tettenhall Towers (or Thorneycroft Towers) had originally been built as a country house by Thomas Pearson (no relation to H.P.) on land previously owned by the Foley family in the late 18th century. The original house was built on the site of an inn known as the Holly Bush, although the remnants of this were demolished to make way for Mr. Pearson's house. In 1820, the house was leased to Judge Uvedale Corbett, who was a County Court Judge for Shropshire, who remained as a tenant for 21 years before the house was let to W. Fleming-Fryer, who stayed there until 1851. It was in this year that Captain Thomas Thorneycroft and his family moved into the house as annual tenants. In 1853, the house and its Tettenhall Wood estate was put up for auction by Major Thomas Hooke-Pearson, who was a descendant of the house's original owner and builder. The whole property was split into 43 lots and Colonel (as he was by this time) Thorneycroft bought lot number 6 (the "mansion") and a number of other lots to make up the rest of the grounds. As his family expanded over the years, the Colonel extended the house, adding the "Towers," which gave it its name in 1866, three years after the College was founded in the house next door.

The Colonel was a wealthy Midlands industrialist and he was also a keen amateur inventor. His main obsessions were ventilation and sanitation, so the house became riddled with the Colonel's own unique ventilation and sanitation systems, which were often elaborate and certainly were reminiscent of the cartoons of W. Heath Robinson. This included over twenty water closets, including one of the Colonel's own invention. He also invented a device that pumped foul air from the sewers, the gas being burned off at the head of a pipe some forty feet from the house.

The Colonel had many industrial enterprises in the area now known with affection of hindsight as the "Black Country," and he found that his house – occupying the high up position that it did – afforded him a wonderful way of keeping an eye on his various businesses interests from home. Once the "Towers" had been added to the main house, the Colonel could communicate with his workforce in the far off Black Country by the use of semaphore flags, which he would wave enthusiastically from the roof of his home, thereby negating the need for daily travel and all the expense this must have entailed. The Colonel didn't know this, but he was really one of the first of what many now consider a new breed of home workers – people communicating with their places of work via an "online" connection. No doubt knowledge of this would have appealed enormously to his much-renowned (and some would say infamous) sense of innovation. Another form of communication popular with the Colonel was the use of rockets of various colours to signify different things, and by all accounts, this spectacle of a heavily moustachioed man frantically waving flags and firing off rockets from the roof of a neighbouring building (viewed through telescopes and field glasses) was definitely an amusing spectacle to both boys and staff of the College alike.

As his family grew, so the Colonel kept adding to the Towers, and so the building became one of those wonderfully eccentric examples of British Victoriana that often serve to characterise the spirit of Britishness at this time. It is no small wonder therefore that generations of Tettenhallians have described the College culture as having a definite eccentric air. Some Old Tettenhallians compare the Towers with the Mervyn Peake creation of "Gormenghast," and others with J.K. Rowling's "Hogwarts," but whatever one's view, no one can say that the Towers does not have a unique character. The treasure of the building is undoubtedly the magnificent theatre at the building's heart, and this remains to this day a cornerstone of College life. Many successive Bursars and Planning Governors have lost hours of sleep over how much money the Towers absorbs, but since it is now a Grade II (Star) listed building, it is definitely here to stay, barring any accidents of course.

Meanwhile in 1943, those in favour of bidding for the Towers argued that the College had made a profit of over £1,000 in the previous year. This money, they said, should be reinvested in new premises to accommodate the increased number of boys. Those arguing against the acquisition said, quite rightly that to raise the sort of money needed to buy a property like the Towers would mean borrowing, and this would meant that the College would be overstretching itself at a time when it had emerged from its early financial difficulties to an era of stability and relative prosperity. Those in favour of buying the Towers countered this by pointing out that there had been a recent bid by the Tettenhall Urban District Council to buy part of the Towers' land to be an annexe to the Parish Church cemetery, and no one, they said, wanted the College's grounds to be adjoining a cemetery. To this, the naysayers had nothing to say, and Governor Alan Stevens then said: "Could the College afford *not* to buy the Towers?"

The answer was clearly "no," but while the governors had been arguing the toss, another potential buyer for the Towers had put in a bid to Miss Thorneycroft in the sum of £15,000. This potential buyer was a Mr. H.R. Clarkson, who had on occasion given money to several local causes, and was also a keen supporter of private education, which is probably why he withdrew his offer when he learned that the College was considering a bid for the property. Eventually, the Thorneycroft Trustees accepted the College's offer of £15,100 and Tettenhall College went from being a modest establishment to full campus academy that now had the potential to expand its services, its students and ultimately its reputation.

The purchase of the Towers was completed in February of 1944, and it is clear that the Second World War had made it increasingly difficult for Miss Thorneycroft to keep such an establishment going. This is perhaps another example of how the College benefited indirectly from the Second World War, although the conflict did take the lives of the following Old Tettenhallians, who are commemorated in the College chapel to this day, along with their compatriots that died in the First World War:

P.A. Annan	G.R. Halbeard	E.C. Miles
P.A.S. Dodd	R.M. Horton	M.K. Parry
L.P. Fidgin	M.O. Howell	P.F. Snape
J.M.C. Garrett	G.H. Livingston	A.J. Thomas

Including the Towers, the College campus now encompassed over 32 acres, and as further development work was carried out using money generously donated by several Old Tettenhallians, the College's finances became increasingly more complex. All of this highlighted the need to employ someone whose sole occupation was to manage the College's increasingly involved finances, so the Governors appointed Mr F.W. Brown as Bursar in 1946.

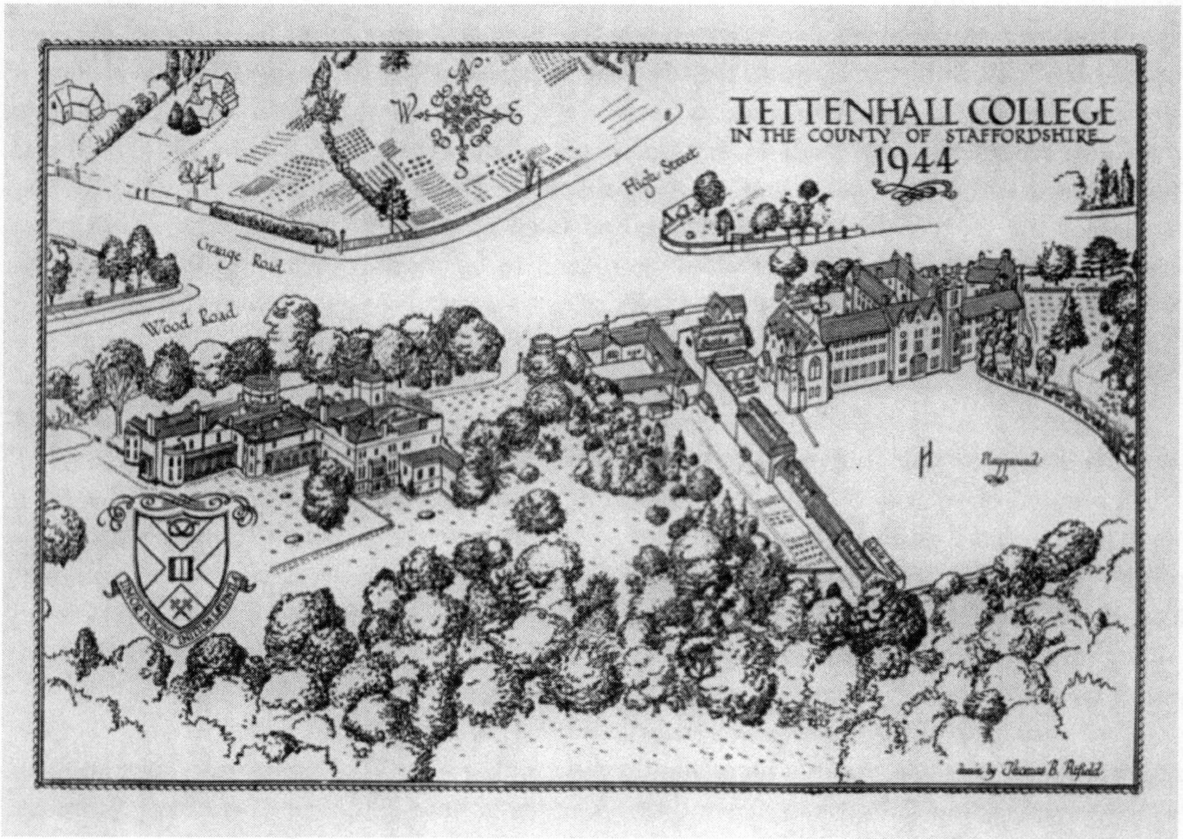

A drawing by Thomas Pitfield of Tettenhall College as it was in 1944 including the newly acquired Thorneycroft Towers

Now that the College had the land it needed, work began almost immediately on creating new on-campus playing fields. There was now some very good ground adjacent to the Henwood Road and an Old Tettenhallian, Mr. F.G. Yorath, was instructed to level the ground out and prepare it for the sports of cricket and rugby. Looking at the fields today, it is easy to imagine that they have been level since before the College had acquired them, but this was not the case. It was necessary to bring in a fleet of bulldozers to level the ground and remove unwanted obstacles. Once this was done, it was necessary to remove many of the stones on the site, as this would then make it viable for sowing fresh grass.

Once the new playing fields were fully grassed over, rugby and cricket pitches were marked out and sport at Tettenhall College moved into a different league. With the advent of increased numbers of boys, especially Day Boarders, the Board invested some money in new changing room facilities for Day Boys and Day Boarders on the site of Colonel Thorneycroft's stables. This sufficed for ten years until in 1962, when there was an additional partitioning of this room into a Cloakroom and Changing Room – the latter extended by the incorporation of the former Scout Room. In 1948, the playing fields at Newbridge were sold and all sporting activities were moved on to the College grounds.

However, by the end of 1952, the need for a pavilion adjacent to the playing fields became apparent, so Mr. Yorath was asked to design and build such a building, with funds being provided by the Old Tettenhallians. Opened in 1953, the Horace Pearson Memorial Pavilion was funded by gifts from Old Tettenhallians, and it was much admired by visiting teams. No doubt the College's vastly improved sporting facilities contributed to the steady rise in numbers that occurred after the acquisition of the Towers.

The Chapel had also felt the pressure of increasing numbers. In 1949 the floor had to be strengthened, and the roof re-laid. In the following year the war-damaged windows were replaced, and in 1953 some stained glass, the work of R.S. Davies, appeared in one of the window lights, and, in the same year, a new memorial to the Old Tettenhallians who gave their lives in the two World Wars was added. Made of Italian stone – Carrera Aurisma – the gift of a parent, the memorial bears the names of all the fallen, and underneath them the words: "Nobis haec otia fecerunt." Increasing numbers also gave rise to the decision to give the younger boys their own morning service in the Towers.

More boys also meant the need for more classrooms. In 1953, work began on the building of the Maurice Jacks Building – the first major building undertaken by the College for nearly ninety years. This was built on the site of a lawned area that had featured several mature chestnut trees. In 1954, the Jacks Block was completed, and the School began to use its five new classrooms and administrative offices. At this time, the main entrance of the College switched from the doors in the Quadrangle to the main entrance of the Jacks Block, with the Headmaster's study situated to the left, the Bursar's office and other administration rooms to the right. This meant that teaching could also be transferred to the new block from Main School and that the newly vacated rooms on the Red Corridor could be used for Boarders' recreation rooms.

It must be emphasised that the Headmaster played a very active role in the building of the New Block. F.W. Brown writes: "…scarcely a brick was laid without his close scrutiny. The whole school sensed that we were gaining in prestige and influence and it was no surprise to us when membership of the Headmaster's Conference was finally granted. With the newly acquired [official] status of a Public School, the Headmaster was hungry for academic successes, and these came in good measure."

In 1953, the playground, which had previously been an uneven grassy area was levelled and asphalted over, and because of the steep camber of the land, the new playground was now on two levels. This allowed better facilities for tennis and basketball, but it also gave rise to more injuries and damaged uniforms as a result of falls and scrapes.

At this time, the science facilities at Tettenhall left a lot to be desired. As has been touched upon briefly before, the Chemistry Laboratory was a somewhat makeshift affair adjacent to the playground, and the Physics Laboratory was situated in a disused dormitory on the top floor of Main School. With increase in popularity of science subjects, the Governors saw the need for better facilities, but the question of how to afford them always proved to be a stumbling block.

It seems that this was a problem facing many schools at this time and the captains of industry were aware that scientific progress depended to a large degree on good science education in schools. With this in mind, a number of companies pooled their resources and set up a fund to improve science facilities in independent schools. Naturally, the award of money from this newly set-up fund was subject to a school satisfying certain criteria, and this had to be done by making a presentation to the committee set up to supervise distribution of funds. The Headmaster and two members of the Governing Body, Mr. K.G. Craddock, and Mr. R. King, successfully put over the School's case for the award of such a grant and the School was given £12,500 towards the cost of a new Science Block. As an added bonus, the College had been given a gift of £700 for the purchase of scientific equipment, so the majority of the award money could go towards building new laboratories.

Work began straight away and the new Science Block was opened 1958 by the chief Assessor himself, Sir Graham Savage. The interior layout owes a great deal to the work of the Senior Science master at the time, Mr. W.P. Davies, and has been much admired, not only by friends of the School, but also by those interested in building similar laboratories elsewhere. It goes without saying that the fact that the College has such a fine building owes much to the energy and tenaciousness of the Headmaster.

Two years later, in 1960, the Governing Body completed the work of improving the

An aerial view of the Towers with the Maurice Jacks Building, Science Laboratories
and Main School.

Science facilities of the College by a new building linking the Maurice Jacks Block and the
Science Block by means of a new Biology Laboratory (now used as an Art Room). Prior to
this, boys who had wanted to study Biology had to go down to the Technical College in
Wolverhampton.

The building of the new Science Block enabled the old Physics Laboratory to be restored
to its original use as a dormitory in the Boarding House. The former Chemistry Laboratory
was modified to serve as the new headquarters of the Art Department under the leadership
of E.G. Hellawell, E. Flegg and J.M. Sankey. It must be said that Art has always been a popular
and successful pursuit at Tettenhall and over the years has enjoyed a great deal of success.
Exhibitions of work on Speech Day and the sets produced for school plays have been much
admired. So too has the work of the Art Department's printing section.

It seemed that as the sixties dawned, Tettenhall College had finally grown out of its
infancy and become a mature academy of learning that could compete well with other Public
Schools such as Wrekin, Repton and such like. It would be easy to put this down to improved

finances, increased numbers and better facilities, but at least some of the reasons for these developments must be down to the Headmaster himself. Mr. Field-Hyde has been described as "stern" and "autocratic" by many who knew him, and one Old Tettenhallian, J.D.P. Walters, said: "Every inch a Headmaster of the traditional mould, he was an autocrat and as much feared by staff as by pupils, or so it appeared. Distant and arch-episcopal, he ruled with an untrammelled air of authority... His cold stare would freeze the most recalcitrant pupil; a sudden glance across the Dining Hall from the Top Table would often produce an instant hush. He addressed his staff by their surnames, and they, in turn, addressed him as "Sir." Yet beneath that stern exterior, kindness and consideration abounded."

Clearly, Mr. Field-Hyde was responsible for much of the progress the College made during his twenty-six years as Headmaster, but the times were rapidly changing. A new, more permissive era was evolving and the values and behaviour prized so much by the College's Headmaster were being questioned by many. The post-war decades had ushered in a new type of moneyed middle class, and with the advent of the technological revolution, the world was becoming a much smaller place. The rise of immigration into Britain from former colonies meant that the needs of the population were changing beyond recognition by those brought up during the first two world wars – and this meant that Tettenhall College would need to change too.

CHAPTER 17

A NEW FOUND STRENGTH

Headmaster: F.D. Field-Hyde Esq.

With the addition of the Towers, Tettenhall College was transformed from a modest sized school to a fully-fledged campus academy. This is probably why many see the year the Towers was acquired as being the year the College came of age. From here onwards, the range of education services the school offered expanded at a vast rate, as did the numbers of boys. The increased space allowed highly ambitious works of development over a long period of time, and it is clear that the board of 1943 were not blind to the potentials the College now had lying before it. In 1941, the property assets of the College were estimated at £29,953. Twenty-one years later, just before the school celebrated its centenary jubilee, these assets were estimated at £118,384. However, these are just material assets, and full credit should be given to the Headmaster and the Board of Governors for developing the College's human resources. In 1948, Messrs Pond, Pine and Theobald were still at the College supporting the new Headmaster, who was determined to enlist as many high-calibre masters as he could to carry the school into what he saw as a new age.

The year 1948 saw the arrival of one of the College's finest and longest serving masters. This was the year when Geoffrey Vernon Hancock stepped off a number 1 trolley bus on to Tettenhall Upper Green and made his way through Tettenhall College gates for the first time. A native of Liverpool, Mr. Hancock was twenty-five years old when he accepted the position of History Master at Tettenhall. He had served in the RAF during the Second World War as an upper-mid gunner aboard a bomber, and from there he went to Exeter College, Oxford. His appointment at Tettenhall was to be a profound milestone in the history of the College for many reasons, but not least of all for his unswerving enthusiasm for College life and his profound grasp and love of history of all sorts. He has that rare gift of being able to transform a potentially dry subject into a pageant of fun and meaningful exploration. In 1963, he published his *History of Tettenhall College* to mark the school's hundred year jubilee, and this book still remains a treasured possession of many Old Tettenhallians to this day.

It was not only in the field of history that Mr. Hancock excelled. Over the many years he spent at Tettenhall, he contributed greatly to the Debating Society, the Chess Club, the History Society, the editing of "The Tettenhallian," the off-campus visits, the organising of the school archives, the preaching in Chapel, the fund-raising and much more. Many Old Tettenhallians will remember his infectious enthusiasm for everything, his firm but fair discipline, but mostly for the respect he engendered in everyone. All of this contributed immeasurably to the fine institution Tettenhall College has become today.

The year 1948 also saw a strong Board of Governors at the College, all of whom gave invaluable support and assistance to the Headmaster. Mr. Maurice Jacks had succeeded Professor Powicke in 1945 and retiring as he did in 1964, much of Mr. Jacks' time as Chairman of the Governors spanned most of Mr. Field-Hyde's time as Headmaster and the two men developed a firm friendship based on the solid foundation of shared educational ideals. "I think you should be warned," wrote Mr. Jacks in his acceptance letter to Mr. Field-Hyde, "that I shall not be an absentee Governor: a good many schools nowadays suffer from these people." In this he kept his word and only illness prevented his attendance at Board meetings. John Chown wrote: "Jacks' willpower and devotion to the school just about saw him through the Centenary Celebrations in July 1963, including a good piece of oratory on Saturday." However, this was Mr. Jacks' final appearance at the College, and following his death on 24th January 1964, what had previously just been known as the "New" block was permanently named the Maurice Jacks Block in his honour.

And so it was that the College started to build on its new-found strength. A strong teaching staff led to good examination results at "O" and "A" level, and two Ministry of Education inspections yielded positive results. In September 1948 (the month Mr. Hancock began) there were a record 324 boys at the College. Increased numbers at the School meant an increase in the size of the Sixth Form, although not to the extent that the School would have liked – too many boys were leaving at sixteen to join family businesses instead of spending two more years studying for "A" levels. Nevertheless numbers did go up in the Sixth Form and this showed itself not only in improved performances upon the games fields, but also in the larger number of Tettenhallians going to the universities or to other places of further education. At that time, there were about 30 Old Tettenhallians at various universities. The favourable terms in which the Education Authorities spoke of the work of the school at an Inspection carried out in 1961 made it clear that these results were largely the result of improved facilities and good quality staff.

Both this report and that of the earlier one in 1954, spoke of the good atmosphere that existed at the school between staff and boys, and many visitors commented upon this. As with previous generations of Tettenhallians, this may be down to the considerable number of extra-curricular activities in which masters and boys meet in circumstances less formal than the classroom. At this time, the Scout troop was flourishing and not only did it promote a spirit of leadership, but it also produced fifteen Queen Scouts along the way.

Another factor was almost certainly the fact that many boys took part in sporting activities. Old Tettenhallian Peter Radford went on to compete in the 1958 European Championships where he won a Bronze medal in the 100 metres and a Silver medal as part of the British 4x100 metres relay team. In the summer of 1960, he broke the world record for 200 metres/220 yards with a time of 20.5 seconds He represented Great Britain in the 100 and 200 metres at the 1960 Summer Olympics held in Rome, Italy, where he won the bronze medal at 100 metres. He then teamed up with fellow British athletes David Jones, David Segal and Nick Whitehead to finish third in the 4x100 metre relay. Despite these tremendous achievements of one Old Tettenhallian, there weren't many other successes in athletics, although in rugby, cricket and hockey, it was a different story. A.R.R. Leonard captained the County Schoolboy side, and M.H. Clarke played for the English Schoolboys against France. The College rugby team beat King Edwards School first fifteen for the first time, and a large number of the College's rugby players contributed to the Wolverhampton Rugby Club. Some expert coaching by Peter Jackson, the former Worcestershire bowler, did much to improve the standard of cricket at the College, and there resulted a memorable victory over the Grammar School. There were many successful sporting personalities during this period although prominent in these is Derek Sage, who excelled at cricket, hockey and rugby. All this contributed to what many refer to as a "happy ship" and there is no doubt that improved sporting facilities contributed greatly to this.

As has been mentioned before, the Headmaster – an enthusiastic sportsman – took a hands-on role in the sporting life of the College. He had previously played rugby for the Harlequins and despite his advancing years, was a formidable player. J. Shenton relates an experience he had during a rugby match when he tackled the Headmaster. "This was one of those tackles which one dreams about," he writes. "I tackled him exactly right and brought him down so heavily that it almost laid him out. He quickly revived, but finished the game looking rather ashen and departed more quickly than usual.

"On the following day I was foolish enough to believe that I was out of his favour and sought to retrieve myself by apologising to him. He was absolutely furious and left me in no doubt that he had, up to that moment, believed that the tackle had been perfectly fair. A perfectly fair tackle required no apology. If, however, he understood from my apology that I was confessing to an illegal tackle, he would feel compelled to beat me for it – unless I agreed forthwith to withdraw my apology… I came away having learned a very valuable lesson."

Another significant staff appointment occurred in 1956. In that year, Old Tettenhallian Leslie Newton Chown returned to the College to teach Mathematics. Always referred to by family and friends as "John," Mr. Chown was born in 1926 and attended Tettenhall College from 1934 until 1943. After leaving the College, Mr. Chown went to Balliol College, Oxford to read Mathematics. Unfortunately the Second World War interrupted his studies and he worked at Bletchley Park from September 1944 right through to VJ Day in August 1945. After the war, Mr. Chown worked for Armstrong Siddeley Motors Ltd. at Coventry and then served two terms as an assistant master at Tettenhall before resuming his studies at Balliol. In 1949 he was awarded a first class honours degree in Mathematics and continued research at Oxford until 1951. After three teaching appointments at Eton, Wellington College and Bury Grammar School, he returned to Tettenhall where he became a much respected and admired master to this very day. Whilst he officially retired in 1986, he still does some part-time tuition at the College. Like Mr. Hancock, Mr. Chown has contributed a great deal to College life both in the classroom and out. It has been said many times that his qualities are very much akin to those of Baldwin Bantock, the College's greatest benefactor. This may be summed up by former Chairman of the Governors, Professor Powicke, who said: "There are two kinds of people in this world, those who snatch and those who enrich, and Mr. Bantock was known to all of us as one of the latter." The same is certainly true of Mr. Chown.

Since its acquisition in 1944, the College has made good use of the Towers. A massive rambling building built on an *ad hoc* basis over a period of several centuries, it was both a source of much-needed extra teaching space and also a veritable "money pit" as far as maintenance is concerned. By the 1960s there were seven forms housed in the Towers, and accommodation for nine resident members of staff. At that time, the Library, Geography Room, Careers Room and Music rooms were there. The magnificent theatre at the heart of the building proved to be reason enough to keep the building going and it formed the nucleus for a long series of dramatic productions that have gone from strength to strength right up until the present day. When it wasn't being used for drama, it doubled very well as a gymnasium, and this allowed the old Gymnasium to be used for teaching. As time has progressed, improvements and modernisations have been made to the building and all evidence of Colonel Thorneycroft's occupation has just about diminished to nothing, although some of the original plumbing still remains.

Mention must be made here of the tremendous work done by F.W. Brown, the College's first Bursar, since it was his financial wizardry that enabled many of the transformations at the College to take place. All records show that there was a lot of mutual esteem between Mr. Brown and Mr. Field-Hyde, and during the College's centenary celebrations, the Bursar's organisational abilities were very much in evidence. At their first meeting, the Headmaster remarked in measured tones to Mr. Brown: "Brown, we shall either make this place hum, or we shall go bust in the process."

It was also down to Mr. Brown to make the Towers into a viable teaching facility, and bearing in mind the poor condition the building was in, it is a tribute to the man's ability that he did just this, and well within the budget allocated for the purpose. Floors were reinforced, ceilings were patched up, the roof was repaired, doors were re-hung, windows were re-glazed and even the magnificent front hallway was given a new coat of polish. All of this gave the building a better cosmetic appearance, but it did little to alleviate the fundamental flaw of the Towers, which was its poor design. There were staircases that went nowhere, rooms with no doors, rambling passages often leading nowhere, limitless roofs, even secret panels by the big fireplace, creaky floorboards, doors and windows. All of this added up to a nightmare for the teaching staff, but for the boys, it was nothing short of bliss. For a term or two after the acquisition, no one actually knew where each class was from one day to the next, so the opportunities for prevarication were endless. That notwithstanding, Mr. Brown did an admirable task of at least bringing the Towers up to the statutory requirements of the day and bestowing some sort of order on what was a vast jungle of a building.

It was around this time that first sightings of the Towers ghost began to emerge. Many rambling old buildings often get the "haunted house" reputation since this notion is very much part of our culture, but over the few decades that the Towers has been in College hands, there have been many very credible eyewitness accounts of the ghost of what is thought to be one of Colonel Thorneycroft's maids. No doubt these stories have been embellished somewhat by the artistic licence of successive fertile imaginations, but sightings still occur even to this day. One Old Tettenhallian recalls walking through the theatre auditorium around 1969 and hearing a noise. On glancing into the wings of the stage on his way down to the auditorium, he saw a lady standing on the stage, but seconds later she was gone.

Likewise another Old Tettenhallian reports walking past one of the music practice rooms after dark and spying an unfamiliar girl playing one of the grand pianos. This was in 1975, in the days when there were only a token number of girls at the College, so the appearance of an unfamiliar female face was a strange sight. The music stopped a second after the boy passed the doorway and as he halted, retraced his steps and glanced back through the open doorway, again the girl had vanished. There are many other such stories to be told, no doubt many of them in various dormitories after lights out.

It was not until after completion of what is now the Maurice Jacks Block that the Towers became a dedicated "Lower School" for younger boys. It will be remembered that the idea of a "Lower School" had first been introduced during Mr. Day's time as Headmaster, although then there had not been sufficient facilities to create a separate school for younger pupils. The acquisition of the Towers solved this problem, and it meant that with the advent of the post-war baby boom and the attendant rise in demand for the education of boys under

11 years old, the College could easily cater for this.

The year 1963 was the year of Tettenhall College's centenary celebrations. It is easy to see why no expense was spared in celebrating this event when we consider the College's first one hundred years of life. The preceding century had been a veritable roller-coaster ride of highs and lows, with plenty of white knuckles along the way. Thus far, the College had survived two major world wars, a crippling period of economic depression, staff and pupil shortages – and other hardships too numerous to recall here but detailed in previous chapters. Despite all of this, the College had always emerged victorious, and so its people saw good reason to celebrate in style. The Jubilee lasted a whole week and was commemorated by the publication of G.V. Hancock's *History of Tettenhall College*, which recounts the College's first hundred years of life.

Guests at the Jubilee Banquet included the former Archbishop of Canterbury, His Grace Lord Fisher of Lambeth, Lord Justice Sellers, Peter Thorneycroft (then Minister of Defence), Enoch Powell (then Minister of Health), the Lord Lieutenant of Staffordshire, the Chairmen of the Baptist and Congregational Unions and the Moderator of the Presbyterian Church. This long list of dignitaries is a measure of the value of the College to its people and to British society as a whole, and it must be mentioned that by then, local people in Wolverhampton had begun to refer to Tettenhall College simply as "The College," such was its reputation as a high quality independent school of high local renown.

Whilst Horace Pearson had been a bachelor, Mr. Field-Hyde was not. This meant that the long hours of work that a headmastership demands also impinged on Mrs. Field-Hyde since a headmaster must always "live over the shop." Inevitably, there are many occasions on a school's calendar that the headmaster's wife is expected to attend and play her part, and Kay Field-Hyde played her part to the full. Her presence at the College was very much in evidence, and the support she gave to Mr. Field-Hyde was tremendous. She was present on every occasion, presenting prizes on Sports Day, supporting drama productions, attending Sunday evening Chapel, entertaining Old Boys, and much, much more. "She was a true Edwardian lady," commented one member of staff shortly after her death in 1980. Despite this, as the sixties wore on, Mr. Field-Hyde was beginning to feel the strain. Whilst he still was physically fit and alert, the need for a headmaster more in tune with the rapidly changing times was getting more and more apparent.

In 1963, the Governors had such confidence in Mr. Field-Hyde that they asked him to remain as Headmaster for a further five years beyond the normal retiring age of sixty. No doubt this was a good thing for the College, but for the Headmaster it was less so. By 1965, the post-war baby boom was tailing off sharply and the birth rate in Britain was also declining. This meant that the school numbers experienced a rapid fall, and this, coupled with the withdrawal of financial assistance from Staffordshire County Council, meant that

Tettenhall College was once again entering troubled times.

However, this time the College was tackling adversity from a much stronger position. As mentioned previously, it had gained an exemplary reputation, and this reputation wasn't just confined to Wolverhampton either. Two years after the centenary celebrations, Mr. Field-Hyde was invited to join the Headmaster's Conference, and this event allowed the College officially to call itself a Public School along with 200 other schools in Great Britain. This achievement had not been easy though. In considering applications to join the Conference, the committee has to assess the degree of independence enjoyed by the school and another crucial factor is the proportion of pupils in the Sixth Form pursuing study beyond "O" level and the number of alumni at the universities. By 1965, it had taken over 20 years to build up a sizeable Sixth Form, and more than 60 of the College's 320 boys were studying for "A" level, with about 30 Old Boys at the universities. Indeed. Between 1943 and 1966, no fewer than 16 Old Tettenhallians had been admitted to either Oxford or Cambridge.

This singular achievement in 1965 helped the College immeasurably, and Mr. Field-Hyde can be justified in his belief that this was one of his greatest achievements as Headmaster. Numbers began to pick up again and the conversion of the old "Carp Shop" into an Art Room and the building of an extension to the Jacks Block to provide a fully equipped Geography Department and two extra classrooms gave the College even greater appeal as far as prospective parents were concerned.

Another legacy from the Pearson era was Miss Hilda Horobin, the Headmaster's secretary. Miss Horobin had held this post for 34 years until her retirement in 1964, and her departure was a blow to the College and the Headmaster in particular. Upon her death a year later in 1965, a memorial service was held in her honour during which the Headmaster was "visibly moved." No doubt this was just one event that helped make up Mr. Field-Hyde's mind to retire three years later in 1968. At that time, he had been the longest serving Headmaster, having been at the College for 26 years.

As with previous Headmasters, Mr. Field-Hyde was instrumental in choosing his successor. It was decided that the new Headmaster would be offered a salary of £3,000 per annum, with a £200 annual expense allowance. The eventual vote was in favour of William John Dale, a graduate of St. Catharine's College, Cambridge – the same college as Mr. Field-Hyde. On the occasion of his last Chapel service, the outgoing Headmaster bade his boys farewell, shaking each one by the hand as they trooped out.

The Field-Hydes left Tettenhall to live in their retirement bungalow at Little Stretton, overlooking the Long Mynd in Shropshire. Mr. Field-Hyde went on to play violin with the Shrewsbury Orchestral Society and become an active member of the Church Stretton Congregational Church. In 1980, Kay Field-Hyde died and the last that most Tettenhallians saw of Frederick Douglas Field-Hyde was at the Old Tettenhallians Dinner the following year when he appeared to be in fine health. However, he died at his sister Margaret's home in Tewkesbury on New Year's Eve of the same year. Shortly afterwards, Margaret brought her brother's ashes to Tettenhall where, in the presence of a small company, she scattered them over the garden at the Headmaster's House. "There," she said. "Douglas is yours."

CHAPTER 18

THE AGE OF TRANSITION

Headmaster: W.J. Dale Esq.

William John Dale was born to a strong Wesleyan Methodist family on 7th September 1933 at St. Agnes, Cornwall. In 1944, he went to Truro School as a Day Boy, and later became a Boarder. At Truro, he demonstrated exceptional talent, and in addition to becoming Head Prefect, he won an Exhibition to St. Catharine's College, Cambridge, a County University Scholarship and a State Scholarship. He went up to Cambridge to read Modern and Medieval Languages in 1951 and was awarded a double first in 1954. In his final year he won the Tasker Prize for the most outstanding modern linguist of his year, and it was at Cambridge where Mr. Dale first met his first wife Rosemary, who was a Classics undergraduate at Newnham College, and who also later became a teacher at Tettenhall College.

Mr. Dale considered various careers including ordination into the Methodist Ministry – he had been an enthusiastic participant in the Truro School Chapel Society and the Cambridge University Methodist Society, so a church career seemed logical. However, he stayed on at Cambridge after graduation in 1954 and spent a year studying for his Postgraduate Diploma in Education, before spending a term at Harrow School as a student teacher. He then served his National Service in the Army Educational Corps, where he taught a number of subjects; and after this, he joined the staff of Clifton College in 1957. Over the eleven years he spent at Clifton, Mr. Dale coached rugby and cricket, was House Tutor at East Town – Clifton's House for Day Boys – and after only four years, he became Senior Modern Languages Master. In 1967 he accepted the Headmastership of Tettenhall College and was present at Speech Day in 1968 when Mr. Field-Hyde announced his retirement. Also present at Speech Day of that year was Dr. Tom Henn, who referred to John Dale as "one of my most brilliant students" when introducing all those present to the new Headmaster.

At the age of 34, Mr. Dale was considerably younger than his predecessor had been when he took up Headmastership of Tettenhall College. Some on the Board of Governors felt that younger blood was needed to cope with rapidly changing times, although others

W. J. Dale Esq., M.A. (Headmaster 1968-1994)

had their doubts. This was the age when Mankind was about to walk on the moon, when the rise of Feminism was changing society's attitudes, and when the Beatles were icons of the new youth-oriented drug culture. It was a decade of student unrest and the advent of a Labour government after thirteen years of Tory rule ushered in a new age of strikes and industrial strife. It was the year when Enoch Powell, Guest Speaker at the College Speech Day in 1967, delivered his controversial "Rivers of Blood" speech at the Midland Hotel in Birmingham to a meeting of the Conservative Political Centre. All in all, it was truly an age of transition that demanded a young man's vision to take the College safely into this new age.

This new Headmaster certainly had a lot of energy and new ideas. He was certainly a man of his time in that he wanted to make a lot of changes and make them quickly. Whilst he was definitely not an anti-traditionalist, Mr. Dale was a firm believer in using old wisdom to temper new ideas. Bearing in mind that he was coming to a school with over a hundred years of deeply entrenched tradition, it is easy to see why there were many who would oppose him. Not only this, but he was stepping into the shoes of a man who, over a quarter of a century, had been the epitome of traditionalist views and who had been revered, liked and respected by many.

This is why there were many die-hards that saw John Dale as a threat to the so-called Public School status quo, but there were also a handful of people that saw the vital need for the College to evolve and embrace the more permissive age that was revolutionising society as a whole. Arguably it was this group of people that were seeking to stay true to the Tettenhall College ethos, which always has been to be "a microcosm of the society prevalent at the time, which exists to serve that society by providing its potential citizens with essential skills to live within it."

This meant that the early Dale years were not necessarily easy ones. To start with, John Dale was most unlike his predecessor in that he was not at ease with formality and stuffiness, and he worked hard to eliminate both, or at least reduce them to what he considered tolerable levels. There was a definite division in the staff, most of whom were loyal to the old values and resistant to rapid reform, and this could not have been easy to live with. Many staff members and Old Boys questioned his commitment to the concept of independent education and even his commitment to the "Establishment" as a whole. Perhaps in a flash of foresight, some even questioned his commitment to single sex education. Little did they know that this liberal quality in the new Headmaster would, in the years to come, save the College from impending doom.

Unlike Mr. Field-Hyde, Mr. Dale did not base his Headship on fear, and he dramatically reduced the incidence of corporal punishment from the very start. Likewise, Mr. Dale did not adopt a magisterial air, and in this sense was far more approachable than his predecessor had been. In later years he was heard to say that out of all his predecessors he would like to meet, he would choose Arthur Angus, and this is not surprising since he shared a lot of Angus' strengths. Just like Angus, Mr. Dale was a charming man, always immaculately presented, and never short of a few words of wisdom. Also like Angus, he was an extremely good preacher and orator and never failed to attract capacity crowds at Speech Day. However, he did not have Mr. Angus' business acumen, but he more than made up for this in scholarly achievement and his exceptional ability as a teacher. In short, he was a man of the people who won many friends by his charm and wit, and this is definitely a factor that contributed to the steady rise in numbers at the College during his time as Headmaster.

Another of Mr. Dale's strengths was that he had an encyclopaedic knowledge of everyone he met, no matter how influential, no matter how small. A master at the College once commented that he "knew more about everybody than even they would be aware of." Consequently, Mr. Dale never went into any meeting without knowing exactly who he was meeting with; he never forgot a face and he never forgot a name. Moreover, being a consummate teacher, he never forgot a question, sometimes coming back weeks later with the answer to the dumbfounded and often bemused questioner – who had probably forgotten that he had ever asked the question in the first place.

In 1970, Mr. Dale's first staff appointment was Mr. R.A. Roberts, who was a talented young History and English graduate fresh from Oxford, and it is perhaps likely that Mr. Dale thought that young blood in the Staff Room would help to quell the traditionalists. In any event, Mr. Roberts became one of the longest serving masters at the College. This and other new appointments were made largely in response to the fact that whilst the College had expanded its physical boundaries, its numbers were also rising rapidly to the point where overcrowding was becoming a serious problem. By this time, Colin Cope had been appointed Master-in-Charge of Lower School (by then firmly established in the Towers), which also was growing.

The Governors endeavoured to address this issue of rapid growth, and in 1970 a proposition was put before the Council of Governors to move the College out of its current premises and go to purpose-built accommodation in the grounds of Wrottesley Hall, which was (and still is) located about three miles out of Tettenhall, just off the main A41 road. At that time, the Hall (the former home of Lord Wrottesley) had been used as a country club. The manor had been owned by the Wrottesley family from the 13th century and it had originally been a moated Tudor house, which was replaced around 1689 with a substantial four storied mansion, comprising a pedimented central entrance block of three bays and flanking wings of four bays each. However, the house was destroyed by fire in 1897 and was replaced with one of more modest proportions, comprising a two storey pedimented three bay building with a central block and single storey four bay wings. Whilst the original estate had been in excess of 2,000 acres, the vast majority of this had been sold off over the years and at the time that Tettenhall became interested in acquiring it, just 52 acres remained.

Following the proposed acquisition of Wrottesley Hall, it was estimated that the new premises would be ready by 1973 and after the move there, the old College premises in Tettenhall would be sold. At this time, many realised that the grounds the College occupied had dramatically escalated in value, and many saw the benefits of moving to other newer premises including Wrottesley Hall as too good to miss.

The Headmaster saw this as a valuable opportunity to make his mark on what would essentially be a new school. It would retain the reputation and the kudos of the old Tettenhall College, but it would also be a new venture on which he could give his own personal stamp. In many ways, a school is defined by its premises, and Mr. Dale thought that this would be as good a way as any other to silence the traditionalists. As such, he applauded the new scheme and worked tirelessly to promote it. He described it to the "Express & Star" on 11 July 1970 as: "a great venture in independent education, which is of national significance." He went on to say that Wrottesley's 52 acre site (as opposed to the College's 32 acre one) would enable the College to "do in three or four years what it would take many more to do on the present site."

"Even moderate expansion in numbers would lead to a shortage of playing field space now," said Mr. Dale. "…the Towers building was far from ideal for teaching small boys: adapting the original building to modern need was difficult and expensive; and in the field of physical education, there were additional facilities, which would be welcome."

The cost of the Wrottesley Hall move was estimated initially as £900,000. However, such a radical solution to the overcrowding problem stirred up a massive hornet's nest. Feelings ran high among pupils, parents, Governors, staff and Old Boys. In fact, everyone with even the vaguest involvement with the College was either absolutely for the scheme or vehemently opposed to it. Very few were indifferent, and this all precipitated a tremendous "civil war" with the Headmaster at its centre. Those in favour of the Wrottesley plan argued that it would be a financially sound move that would make the College a lot of much-needed money to invest in premises, staff and equipment that would far outstrip the competition from other independent schools. Not only this, but it would be a new and exciting venture where the College could be moulded to suit that society it now found itself in. It would still be located in the same general area as before, so Day Boys and Day Boarders would not be lost.

Those against the scheme quite rightly pointed out that Tettenhall College could not call itself Tettenhall College if it was not located in Tettenhall. Not only this, but much of the College's history had its roots in the old premises and if it moved elsewhere, all of this would be lost. This, in turn would tarnish the College's reputation as an established school and much of the goodwill it relied upon to flourish would be lost. Those opposing the scheme pointed out that moving to an ostensibly rural area like Wrottesley might mean that many "foot" pupils from Tettenhall would be lost since these then made up a substantial portion of the College's Day Boys and Day Boarders. Moreover, since the Perton housing estate was still several years in the future, it was feared that the College would lose its ability to attract such pupils altogether, since Wrottesley could only be reached by road at this time.

Those against the scheme also questioned the financial viability of the move, saying that it could end up as a disaster that would certainly kill the College. They said that in the past, the College had relied heavily upon the support of its Old Boys and with new premises, those Old Boys would no longer see the College as "the place where they went to school."

However, the war was effectively ended when the whole scheme had to be scrapped when financial backing to develop the site was withdrawn in 1971. The College had been relying on bridging finance, originally promised by the Vehicle and General Insurance Company, which was never materialised due to the company's collapse, and all plans to develop the Wrottesley site had to be scrapped. This was a tremendous blow to those who had supported the scheme, especially the Headmaster, and whilst the traditionalists breathed a sigh of relief, life resumed at the College – although more controversial change was yet to come.

Following the Wrottesley scheme, Mr. Dale had to do a public about-face and convince many people that it actually was in the College's best interests to remain in Tettenhall. He also had the unenviable task of managing the College's recovery from this crisis so that all appeared to be well with the outside world, and it is a tribute to his public relations skills that the outside world did not notice the bitter battle that had gone on within the College walls. The then Vice-chairman of the Governors, Bob King said to the *Express & Star* on 23rd March: "There is no question of us looking over our shoulders to Wrottesley. The move is definitely off."

At this point, the College had actually acquired Wrottesley Hall and its 52 acres of land, but it now lacked the funds to develop it for school purposes. It had been rumoured that the College was going to sell off part of the Henwood Road playing fields, but these rumours were vehemently denied. Many thought that the grounds of Wrottesley Hall would make better playing fields, so this is probably how these rumours originated. In any event, the Wrottesley Hall site had to be sold, and the Governors turned to ways of expanding its existing premises in Tettenhall. With this in mind, in July 1971, the College announced long-term plans to extend the Dining Hall and improve kitchen facilities, improved boarding accommodation, a new Music School, an Upper School Theatre, a new Art School, Language Laboratory and new domestic wing. Mr. Dale said to the "Express & Star:" "Of course we realise that we are here concerned with a long-term plan covering perhaps 15 years."

These goals would not be achieved without finance though. By July, a College Development Trust had been set up and it had accumulated over £50,000 to help improve school facilities. This included £20,000 from the Goodyear Tyre and Rubber Company Ltd., and the remaining £30,000 from Governors, parents and members of the Old Tettenhallian Fund Raising Committee. Later that year, Wolverhampton millionaire and philanthropist Charles Hayward donated a sum of £10,000 to the College to help with improvement work on the kitchen and dining facilities, which allowed work to begin immediately. Mr. Dale went on record as saying: "I want to make Tettenhall College an independent school with a wide variety of courses to meet the needs of its pupils."

One thing Mr. Dale valued greatly was the need to keep abreast of current ideas and concepts. During the Field-Hyde era, Tettenhall College was very much the epitome of a British Public School. Everyone followed the Headmaster's example and used only surnames (even in private), beatings were dished out to enforce discipline, and short haircuts were mandatory. However, Mr. Dale relaxed this regime, and whilst surnames were used in the classroom, he turned a blind eye to Christian names being used outside the school walls or in private. As the seventies dawned with its long hair and flared trousers, boys were allowed to grow their hair down to their collars (but not beyond), and they were also allowed to wear fashionable trousers and shoes as part of their uniform, providing they were black. However, shirt buttons had to be kept fastened at all times and the wearing of shirts outside one's trousers was definitely not allowed. All of this colours Mr. Dale as a man of the times who saw the need for the College to adapt to these times, whilst not compromising on traditional values of discipline and hard work. Moreover, Mr. Dale wanted his pupils at least to feel that they were a part of the world outside the College gates, and in an age where television, radio (and eventually computers) kept people much better informed than they had been in previous generations, this he thought was essential.

Very early on in his Headmastership, Mr. Dale introduced Parents' Evenings when parents could meet with masters to discuss their children's progress and raise any issues they might have. This in turn led to the forming of a Parents' Association whose main function was to raise funds for the Sixth Form, and also to be a lobbying group for any changes its members thought would benefit the school. One can imagine that if Mr. Angus had been Headmaster in 1969, he would have introduced such an idea, keen as he was to listen to the needs of his customers.

In 1969, at around the same time as he introduced the much-needed Parents' Evenings, Mr. Dale – amid much controversy – invited two girls to join the Tettenhall College Sixth Form. This was done largely in response to girls' school Brewood Convent not having a Sixth Form and the increasing number of girls there wishing to sit "A" levels and not wishing to go to a state run college to do this. Naturally, the staunch traditionalists were vehemently against this move, and it is a credit to Mr. Dale that he managed to quell this faction and go ahead with including girls in the Sixth Form anyway. The College's first ever girls were

Vanessa Corbett and Louise Champion, and private female toilet facilities and a changing area were provided for them adjacent to the main changing rooms. One can only imagine what it must have been like for these two girls, being the only females in a school of over 300 boys and an almost entirely male teaching staff.

This idea proved to be a success and over the following years, the numbers of girls grew larger, and the fact that many of them achieved good results should probably speak for itself. It must be noted though that Marlborough School was the first H.M.C. boys' school to introduce girls into the Sixth Form, and no doubt Mr. Dale followed their example in an effort to introduce an innovation that would not only increase numbers but would also help the Sixth Form boys and girls to learn how to manage in a mixed environment. One criticism that is always levelled at single sex schools is that the older pupils cannot learn how to cope with the opposite sex and this in some cases leads to problems later on in life. Clearly, Mr. Dale was aware of this school of thought and in the light of changing inter-sexual attitudes, he strongly believed he was doing the right thing for his older pupils. With the benefit of hindsight, many say that it was a good move, since it also paved the way for a later, much more controversial move to turn the College into a fully co-educational school for both boys and girls.

In 1969, the Governors decided that the old Thorneycroft stables would make an excellent Library. The building was not in a very good state of repair, so extensive work was needed to convert it to a Regency-flavoured room with plenty of space for bookshelves and desks. The lawn and terrace outside this building also proved useful as a venue for College summer plays and other social events. The Library was contained only in the main stable block directly facing the Maurice Jacks Block and the wing on the building's left side was converted into a Woodwork Room in the following year.

In 1971, another Tettenhall College tradition came to an end. On 2nd May, the Queen Street Congregational Church held its final service, and 50 boys from the College marked the occasion by following tradition and walking the three miles to the church to attend this event. The church had been founded in 1809, and it will be remembered that most of the College's founding fathers had originated there. Even though there was no one left to remember the first years of the College, many marked this event as the end of an era.

But the College continued to move forward. Mr. Dale had been at Tettenhall only four years before he introduced the notion of an annexe nursery school for very young children. Supporters of this scheme argued that if the College could provide an entire education package from the age of five through to eighteen, it would not only increase numbers, but it would also mean that boys would be more likely to stay on from Nursery School, through to Lower School and finally to Upper School. It was also argued that having a child at one school from an early age to maturity would be less stressful upon the child because he would not have the trauma of moving to a different school for each stage of his education.

This idea proved to be popular, and The Drive School was opened in 1972 under the direction of Headmistress Mrs. Molly Grosvenor. There was no room in the main College campus for the new school, so a large house had to be purchased in Tettenhall just off Wrottesley Road for this purpose. Fortunately the house had previously been used as a school (Miss Marjorie Hill's Preparatory School), so did not need a great deal of conversion. Looking back, we can see that the Drive School was a success in that it managed to attract a comparatively large number of pupils, but in terms of logistics it was less successful than it might have been had it been located on the main College campus. Meals for the younger children had to be ferried from the kitchens at main school, and on the frequent occasions when the younger children had to avail themselves of the facilities on the main College campus, this entailed a long walk from Wrottesley Road and the potential danger that this entailed. However, there were insufficient funds and space available to do anything about this at that time, and it would be many years before the Drive School was finally moved to the comparative safety of the main Tettenhall College campus.

Another significant staff appointment occurred in 1974 when Economics master Mr. A.R. Mottershead joined the College. Whilst Economics had been taught for some years previously, the need for this subject became more apparent with the advent of polytechnics and universities requiring Economics subject as the basis for the numerous varieties of Business Studies degrees that were gaining in popularity. Mr. Mottershead was another talented young man fresh from Keele University, and he wasted no time in revolutionising the Economics Department with his boundless enthusiasm and drive. Both he and Mr. Roberts later went on to obtain PhDs, and no doubt Mr. Dale was quietly pleased to have two such well-qualified members of staff on his team.

Music at the College thrived during Mr. Dale's time. Looking back over the College's history, we can see that music has always been an important part of school life, and this Headmaster was equally as determined as his predecessors to maintain the tradition. A Concert Club was started and instrumental tuition at the hands of professional musicians was revived. Whilst instrumental tuition was not compulsory – it was popular – and most pupils at the College could play at least one instrument. The House Music Competition was also popular, and musicians of all standards were invited to win points for their House. The tradition of having an annual musical show drew in pupils of all ages, and every year the resulting production played to packed houses. Pupils not only sang on stage, but they also made up the orchestra too. Lower School master Tom Blacklock penned an original musical himself named *The Wotsit* and this was performed at the end of summer term. Its follow up, *Samson and Delilah,* also written by Mr. Blacklock, proved popular as well. As each year passed the productions became more and more professional and on several occasions even the usually acerbic theatre critics at the "Express & Star" gave glowing reviews.

The Tettenhall college campus in 1974.
The Towers and the Maurice Jacks Block with Main School in the background.

A thriving Gilbert and Sullivan Society also played to packed houses, with the Headmaster often playing an active part. Most memorable of these was *The Gondoliers* in 1974. In fact, many Tettenhallians at this time went on either to study music at university or become professional musicians. The name that springs easily to mind here is Julian Trafford who is now a professional violin player, having played with many orchestras including the English Chamber Orchestra, the BBC Symphony Orchestra and the London Mozart Players.

Non-musical drama was also given a shot in the arm during Mr. Dale's time. A tradition of performing an annual play by Shakespeare was seen to be an excellent way to "educate and delight," since this play was usually the one being studied at either "O" or "A" level. Another tradition started at this time was the annual play performed in the open air outside the Library (now the Sixth Form Centre). This was usually a much lighter offering than the Shakespeare play and these often took the form of comedies or farces such as *Hay Fever* and *Blithe Spirit*.

Reading through the earlier chapters of this book, it is obvious that Tettenhallians have always been keen on sport. Whilst the more traditional games of rugby and cricket were played no less enthusiastically than they had been in previous years, the introduction of squash in the early seventies proved very popular, and on several occasions the College Squash Team did extremely well at a national level, some Tettenhallians even gained national recognition for their game. Whilst in-campus squash courts were not introduced until 1978, many pupils at the College took advantage of the courts at the Wolverhampton Lawn Tennis and Squash Club at Newbridge. Nick Jeavons was already making a name for himself in the field of athletics and rugby, cricket and swimming. He would go on to become a rugby union player for England, and in 1983, he toured with the British Lions on their tour to New Zealand while playing club rugby for Moseley.

Just like in previous years, all kinds of extra-curricular activities were encouraged and John Dale was no less enthusiastic in promoting these than his predecessors had been. Mr. Dale often spoke of the "whole man" type of education, in which a person should be educated at all levels of activity to become as fully rounded an individual as possible. Following from this, he was also keen to engender an adventurous and questing spirit, and many Tettenhallians at the College during Mr. Dale's time have commented to this effect. This meant that there were even more school trips than before, and one is reminded of Mr. Angus' excursion to London some sixty years earlier.

It has been said by several people over the history of Wolverhampton that if you want your child to go to university, you send him to the Grammar School, but if you want him to play rugby, you send him to Tettenhall College. John Dale worked very hard to refute this contention, and his holistic approach to education meant that the academic side never played second fiddle to sport or pastimes. No fewer than 17 Tettenhallians went on to either Oxford or Cambridge during the Dale years, including Mr. Dale's son Stephen, who won an Exhibition to his father's *alma mater*, St. Catharine's College, Cambridge.

As numbers (especially in the Sixth Form) continued to rise towards the middle of the seventies, the need for more classrooms became all too apparent. The Council of Governors realised that the College was under a tremendous amount of pressure to expand, and it was just a question of how this expansion could be achieved? The obvious answer was to extend the Maurice Jacks Block and the only logical way to do this with a minimal amount of disruption was to build another storey on top of it. It was decided that this would be a cheaper alternative to creating extra buildings and a more permanent solution than prefabricated buildings might be, so work began in 1974 and was completed in that same year. The new storey proved to be a very useful addition, as it provided a purpose-built Staff

Common Room and several large classrooms that had movable partitions to make them smaller if desired. The new storey was used only for Sixth Form work at first, although the usage of these rooms has changed many times over the years.

In 1977 the Headmaster called an end to Saturday morning school. Up until this time, all pupils had been required to attend school on Saturday mornings, and it was felt in earlier years that this would provide Day boys and Day Boarders with greater integration with the Boarders. As time wore on, and Day Pupils and Day Boarders had increased in proportion, it was decided to relegate this custom to history, much to the relief of teachers who had to commute long distances to work. This was also the same year when the traditional formal ritual for meals was replaced by improved kitchen facilities and a canteen system.

Following the College's unprecedented success at squash at national levels, it was decided in 1978 to build some squash courts on the College campus. There was some debate over where these should be built, but in the end, it was decided that the best site would be the Towers rear lawn adjacent to the woods on the site of the existing hard Tennis Courts. Work was completed relatively quickly, and it is disappointing to note that with the lessening in popularity of squash, these courts have become very under-utilised in recent years. It must also be noted that the new Squash courts also incorporate an external "Tettenhallian" fives court – a sport that thankfully still remains popular at the College.

The year before the Squash Courts were begun saw the retirement of Harold Parker, the College Groundskeeper. In his place came Alex Poile, who was to make tremendous improvements to the College estate in the years to come. Up until this point, all the various Groundsmen had done was mostly maintain what was already there, but Mr. Poile introduced such things as an adventure playground on the Towers lawn and numerous marked out nature trails in the woods. He also revived the old College tradition of pet's corner and provided hutches, stables and other accommodation for animals ranging from hamsters to horses. Of course, all of this had Mr. Dale's blessing, although there were a few Old Tettenhallians who were horrified to see the Towers lawn with an adventure playground on it.

As the seventies ended and a new decade dawned, we can see from Mr. Dale's first twelve years as Headmaster that there had been much progress at the College. In spite of those to whom change was anathema, Mr. Dale remained steadfast to his belief that the College had to move with the times. He was certainly aware that this had often been one of the factors that had saved the College in the past, and it is to his credit that he perceived the essential wisdom that we can only get from history. He had behind him a truly remarkable team of supporting staff including Dr. A.R. Mottershead, Dr. R.A. Roberts, Mr. L.N. Chown, Mr. N.A. Gratton, and last, but by no means least, Mr. G.V. Hancock, and it seemed that the College could only go from strength to strength – although this would not be possible without a lot more radical change.

CHAPTER 19

THE BOOM YEARS

Headmaster: W.J. Dale Esq.

M any remember the eighties as a "boom" decade where there was low unemployment and plenty of prosperity. Everyone seemed to have money in their pockets and many of these people had seen fit to spend that money on a private education for their children. Along with this prosperity came greater competition, and this meant that companies needed to spend large amounts of money in analysing their markets so that they could secure as many customers as possible. In 1982, this was no less the case for Tettenhall College. It must be remembered that whilst the College had enjoyed the help of several wealthy benefactors in the past, it had no endowments whatsoever. This meant that it had to pay a lot of attention to marketing in order to secure more pupils and more much-needed revenue. The College's arch-rival the Wolverhampton Grammar School had gone independent in 1979 and admission levels at Tettenhall had suffered as a result. The only thing that Tettenhall could offer that the Grammar School could not was boarding facilities, and since the whole concept of boarding school was becoming less popular, this was a slowly diminishing edge. Tettenhall also had the advantage of offering an education to all ages and to all abilities, whilst the Grammar School was still just a secondary school for "high fliers." This helped the College's fortunes quite a lot, but it must not be forgotten that the majority of pupils (and therefore the majority of the schools' revenue) lay in Upper School, and clearly long-term financial success was also linked to the number of "high-fliers" who would bolster the College's reputation for excellence.

Another competitor was the Royal Wolverhampton School, which, like the Grammar School, was very well endowed by numerous charitable concerns. This school had shaken off its "Wolverhampton Orphanage" image and presented serious competition for Tettenhall, since it too could offer boarding facilities. So, in the first years of the eighties, with all that lovely extra disposable income in people's pockets, the College had to find a way to get its hands on some of it – and in the face of some very stiff competition.

In 1982, Wolverhampton was home to just a little over 255,000 souls, of which only a small percentage had a sufficient income to afford a private education for their sons. It is obvious then that Wolverhampton's thee independent boys' schools were fighting over far too few customers to go round. The stark fact was that there simply was not enough room for three boys' schools in Wolverhampton. In response to this, the College invested in a marketing campaign, which involved establishing links with local and foreign communities and exploiting the press at every opportunity, so that the College would be kept in the public eye. These efforts were successful in securing more pupils from the Far East, notably from Hong Kong, but the local market was proving to be very difficult indeed. Despite everyone's efforts, there was little doubt that the College was losing ground.

There were also movements afoot in Whitehall to abolish independent schools completely, and this had caused an understandable amount of reluctance for parents to send their children to such schools. Mr. Dale said at the time that the abolition of independent schools would be "an act of destruction on a scale of King Henry VIII's dissolution of the monasteries." He went on to say: "Our anxieties can be survived, and the best cure for uncertainty is to get on with the job." These were brave words, but it didn't lessen the severity of the potential threat. With 476 pupils on the College register and the economic need to expand even further, it was difficult to see how to do this in the light of fierce competition.

It is easy when recounting the history of an institution like Tettenhall College to see either the College itself, or indeed Wolverhampton, as isolated from the outside world. This has never been the case, and whilst the College's fortunes have in the past been geared to the economic fortunes of the West Midlands, all this was changing. The computer and technological revolution had just begun, and economic expansion was rife. International travel and trade were becoming more commonplace, and the concept of the "Global Village" was taking shape.

On 19th March 1982, at a time when the Cold War with the Eastern Bloc had reached new levels of paranoia, the military forces of Argentina invaded the British territory of South Georgia in the South Atlantic Falkland Islands, and whilst war was never officially declared, all British armed forces were mobilised to meet this potential threat. This meant that with the absence of tens of thousands of British servicemen and women, the need for schools with boarding facilities for both boys and girls had been reawakened overnight.

At about this time, Mr. Dale put forward a carefully thought-out proposition to the Council of Governors that Tettenhall College should go fully co-educational. Up to this point, there had only been a handful of girls in the Sixth Form and the proposition was that girls should be admitted throughout the entire school. Naturally, this ignited a heated debate among the Governors. On one side were those that said that Tettenhall College had been a boys' school for 120 years and that it should continue to be so. The other faction, led by the Headmaster, argued that not to do this could mean the end of the College due to increased competition. The Headmaster pointed out that with the advent of more and more military and diplomatic service personnel seeking boarding schools for boys and girls, the move to co-education would allow families of brothers and sisters to remain together, and this would allow them to support each other while their parents were away.

Mr. Dale also argued that the introduction of girls would increase competition in a way that the College had never known before, and that both sexes would push each other to new levels of achievement by means of "natural competition." He also argued that the introduction of the female perspective would give learning at the College a dimension that it had hitherto lacked.

This proved to be a convincing argument since the vote came down strongly in favour of the motion that the College should go co-educational. The only problem was that the Governors would have to take immediate action to provide more female toilet and sports facilities, not to mention hiring more female members of staff. There was also the obvious problem of where to put girl Boarders.

The move to co-education was announced in July 1983, and the press were told that girl pupils of all ages would be admitted from the autumn term onwards, although it was stressed by the Headmaster that this would be a "phased development over the next few years." This meant that the Governors had to act quickly. They had only a few scant months to prepare for a potential influx of female pupils, and rapid alterations to the school premises needed to be made. Pre-fabricated classrooms were hastily erected at the rear of the Maurice Jacks Block, and the Headmaster and his second wife Lydia said that girls could stay at the Headmaster's House until more permanent accommodation could be found. Extended girls' toilet facilities were added to the existing ones adjacent to the main changing rooms and the former cycle sheds were converted into a Home Economics Room. A hockey pitch was hurriedly marked out and it was decided that the all-male facilities in the Pavilion would have to wait their turn to be converted to unisex.

By all accounts, the first years of co-education were not easy ones, with girls and their attendant toilet and laundry needs being shared between the Headmaster's House and the Towers. While all this was going on, the Governor's Planning Committee was given the task of building a dedicated Girls' Boarding House on the school grounds as soon as it could. Architects Butler Wones were asked to design such a building and after much consultation, work began on a new girls' boarding house in the woods adjacent to the garden of the Headmaster's House. It seems also that the College's guardian angel had decided to give its blessing on the move to co-education, because a large four-bedroomed house suddenly came on the market in College Lane only a few seconds walk from the College gates. The Governors lost no time in acquiring this property, and it eventually did a wonderful job of housing several girl pupils under the supervision of a resident member of staff.

The year 1983 was also the year when the Sports Hall was built. This had stemmed from a need to provide children with a covered area to play games in during wet weather, and the Governors' Planning Committee had discovered that it was more cost effective to build a basic shell with a concrete floor, basic lighting, heating and walls – rather than just a simple canopy. This "Sports Hall" was erected in its basic form in 1983, but it would be many years before it was equipped with a Granwood floor, proper lighting and heating. In the early days though, it served as a dry area for games. Like the Squash Courts, the Sports Hall was located on the site of the former hard Tennis Courts adjacent to the woods behind the Towers lawn.

In January of the following year the Governors gave the go-ahead for a new Technology Centre. By this time, the computer age was with us to stay and educational establishments, like many other organisations, were under pressure to "be there or be square." Information Technology was progressing in leaps and bounds and Tettenhall College wanted to embrace it fully. At Speech Day of this year, the Headmaster heavily underlined the need for computer skills in a world where Information Technology would be at the cornerstone of practically every career path. The Technology Centre had actually been two years in the planning and a fund to raise about £750,000 had accumulated about £220,000, so the green light was given to start phase one, which was work to modernise the buildings fronting the Playground and adapt them for high-tech use.

And so, as work commenced on permanent new boarding facilities for the girls and the new Technology Centre, Mr. Dale was delighted to be elected as Chairman of the Society of Headmasters of Independent Schools (SHMIS). This, of course, meant that the College would enjoy a greater profile in an organisation whose purpose was to further the interests of independent schools. Whilst appointments of this kind do tend to eat into the time of a headmaster, being Chairman of SHMIS didn't take Mr. Dale's finger off the College pulse. While maintaining his twelve-hours a week teaching routine, he still found time to monitor progress on all the developments to the school premises.

Meanwhile, the College Operatic and Dramatic Company were making headlines with their production of *I Pagliacci*, which won rave reviews in many periodicals. This was largely down to the enthusiasm and drive of Allen Roberts, Olwynne Hutt and Chas Rimmer, who moved musical drama at the College into a completely new league. Previous performances of *Carmen* and *Orpheus in the Underworld* had led up to this momentous performance.

In 1984, the College became aware that the Headmaster's House was in severe need of repair. The house where it had all began had become infested with Death Watch Beetle and the costs of remedying this were extremely high indeed. The Governors balanced on one hand the high cost of putting the house right, against the other option of housing the Headmaster elsewhere and disposing of the old Headmaster's House, beetles and all. Eventually, the Council of Governors reached the painful decision to sell the house and acquire new accommodation for the Headmaster. Fortunately, an American buyer took the old house readily enough in 1988, paid the costs of de-infesting it and proceeded to move in. Meanwhile, the College's guardian angel had not been idle, and a house came on the market in Tettenhall High Street just a few seconds walk away from the College, and the Governors lost no time in buying it – no doubt to sighs of relief all round.

By this time, Alex Poile had worked wonders with the College grounds and his open days for the public to take guided walks around the estate were proving to be very popular. Favourite among these was the "Bluebell Walk" held in May, and this succeeded in raising the College's profile among many prospective customers. Not only this, but Mr. Poile was also asked to appear on BBC TV to talk about his work at the College, and there is no doubt that this could only have had a positive impact on the school's public profile.

Dr. A.R. Mottershead had, by this time, introduced the College May Ball, which was held at a similar time to Alex Poile's "Bluebell Walk." This is an event that has proved to be tremendously popular among students at the College. The event was along the lines of a university May Ball where students could celebrate the end of the school year and review their various achievements. The early May Balls were held at the Towers, but in recent years, the event has been moved to venues outside the College due mostly to the popularity of the event and the escalation since this time of numbers at the College. Now that girls formed a part of College life, the concept of having dance socials like this among College students was a completely new thing that could only improve morale considerably.

In the light of all these advances, it must be noted that standards of discipline at the College had not been neglected. By July 1986, six pupils had left the College (four of them expelled) due to breaches of discipline. The Headmaster accused some parents of failing to back school discipline and in an address at Speech Day, he said: "A few parents, however many privileges are given, always want more. A few parents apparently cannot understand that it is not possible to operate the whole establishment for the benefit of their particular offspring.

"Most parents take a keen interest in pupils' progress and welfare, giving the College every encouragement. On the other hand, a minority is prepared to conspire with their children to outwit school authority."

This is evidence indeed that in spite of its willingness to embrace newer and perhaps more liberal ideals, the older traditions of discipline and respect had not been neglected, and the College's "zero tolerance" of flagrant breaches of discipline was still being enforced in ways that would have done Mr. Field-Hyde proud.

In 1986, after 38 memorable and magnificent years of service to Tettenhall College, Mr. G.V. Hancock announced his retirement. He used no notes when making his address at a packed-to-capacity marquee on Speech Day, and he said that his most cherished moment of his 38 years at the College since his arrival in 1948 was the moment in 1953 when he persuaded the new Assistant Housekeeper to marry him. Everyone then joined in for a rapturous applause to wish both Mr. and Mrs Hancock a very happy retirement. There is no doubt that Mr. Hancock's infectious enthusiasm for history turned what could have been a very dry subject into a much looked-forward-to journey involving colourful characters, intriguing machinations and hilarious exploits, which have enthralled generations of Tettenhallians who were fortunate enough to have been taught by him. His firm-but-fair avuncular discipline always garnered a great deal of respect, and there is no one that could ever fail to like Mr. Hancock. There is no doubt that without his expert teaching and advice, this book would never have been written. An honorary Old Tettenhallian since 1980, Mr. Hancock is still an honoured guest at Old Tettenhallian events, and now devotes his time between his family and his cherished studies of the history of Wolverhampton.

It was also in July of 1986 when the Headmaster and his wife Lydia attended the Queen's Garden Party at Buckingham Palace. The drama of losing their invitations between leaving Euston Station and the Palace Gardens caused them some anxious moments, but they both recall the day as being one of the most memorable ones of their entire lives. Mr. Dale recalls that the guards at the Palace reminded him of Gilbert and Sullivan's *The Yeoman of the Guard*, and both were amused at the way the Queen took her tea from a gold urn, or samovar. In any event, the day proved to be a success for the Headmaster and his wife, not to mention excellent publicity for the College. This was the first of two such visits to the Palace for Mr. And Mrs Dale, and both events proved to be a resounding success both for them personally and for the College.

A glance through the earlier chapters of this book will reveal that the standard of school food at Tettenhall in its early days was perhaps not of the highest. By the late nineteen-eighties, this had all changed. As has been mentioned, the old meal ritual of a Top Table, long benches and servers had long since been replaced by a canteen system, and pupils at the College had for a long time enjoyed a wide choice of excellently prepared meals. In fact, the local paper the "Express & Star" published a feature article on meals at the College which said: "Hot meals such as egg on toast, steak and kidney pie and vegetable lasagne are served for tea and there's a supper trolley stacked with sandwiches, cakes, biscuits and toast. Semolina and stodge were my memory of school dinners, so it was pleasant to find a lunch menu including tasty lamb hotpot, containing chunks of lean, tender meat, served with crisp broccoli followed by a raspberry yoghurt full of fruit and not too sweet.

"A nicely presented array of fresh salads including bean sprouts and peppers complemented the hot menu.

"'The most significant change we have made is a switch from convenience to fresh foods,' said Mr. Baizley [the Bursar]. 'Frozen food is used only as a last resort, all vegetables and fruit are fresh, sweets homemade and we never use soya substitute.'

"Chips he admitted ruefully are the one item 'rationed.' Children are not allowed to serve themselves."

All of these advances were due in no small part to a strong and competent teaching team, as well as one of one of the best Council of Governors the College has known, headed up by Peter Brown OBE. In 125 years, the College had come a long way from its religious roots, and by now its doors were open to boys and girls of any religious background. Despite this, the ritual of morning Chapel remained no less a part of the school day than it had in the early years. Even the College Swimming Pool had undergone many renovations and improvements over the years and it was in the late eighties a far cry from the murky pit that it had been at the beginning of its days in 1876.

However, despite all these advances, the numbers at the College began to slip and it became clear as the eighties came to a close that despite the changes, the College facilities were beginning to look a little dated. Lower School was still in the rambling Towers building and the Drive School was still in its remote annexe on the other side of Tettenhall village. Whilst all this was happening, other independent schools were offering ever better on-campus facilities. Economic tension began to grip the country as it slid into yet another recession, and anxieties were felt among Governors, staff and parents alike as to how the College would cope with the hard times that would inevitably come.

The first measure that caused a sigh of relief for many was the long-awaited and much-needed opening in 1989 of Thorneycroft House, the new girls' boarding house. This building provided all new modern facilities for up to 24 girls, and it was seen as a major coup in the quest to get the College numbers up again. However, ever since girls had been admitted to the College, the need for extra security had become more and more apparent as each year went by. The girls' boarding facilities especially needed extra vigilance, and extra money had to be found to make the College's premises much more secure than they had been in previous times.

The new Thorneycroft House proved to be a resounding success however, and Sally Nowell, one of the first girl Boarders there wrote: "Being both a first time Boarder and a newcomer to Tettenhall College, I was a little uneasy to say the least, at what was in store for me. But I was soon reassured by the sense of belonging that struck me as I walked through the door, and being accepted as a member of the community.

"It was obvious that a lot of time, thought and effort had been put into the construction of the new girls' boarding house, from the comfort of a kettle and toaster in the recreation room to the sanctuary of a hot shower.

"A lot can be said for boarding at Tettenhall College. I for one found that you receive a lot more out of school life, not purely academic but certainly educational. Bering made to respect different aspects of discipline are accepted and once mastered stand us in good stead for the rest of our future lives."

Thorneycroft House: Boarding House for Girls

In 1991, the College achieved an 80 per cent pass at "A" levels with a high proportion of "A" grades. University admission was high and it seemed that the College was thriving. However, during the 1980s the government had allowed the economy to expand at a significantly higher rate than its long run trend growth rate. This was because they felt there had been a "supply side miracle". They argued that its supply side policies enabled the economy to grow at a faster rate than before. Therefore the government kept interest rates low and cut income tax. Also during the 1980s there was a boom in the housing market, the increase in prices lead to an increase in consumer spending and this in turn had led to a big increase in consumer confidence.

Unfortunately, most of the growth was caused by consumer borrowing and spending, the effect of which was to cause higher rates of inflation and a large current account deficit. To reduce this double digit inflation, the government joined the European Exchange Rate

Mechanism (ERM) in 1990, since it was felt this would bring inflation under control. Market forces kept speculating the pound would fall. To maintain its value the government had to use its foreign currency reserves to buy sterling (the UK lost £21 billion in the ERM) and increase interest rate to 15 per cent.

Despite these measures, Britain was forced to leave the ERM and devalue. Meanwhile, the high level of interest rates had caused the country to fall into a deep recession, which, in turn, caused a fall in house prices and many people who had borrowed heavily to fuel the "boom" years of the '80s were now crippled with high interest rates; jobs were lost and disposable income fell. In short, there was less money to spend on private education, and the College had to face up to the prospect of falling income and therefore less to spend on much needed improved facilities.

Despite the gloomy economic outlook, the College was able to count its blessings though. The Council of Governors was still under the capable chairmanship of Peter Brown and the supporting Governors were all men and women of the highest calibre. Despite the fact that Mr. Dale had lost his strongest right hand man five years previously, the teaching staff were continuing to produce good quality results. However, the onset of recession was causing a fall in numbers and as pupils left the College, they were not really being replaced in large enough quantities. By now, the Grammar School had gone co-educational and potentially adverse market forces governing the supply of both boys and girls needing independent education were rearing their ugly heads once again. By the end of 1991, exam passes at "A" level had fallen 3 per cent over the previous year, and while the Headmaster publicly said that he was "quite pleased," many felt that the time was fast coming to take measures to prevent any further "slippage."

As the recession took a firmer grip, funds to complete the proposed Technology Centre had dried up and whilst the College had well and truly moved into the computer age, it did not quite have the facilities to provide the fully fledged IT Department that it had previously hoped for. However, whilst the Technology Centre never got past phase one of development, it did focus all minds on the need for technological awareness

In his 1993 address at Speech Day, the Headmaster reaffirmed his belief that the teaching staff was the College's greatest asset and whilst improved facilities were high on the priority list, keeping good staff was even higher, and in order to maintain a happy staff, a modest pay increase (whilst keeping fees on an even keel) was far more important than investing the money in school infrastructure. At this time, over 70 per cent of the College outgoings was on salaries, and high interest rates had prevented the College borrowing any more money for building improvements, so the subtext of Mr. Dale's speech on this occasion was that we all had to "tighten our belts." Despite this, 1992 had seen a dramatic rise in "A" level pass rates to 85 per cent and whilst this may have reaffirmed confidence in the Headmaster, to use his own words, everyone was "walking a tightrope."

By this time, the economy was beginning to recover and the advent of the Internet and the communications revolution was truly reducing the world to just one "Global Village," it must have been difficult for Mr. Dale (and indeed many of his staff) to come to terms with the fact that they had simply not grown up with this new phenomenon that was fast becoming a part of everyone's lives. The need to have a full understanding of computers and their uses was becoming paramount over the incentives to learn using more traditional methods. By then, everyone was aware that they had to either embrace this new "cyber-world," or make way for those who could.

With the bottoming out of the recession and the need to invest large quantities of money on College facilities, the traditional mores of "living within one's means" were beginning to look dated. Increased competition from other schools was deeply underlining the need to provide a newer Lower School and even an on-campus Drive School, although in 1993 it was not clear where the money was going to come from to provide this. Yes, there were new girls' changing facilities in 1993 and a new Home Economics Room in 1989, but the need for the College to expand beyond these small extensions and adaptations was all too apparent.

In 1993, Mr. Dale announced his retirement. This surprised many people since at the time he was only 60, but rapidly changing times must have been a constant reminder to him that he was no longer the young new Headmaster brimful of new ideas, and that it was time to admit that the changing world would need a changed College. To usher in this new age, he felt that a new Headmaster was what the College needed.

Mr. Dale retired back to his family home "Chinale" at St. Agnes in Cornwall, and left behind him a strong Tettenhall College that had weathered the storms of two major recessions with vigour. During his retirement in Cornwall Mr. Dale endeavoured to keep abreast with developments at the school to whom he had devoted such a large part of his life and career. He took pleasure and pride in following the careers of many of his former pupils, and despite spirited fights against aphasia and skin cancer, everyone who knew him were saddened to learn of his death on 19th November 2007. His passing was commemorated at the St. Agnes Methodist Chapel and he is interred at St. Agnes Cemetery in his much-loved home county of Cornwall.

The final word on the Dale era should belong to Jeremy Walters, Old Tettenhallian (from the Field-Hyde era) and close personal friend of Mr. Dale's, who said: "John will be remembered as a man of fertile ideas and fresh thinking, who ploughed many new furrows and planted firm-rooted saplings, which are already bearing fruit."

CHAPTER 20

A New Broom

Headmaster: P.C. Bodkin Esq.

After Mr. Dale's retirement, there was still a strong core teaching staff at Tettenhall, although it was clear that despite many improvements, much more needed to be done to the College facilities in order to make the school more competitive. Undoubtedly the Governors knew this when appointing Mr. Dale's successor because they unanimously chose a man who had his eyes fixed on the future and his feet planted firmly in the present.

The new Headmaster, Peter Charles Bodkin, was born in London on 15th June 1953, the eldest son of a doctor. He attended Bradfield College where he soon won his colours in cricket and soccer, and was eventually appointed Head Boy. From Bradfield, he went to St. Andrews University, Scotland to read Botany in 1972 and was awarded a BSc. degree in 1976. He was also awarded a scholarship to research for a PhD in freshwater ecology of aquatic plants. His research for this degree included six months at Guelph University, Ontario, Canada, for which he was awarded a Carnegie Grant. Upon returning to Britain, he captained the Scottish University Cricket Team for the 1978/9 season and was awarded his PhD in 1979. In the same year, he was invited to teach at his old school, Bradfield College, where he became Housemaster of Hillside House at the age of 29. While at Bradfield, he coached the First Eleven at soccer and eventually was offered the Headmastership of Tettenhall College in 1994. A talented and enthusiastic sportsman, Dr. Bodkin was keen to take the Headmastership of a school with boarding facilities, as he remains committed to the concept of boarding schools, since his own personal experience has shown the benefits that this type of school can bring to children of all ages. Quite early on in his association with Tettenhall, he saw the tremendous benefits of the tight family atmosphere that prevailed at the College, and felt that this was the school that would most benefit from his strong business skills and desire to succeed.

There is no doubt that the new Headmaster brought with him the winds of change to Tettenhall College. In the last years of the twentieth century, affairs in practically all circles were moving at a much swifter pace than they were in the days of the school's infancy. This

P. C. Bodkin Esq., BSc. PhD

necessitated a greater need to take on board more rapid changes in methods, techniques and attitudes. In times such as these, the people most likely to prevail are those who can easily adapt to, and indeed predict, future trends. It is obvious that the Council of Governors chose their new Headmaster for his proven ability to do just this.

Some may argue that several of the changes that Dr. Bodkin brought to bear were gratuitous, but few can deny the positive effect that many of them have had upon the College's standing as a modern, forward thinking academy of learning. Change is feared by many and avoided by most, but Dr. Bodkin, apparently fearless, lost no time in embossing his own business-like stamp of efficiency upon almost every aspect of College life. One of the first items to go were the varying terms of engagement of the College's staff. Hitherto, teachers and other staff alike were engaged on differing terms, obviously the result of negotiations carried out at the time of each individual engagement. In their place, Dr. Bodkin introduced a new standard Contract of Employment that all staff would now have in common. While items such as remuneration and duties varied from individual to individual, terms such as notice period and such like were standardised. The argument for this was that the old differing contracts caused many managerial problems as well as friction between individuals. Under the new standardised system, at least everybody knew more or less where they, and everyone else, stood. The result was that the College lost several members of staff who, for varying reasons, didn't like the new system, but the long-term benefits were that there was less one-upmanship, and a "flatter" hierarchical structure where rank mattered less than individual respect for one another. Although this was not ostensibly a popular move, the benefits gained by reducing staff management headaches greatly outweighed the birth pains of this brave new world.

The next item that greatly impressed the Council of Governors was the Headmaster's production of a formal Business Plan for the College. This was an extremely well thought out and progressive document that outlined in fine detail the College's way forward. The Plan included such things as College building development, funding, staffing levels, marketing, student numbers, investment options, and much, much more. Written in a positive and business-like style, the document was later used to great effect to sway the decisions of financiers, inform the decisions of professional advisors, and generally impress all those who wanted a taste of the mettle of the man now in charge. A weighty document, the Business Plan provided a series of goals for the College to aim for that have greatly helped to motivate both Governors and College staff alike. While Dr. Bodkin, as the new broom, may not have been too popular in certain, more reactionary quarters, the written definition of his Vision for the College certainly engendered a great deal of respect from everyone who had even the slightest interest in College affairs.

Another completely different type of goal provided by Dr. Bodkin was of the type found on the soccer field. For many years, rugger had been the staple of all College winter sporting activities, and whilst this was to some degree ameliorated by the introduction of co-education (and the additional female-oriented sports this ushered in), no one really had played much in the way of properly organised soccer until it was introduced into the School curriculum by Dr. Bodkin shortly after his appointment as Headmaster. A skilled soccer player and referee, the new Headmaster led from the front with his enthusiasm for the sport, and now soccer has proved to be as popular at the College as rugger and cricket ever had been. It is interesting to note that since 1995, the College has been doing extremely well at soccer and has achieved major successes in national school leagues.

One of the first challenges to confront the new Headmaster was the fact that there was not a properly equipped Lower School in that the facility was still located in the rambling corridors of the Towers. Not only this, but the old and essentially improvised nature of this building meant that the younger pre-secondary pupils could not receive the full benefit of a modern thoroughly planned high-tech education. Moreover, the Drive School was located on the other side of Tettenhall village and as such, neither the teaching staff nor the pupils felt that they were a part of the College at all. This meant that many Drive School pupils were leaving to go to other schools, whereas they might be tempted to go on to Tettenhall College's Lower School and Upper School if they felt they had already been a part of those institutions in the first place.

This meant that the first priority for the new Headmaster was to build a new Drive School on the main College campus. This he set about in earnest and, assisted by his Planning Committee, drew up detailed plans of how this was to be achieved. A mortgage was taken out on the College premises to pay for the project and it was proposed that this should be paid off by the improved revenue brought in by better Drive School facilities.

While all this was being put in motion, the Headmaster set about making changes to many of the school systems and methods. The Library was moved from the old Thorneycroft stables to what was formerly known as Big School. This meant a far larger Library under the supervision of a permanent staff of librarians. The Chapel, which had in 1994 still featured its original (much carved-upon) pews from the school's early days was refurbished and (much to the chagrin of many OTs), the old pews were replaced by interlinking padded chairs. The newly vacated Library was converted to a Sixth Form Centre and what used to be the old Woodwork Room was refitted as a Sixth Form Café, named appropriately Café Six. The old Geography room at the end of the Maurice Jacks Block was eventually converted into a common room for non-Sixth Formers, and additional vending and other related facilities brought the College's amenities more in line with the needs of a modern competitive environment.

Another modernisation that horrified many Old Tettenhallians was the removal of all the old desks from classrooms and the replacing of them with modern desks and chairs. The old desks had been ancient things made in one piece with an iron frame featuring a tilt-up shelf as a chair and a sloping desk surface that opened to a compartment for storing books and such like. It will be remembered that these desks had been provided at the end of Mr. Pearson's time as Headmaster, and as such, were regarded as a solid symbol of these times by many OTs who could remember that far back. Despite this, all of these relics of a bygone era were swept away along with the traditional platforms at the front of classes, which had until then given the teaching staff a more panoramic view of the class. All the remaining chalkboards were eventually removed and replaced with modern whiteboards and marker pens. These were then augmented by more modern overhead projectors, which gave the staff the facilities to present classes from laptop PCs or other multimedia equipment on pull-down white screens mounted in front of the whiteboards.

School timetables were reorganised, and the old form structure was scrapped in favour of a more modern nomenclature. Whereas before, Drive and Lower School had their own form structure with Upper school being divided into Upper Fourth, Lower Fifth, Upper Fifth, Lower Sixth and Upper Sixth, everyone was now placed in sequentially numbered years – One (Drive School) through to Eleven (at age 16) and finally Sixth Form for 17 and 18 year-olds. All of this gave the College a unity that it had not enjoyed before. Under previous regimes, Drive, Lower and Upper Schools all had their own identity and, to a large extent, autonomy. In bringing them all together under a collective umbrella, they all became more unified and part of the integral whole. This made management of them all a much easier affair and the introduction of Departmental Budgets by new Bursar Charlotte Jones meant that spending could be kept within carefully crafted guidelines.

In the final years of the twentieth century, the College's computer facilities were greatly enhanced, and the skylines over the various College buildings became increasingly crowded with overhead cables as various College computer networks grew and developed in sophistication. The advent of the Internet as a major force in how businesses were run and marketed gave rise to a Tettenhall College website that has developed from its original concept of an "online brochure" to an online resource of Tettenhall College culture.

Security at the College was brought right up to date with electronic CCTV, passkey fobs and pass code keypads for all areas. Gates were erected in front of the Quadrangle and an additional entrance, drive and car park was built around the Wood Road entrance to the College, thereby allowing access to the proposed new Drive and Lower Schools as well as to the Maurice Jacks Block at the end of Tettenhall High Street and the beginning of College Lane.

Security on the Henwood Road was also tightened up. In previous years, local residents had taken to exercising their dogs on the College Playing Fields – some even believing that

College grounds were public property! In the light of public liability issues in an increasingly litigation-conscious society, not to mention the potential health and hygiene nightmares when putting together uncontrolled dogs and children, this practice was ended forthwith and the Henwood Road gates and borders were modernised and made more secure. A strict system of visitor signing in and out was introduced to College reception and all non-staff members now need to carry identification at all times. The advent of female Boarders at the College had necessitated a lot of these additional security measures, as had the presence of a lot of high-tech hardware on the premises. Many OTs remember with nostalgia the days when the College was open to the world at most times of day. Unfortunately, a more crime-laden society had brought all this to an end.

While all of this was taking place, the new Drive School was taking shape on what had been the old Towers playing field. Under the supervision of Chairman of the Governors' Planning Committee, the new building was completed during the summer period so that the school would open at the beginning of the autumn term and within budget. The new entranceway to Wood Road provided a good vehicular access to this new facility and it was by then proposed to build a new Lower School behind the new Drive School that would also be able to take advantage of the new improved access. At around about this time, the Nuffield Hospital, now the College's next door neighbours on Wood Road, proposed a shared car park facility for both hospital and school, but agreement was never reached and this idea never reached fruition.

A worthwhile project that did reach fruition on the other hand, was a fund for continued staff professional development. While the College had always sought to help staff achieve professional development in the past, this practice was formalised under Dr. Bodkin and was accordingly allocated a budget. This meant that staff could now apply for assistance in achieving further qualifications if they can make a case to support the belief that this would benefit the College.

As the new Drive School reached completion in 1998, the Governors placed the old building in Wrottesley Road on the market and it was sold very quickly. Most of the old fittings and equipment that had existed in the old Drive School were thrown away and the new building benefited from all new fixtures and equipment. As soon as the new school was opened, it must have been gratifying for the Headmaster and Governors to see Drive School numbers swell to over one hundred. Another welcome addition to Drive School facilities was the addition of a nursery for children under the age of five, and this helped to increase numbers even further.

All of this gave the Governors the incentive to invest in an all-new Lower School. The success of the new Drive School enabled suitable financial backing to be readily available for this project, and work commenced almost immediately with a projected completion date of 2002. Again, it was proposed that the new Lower School would have all new equipment and fittings, and that it would have a physical connection with the Drive School and the existing Sports Hall, which by now had been completely fitted out with state of the art facilities and fixtures. This meant that this building could easily be used for College gatherings such as the renamed "Annual Prizegiving," which had formerly been known as "Speech Day."

When Dr. Bodkin began his Headmastership, he had originally intended to continue his predecessor's practice of devoting at least some hours of the week to teaching, but it soon became apparent that the complex machinations of managing the extensive development work on the College campus were making this impossible. The need for regular meetings with planners, builders, architects and the like were an essential part of keeping a hands-on role in the College's physical evolution, so the Headmaster decided to leave the task of everyday teaching to his more than competent staff, reasoning that his talents would be better

The new Lower School.

The building of a new Lower School allowed for the Towers to be put to other uses

used in providing everyone with the facilities, which they needed and deserved.

As the end of the twentieth century neared and the new Lower School came closer to reality, the Headmaster had embarked upon a programme of appointing new teachers to swell the growing demand that increased numbers were bringing. By now, the designation of "master" had been dropped from general parlance as a generic reference to a member of the teaching staff, and the word "teacher" had been substituted as a more apt description of a member of the College's academic staff. Since the advent of co-education, the practically all male staff had been augmented by increasing numbers of female teachers until the point was reached where the College could truly offer the full range of co-educational facilities that would satisfy even the most stringent Equal Opportunities regulators at Whitehall.

As in the past, Tettenhall College had moved to cater for rapidly changing times, and as the twenty-first century dawned, the future looked brighter than ever.

CHAPTER 21

A TWENTY-FIRST CENTURY COLLEGE

Headmaster: P.C. Bodkin Esq.

There are times in the life of every individual, and indeed every organisation, when fate has a way of dealing an unexpectedly poor card. As can be seen from the pages of this book, the College is no exception here, and has received, some would say, rather more than its fair share of bad fortune over the years. However, a seemingly equal share of good fortune – usually arriving at the eleventh hour, has usually come to our aid! This was certainly the case in 2000 when the College woke up to find that a strong gust of wind had caused a very large tree to fall down and completely crush the Sports Pavilion. One cannot legislate for the vagaries of Mother Nature, and in this instance it was clear to everyone, including the College surveyors, that the "Pav" had been destroyed beyond all hope of repair or rebuilding. However, not to be daunted, the College's insurers insisted that it obtain a quote for repair; but once they had sent representatives to inspect the devastation, even they were forced to admit that there was no hope of restoring the Pavilion that had, in 1953, been a gift from the Old Tettenhallians, given in recognition of Horace Pearson's achievements for the School.

Matters were made even more distressing bearing in mind the fact that the College had just paid £15,000 on having the Pavilion refurbished and newly re-decorated. Obviously, this money had to be completely written off, and all the College could do was smile and absorb the loss with what stoicism it could muster. Not to be daunted though, the Governors quickly decided that the College could definitely not do without its Pavilion and that the money had to be found to build another. It was quickly determined though that it would cost at least £250,000 to replace the old Pavilion, and after much "horse trading" with insurers, the College settled in the end for a restitution sum of £165,000, which would at least go some way to replacing the Pavilion, so beloved of many generations of Tettenhallians and Old Tettenhallians alike.

But the problem didn't end there though. Obviously the College wanted to build its new Pavilion on the site of the old one, which would have negated the need for Planning Permission and kept other costs to a minimum. The problem was that there were some badger setts near to where the old Pavilion stood, and carrying out works of building on this site would disrupt the badgers and therefore contravene the law, since badgers are a protected species. It seemed that the College would have to think again.

After turning over various possible alternatives, the Council of Governors decided to build the new Pavilion on another site. Various possibilities were considered, including the positioning of the new building on the Henwood Road side of the Playing Fields, although it was felt that this would be bad from a security point of view, and eventually everyone settled on a site that was on the same side of the Playing Fields as the original, only further along towards the College's western boundary. Rather than build a similar building to the old Pavilion, it was decided that since the new structure would be lower down, at field level, and unlike the original, it would take the form of a two-storey building with a balcony. Many felt that this design was best, so that sports matches could be viewed from a "grandstand" point of view. Since an identical pavilion could not be built on the original site, there were no other sites suitable for a replica of the original. After considering many alternative designs, the College Governors settled on the two storey "grandstand" concept, and ordered that work should begin on the new Pavilion, although at the outset it was not completely clear where all the money was going to come from to complete it. Sure enough, as the building neared completion it was realised that there were not enough funds left to build the balcony area, and it was feared that this part of the design would have to be scrapped, or at least put on ice until the necessary funds became available. As usual, Tettenhall College's guardian angel smiled down in this time of need and provided the school with a timely and generous anonymous donation of £10,000 to allow the balcony area to be completed on time.

It must be remembered that when the old Pavilion had been built in 1953, there were only male toilet and changing facilities, since the College had been an all-boys school at this time. Exclusive male changing and toilet facilities had created many obvious problems after the College went co-educational, and whilst much money was lavished on providing facilities for girls and female members of staff in the main areas of the campus, the Pavilion had been rather neglected in this regard. The building of a new Pavilion, though, had allowed the Board to rectify this problem by furnishing the new premises with unisex facilities, which, in turn, now allows the College far more latitude in hosting visiting teams of either gender. Shakespeare said: "Ill blows the wind that profits nobody.[2]" In this case, he was right!

All of this happened the year after the new Lower School opened its doors for business. Work on the latter had been completed in 2002 and, like the new Drive School, which had opened four years previously, it proved to be a resounding success. The site of the new building was to the rear of the Drive School adjacent to the woods, with its entrance path

2 3 Henry VI, II, v

The new Sports Pavilion

siding on to the old Towers rear lawn, which by then had been adorned with a wood-built adventure playground. Also built at this time were new hard Tennis Courts located between the Drive School and the road leading to the new Wood Road entrance.

The original Head of the Drive and Lower Schools had been Mr. Paul Cochrane, who had given a lot of energy and authority to the task, and the foundations had been well and truly laid for solid nursery and preparatory facilities on Tettenhall College campus. However, Mr. Cochrane decided to pursue his career elsewhere, so shortly after the new Lower School building was completed, Mr. Philip Meadows was appointed new Head of the Drive and Lower School. This meant that not only did the College get a new building for both institutions, but it also got a new vision to go with it. By this time, the collective population of both Drive and Lower Schools was in excess of 200 and rising.

This all meant that the Towers could now be put to other uses now that Lower School had its own dedicated building and facilities. Whilst it is no less a "money pit" now than it has been in the past, the building is still of tremendous value to the College. The magnificent theatre has had money spent on it to turn it into one of the school's greatest assets. Every year, it is the venue for many highly professional productions put on by staff and College students, under the supervision of music director Ian Wass, and without it, there is no doubt that drama and music at Tettenhall would not be as well developed as they are.

With all of this new development of the College campus, one could be tempted to think that the Headmaster had done enough. Indeed, lesser men would probably have been tempted to sit back and rest on what they had achieved this far. But not so in this twenty-first century Tettenhall College! With seemingly boundless energy and enthusiasm, Dr. Bodkin and his Governors set about putting together plans to refurbish the Swimming Pool, to modernise the existing boys' boarding facilities, and – a project close to the Headmaster's heart – augment the Maurice Jacks Block with some completely some new science laboratories that would well and truly put Tettenhall College on the map as far as state of the art twenty-first century science facilities were concerned. It must be remembered that the original science laboratories had been built back in 1958, and they were definitely looking a trifle dated nearly fifty years later.

The success of the new Drive and Lower Schools had improved the College's overall fortunes no end. Whilst Lloyd's TSB, still the College's bankers, had originally looked at the school with some disdain, and had originally only deigned to take on the account to pacify Mr. Baldwin Bantock, they were, by the early twenty-first century, one of the school's closest allies. Whilst seemingly tireless efforts were made to raise funds for the new projects, it soon became clear to Lloyds that the sooner these schemes were implemented, the sooner the College would benefit, and they too would reap the rewards of the many decades of patience and risk they had shown when the College's fortunes had not been so potentially profitable.

From fairly early on, the Headmaster had seen the need to spread the College catchment net as widely as possible and during the early years of his Headmastership, the school had gained a greater percentage of pupils from China and the Far East. With the advent of the Internet and the proliferation of English language websites, the need to speak English among non-native speakers has grown exponentially. This, in turn, has created a far greater need for teaching English as a Foreign Language (EFL), and thanks to the expert guidance of Dot Stone, this subject is one of the College's major strengths, and certainly one of its greatest selling points as far as foreign students are concerned.

Meanwhile, the College's attention to more traditional subjects has never wavered. English teaching has taken many strides ahead, and with the Headmaster's determination to take Drama and Music to new levels, all of these subjects have been benefitting from each other's strengths.

Another change introduced by Dr. Bodkin to the staff structure was the creation of the role of Deputy Headmaster following the retirement of Dr. R. A. Roberts as Second Master. This post was awarded to Mr. H.R.J. Trump, a History teacher, who has been fulfilling these duties with dedication ever since his appointment to the role.

All through this, "The Tettenhallian" has never failed to keep a constant chronicle of events. Whilst more recent issues have lost the often acerbic and satirical quality of the earlier editions, the magazine has kept going through thick and thin. Advances in desktop publishing and printing techniques have meant that the glossy and slickly produced magazine we have now is a far cry from the black and white pamphlet of earlier years, but it still maintains a record of the school's progress with clarity and precision.

In 2004 one of Tettenhall College's oldest and most loved assets – the Swimming Pool – went through a much-needed makeover and refurbishment. Already a far cry from the muddy pit that it had originally been, it was re-lined and re-marked. After this, it was completely re-tiled and heating was added to the pool-hall itself. The changing rooms were then modernised and re-fitted and the heating system renewed. In addition to this, some of the extra space created allowed the provision of a small spectator area, thereby allowing uninhibited viewing without direct access to the poolside and any attendant contamination of the pool itself. No one can argue that this squeaky clean example of modern sporting hygiene has now come a long way from the days when it was a punishable offence to stir up the mud at the bottom of the pool!

At around this time, the boys' dormitories had more or less been as they always had been, and the need to modernise them was now acute. In response to this, the old cubicles were removed in favour of individual rooms with washbasin facilities. These were augmented by completely new shower and sanitary facilities. One dormitory was even converted into a common room area with a television and self-catering facilities. Whilst this was not an absolutely perfect solution bearing in mind modern needs, it must be remembered that this building had been constructed over a hundred years previously when needs were very different indeed. Many see these modernisations as a halfway house to constructing whole new unisex facilities without the need for common sanitary facilities. However, this will have to remain, for the time being, in the conceptualisation stage as the College campus evolves.

At the same time, it became necessary to replace the windows in Main School, since these were the original windows that had been there since the building was first constructed in the early days of the College. Many of these were rotten and needed new glass, so the project to replace them all with modern double-glazed units was begun in earnest. Because the building is a listed building, the College was not allowed to replace the original sash windows with modern PVC equivalents, so each frame had to be reconstructed using wood and then double glazed. Needless to say, with over 266 windows, this took several years to complete.

One of the Arthur Harden Science Laboratories offering modern facilities – a far cry from the original Chemistry Laboratory pictured in Chapter 3.

In 2005, planning permission was granted to build extra facilities on the first floor of the Maurice Jacks Block. The first phase of this was to include two brand new science laboratories with more teaching facilities. The Weedon Partnership of Birmingham was instructed to design the new laboratories, and work was completed in 2007. It was named after the Old Tettenhallian Nobel Prizewinner Arthur Harden, who, it will be remembered, won his Nobel Prize in 1929. The facility was opened in September by world-renowned scientist and Chairman of the Lister Institute, Dame Bridget Ogilvie. The addition of these facilities has allowed the old Biology Laboratory to be used as the new Art Department.

Tettenhall College has come a long way in its almost one hundred and fifty years of life. It has been through many changes, both in its people and in its buildings. But the very spirit that drives it remains there, as unwavering as ever. Few Tettenhallians fail to catch the spirit of the place, and fail to understand what Mr. Pine meant at one reunion dinner when he looked about him and remarked: "There's something you've got. I don't know what it is, but it's there, and each of you here has it."

But one thing that embodies the spirit of the College hasn't really changed much at all in nearly 150 years. Out of all the aspects of College life that compete to be the most memorable, just one daily event has come to mean a lot to successive generations of Tettenhallians, and that is the morning Chapel Service. Following pretty much the same format that it always has, it begins with a hymn, and then is followed by an exposition by the Headmaster or Chaplain after a reading from some work of a religious nature, and finally prayers to make up this daily morning service. Although it would be rash to assume that in these more secular or multi-cultural times, all pupils benefit alike from what they hear, there is no doubt that many Tettenhallians, at any rate, find that this morning service fills a prominent place in their memories of the College for a long time after they have left it.

Simon Whild was brought up in the Midlands of England and was educated at Tettenhall College, followed by the universities of Reading and Wolverhampton. After several years in the property business, he became a full-time writer, editor and journalist. He was Editor in Chief of the Shell International intranet publication *Silent Dialogue* and then Editor in Chief of *Nuclear Europe Worldscan* – one of Europe's leading scientific journals.

Simon Whild is now a freelance writer and journalist, and currently lives in England. He is the author of a volume of poetry entitled *Pictures of the Floating World*, also published by Matador.

Printed in the United Kingdom by
Lightning Source UK Ltd., Milton Keynes
141924UK00001B/64/P

9 781848 761247